SILVER BURDETT SCIENCE

Centennial Edition

GEORGE G. MALLINSON
Distinguished Professor
of Science Education
Western Michigan University

JACQUELINE B. MALLINSON
Associate Professor of Science
Western Michigan University

WILLIAM L. SMALLWOOD
Head, Science Department
The Community School
Sun Valley, Idaho

CATHERINE VALENTINO
Former Director of Instruction
North Kingstown School Department
North Kingstown, Rhode Island

SILVER BURDETT COMPANY
MORRISTOWN, NJ
Atlanta, GA • Cincinnati, OH • Dallas, TX • Northfield, IL •
San Carlos, CA • Agincourt, Ontario

SILVER BURDETT

SCIENCE

Centennial Edition

GEORGE G. MALLINSON

JACQUELINE B. MALLINSON

WILLIAM L. SMALLWOOD

CATHERINE VALENTINO

THE SILVER BURDETT ELEMENTARY SCIENCE PROGRAM
1-6 PUPILS' BOOKS
AND
TEACHERS' EDITIONS LEVELS K-6

ISBN 0-382-13106-1

CONTENTS

Discovering the Plant and Animal World

There are many different kinds of living things in the world. Scientists group these living things by the ways in which they are alike and different. Look at the drawings and pictures of the living things. Into what two groups could you divide these living things?

How are these living things alike? How are they different? What can the cactus and the tulips do that the other living things cannot? What makes the snake, the bat, and the fish different from the butterfly? These and many other questions will be answered as you study this unit.

Chapter 1

Activities of Green Plants

In the spring the weather becomes warm, and green plants begin to grow from the soil. In a few weeks many plants produce beautifully colored flowers. The picture shows the stages in the opening of a daffodil flower. Flowers such as the daffodil do more than add beauty to the world. They are an important part of the plant. Without flowers many plants could not produce more of their kind.

Producing new plants is one special activity that green plants carry out. What are some other special activities of green plants? How do the parts of green plants help them carry out these activities? You will find out in this chapter.

── LIVING THINGS ARE ALIKE ──
In what ways are living things alike?

All living things are alike in many ways. One way in which they are alike is that they are made up of cells. A **cell** is the basic unit of all living things. Cells are sometimes called the "building blocks of life." The cells that make up plants and animals can be compared to the bricks in a building. Many bricks are needed to make up a building, just as many cells are needed to make up most plants and animals.

Most living things contain many different kinds of cells. The cells in your brain are different from the cells in your heart. The cells in the roots of a plant are different from the cells in its leaves. But no matter what kinds of cells they are, all cells are very small. They can only be seen by viewing them through a microscope.

Onion skin cells

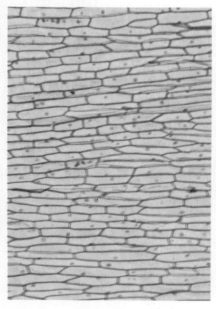

Elk

Giraffe

Living things are alike in another way. All living things need certain things to stay alive. You are a living thing. What do you need to stay alive? Three things you need are food, water, and air. Plants and animals also need these things. What needs are being met by the animals in the pictures?

To meet their needs, living things must carry out life processes (pros'es iz). **Life processes** are the activities that keep living things alive. This is another way in which all living things are alike.

The life processes carried out by all living things are listed in the chart.

LIFE PROCESSES OF LIVING THINGS

Life process	What it means
Getting food	Most living things get food from plants and animals. Green plants make their own food.
Releasing energy	Living things break down food to release energy stored in food.
Removing wastes	Living things get rid of waste materials.
Growing	Living things grow in size; they also replace old, worn cells by growing new cells.
Reproducing	Living things produce more living things of the same kind.

5

— TRANSPORTING MATERIALS —
How do green plants transport the materials needed to make food?

You have learned some ways in which living things are alike. One way in which living things differ is in how they carry out some of the life processes. Most living things get food by eating plants and animals. But green plants do not eat food—they make it.

Green plants need three things to make food. They need (1) water, (2) carbon dioxide (kär'bən dī ok'sīd), and (3) light energy. How do green plants get these things? Food making usually takes place in the leaf cells of green plants. So the things needed to make food must be transported to these leaf cells by the roots, stems, and leaves.

Roots play an important role in transporting materials for food making. The picture shows small hairlike parts growing out from the sides of

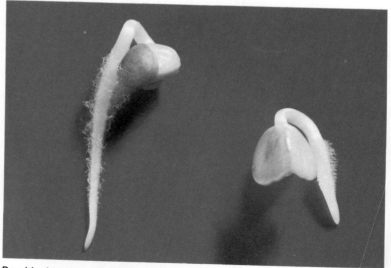

Root hairs on radish seedlings

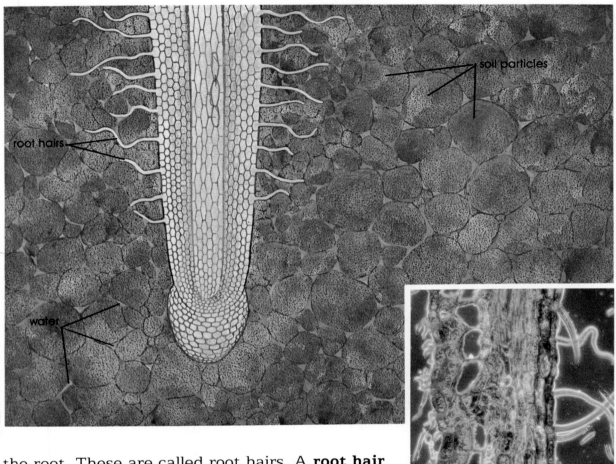

root hairs

soil particles

water

Root hairs under a microscope

the root. These are called root hairs. A **root hair** is part of a single cell that grows from a root into the soil. Root hairs grow near the tips of roots. Almost all the water taken in by roots is taken in by the root hairs. The rest of the root helps to anchor the plant in the soil and to store food.

The small root hairs enter spaces between bits of soil. The water in these spaces is taken in, or absorbed, by the root hairs. There are millions of root hairs on most plant roots. The more root hairs there are, the more water the root can absorb. The picture shows how root hairs look under a microscope.

What do root hairs look like?

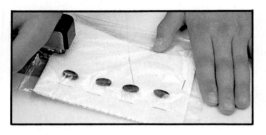

Materials   paper towel / self-sealing plastic bag / 4 radish or bean seeds / stapler / 2 pushpins / jar / hand lens / scissors / tweezers / microscope slide / microscope

Procedure

A. Fold a paper towel in half and put it in a plastic bag. Place the bag on a table.

B. Place four seeds on the paper towel inside the bag. Staple the bag and towel beneath each seed as shown. Then staple the sides of the bag.

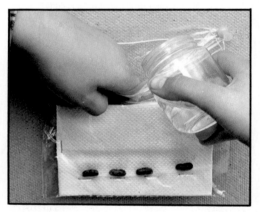

C. Use two pushpins to put the bag on a bulletin board. Open the bag and carefully pour some water behind the towel. The water level should not go above the staples beneath the seeds. Seal the bag.

D. Check the seeds each day. When the roots are about 3 cm long, take the bag down. Carefully remove the seeds from the bag. Examine the fuzzy areas on the roots with a hand lens.
   1. Describe what you see.
   2. Draw a root and show where the root hairs are. Label the drawing.

E. Use scissors to cut off one root from a seed. Carefully pick up the root with tweezers and place it on a microscope slide. Examine the fuzzy areas of the root under a microscope.
   3. Make a drawing of the root hairs as they look under a microscope.

Conclusion
1. Describe what the root hairs look like.
2. Why is it helpful for a plant to have many root hairs?

Using science ideas
Many plants that live in water do not have root hairs. Why don't these plants need root hairs?

From the roots, water is transported to the stem. The stem is the part of the plant between the roots and the leaves. The stem transports water and food to all parts of the plant through tubes.

The picture shows the inside of a stem. Notice that there are two kinds of tubes within the stem. Both kinds of tubes occur in bundles. One kind of tube transports water upward from the roots to the leaves. The other kind of tube transports food from the leaves downward to all parts of the plant. Look at the bundles of water-carrying tubes. In what direction does water move through the stem? Where does it go?

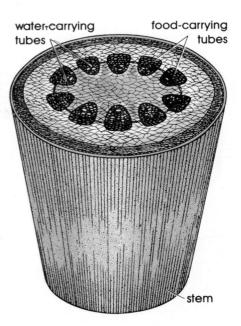

water-carrying tubes
food-carrying tubes
stem

Do you know?

As they absorb water from the soil, plants also take in minerals. Minerals are needed by plants to perform life processes. Most plants that live on land get minerals from the soil. But a few green plants get minerals by eating insects!

Different kinds of insect-eating plants have different ways of trapping insects. One kind, the Venus's-flytrap, uses its leaves. As an insect crawls onto a leaf, the leaf presses together, trapping the insect. The leaf then gives off special juices. These juices break down the insect's body. Minerals from the insect's body are then used by the plant.

Venus's-flytrap

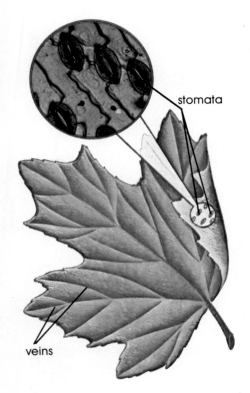

stomata

veins

Water is transported from the stem to the leaves. Most leaves contain small thin tubes called **veins** (vānz). The veins are much like the tubes in the stem. They carry water and food to and from leaf cells.

Besides water, leaf cells need carbon dioxide to make food. Carbon dioxide is one of the gases in air. How does air get into a leaf? The picture shows the underside of a leaf as seen through a microscope. Notice the openings in the leaf. These openings are called **stomata** (stō′mə tə). Air enters a leaf through these stomata.

Light energy is the third thing needed for leaf cells to make food. Most leaves are flat and thin. This allows light to reach the food-making cells inside the leaf.

Finding out

Where are the water-carrying tubes in a stem?   Put several drops of red food coloring in a glass three-fourths filled with water. Stir the water. Get a celery stalk with some leaves still on it. Cut about 3 cm off the bottom of the stalk. Place the stalk in the colored water and allow it to stay overnight.

The next day examine the leaves. What has happened? Why did this happen? Take the stalk out of the water and cut off another 3 cm. Look at the bottom of the cut stalk. Where are the water-carrying tubes? How do you know?

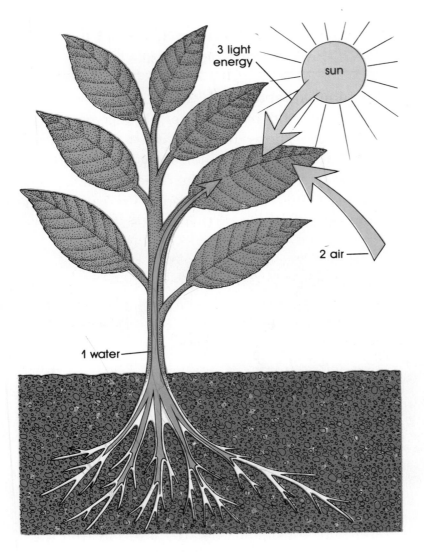

How a plant gets materials for food making

The drawing shows how a green plant gets the things it needs to make food.

1. Water enters the roots and moves through the stem to the leaf.

2. Air, containing carbon dioxide, enters the leaf through the stomata.

3. Sunlight striking the leaf provides the energy that leaf cells need to make food.

— FOOD MAKING IN A LEAF —
How do green plants make food?

Imagine a factory in which bread is made. Flour, milk, and other materials are needed to make bread. These materials must first be transported to the factory. Then they must be mixed together to form dough. The dough is then baked in ovens. Heat energy is needed for baking. The product that is made by this process is bread.

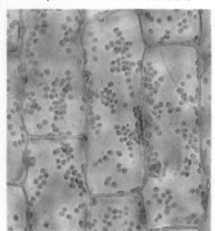

Chloroplasts in elodea leaf cells

The leaf of a green plant is much like a factory. Water and carbon dioxide are materials that must be transported to the leaf factory. Sunlight provides the energy to make the product. Food, in the form of sugar, is the product that is made. The process by which green plants make food is called **photosynthesis** (fō tə sin'thə sis).

To better understand photosynthesis, you should first know what the inside of a leaf is like. You can see chloroplasts (klôr'ə plasts) in the cells of this leaf. A **chloroplast** is a small green body in

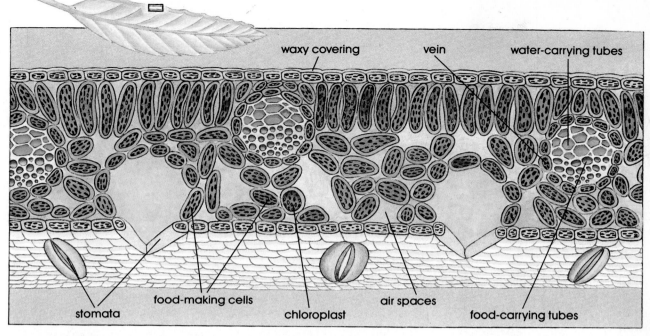

waxy covering · vein · water-carrying tubes · stomata · food-making cells · chloroplast · air spaces · food-carrying tubes

Leaf cross section

plant cells. The green color comes from a special material that is needed by the plant to make food. This material is called **chlorophyll** (klôr′ə fil).

The drawing shows how the cells inside a leaf would look under a microscope. Notice the waxy covering on the top and bottom. Beneath this covering is a single layer of cells. These cells help protect the leaf from damage. Usually these cells do not contain chloroplasts. Find these cells in the drawing. Notice the stomata in the bottom layer of these cells. As you learned, gases enter and leave the plant through these openings.

The food-making cells are in the middle part of the leaf. There are a great many chloroplasts in these cells. Around the food-making cells are air spaces. These air spaces are connected to stomata and allow carbon dioxide to reach the food-making cells. The vein contains cells that carry water to the food-making cells.

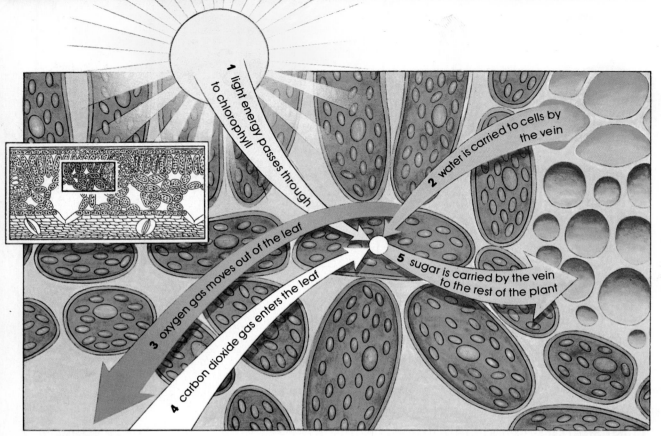

On the image:
1 light energy passes through to chlorophyll

2 water is carried to cells by the vein

3 oxygen gas moves out of the leaf

4 carbon dioxide gas enters the leaf

5 sugar is carried by the vein to the rest of the plant

Food making in a leaf

You have seen how the food-making cells get the water and carbon dioxide they need to make food. Now you will see how food is made in these cells. Refer to this drawing as you read the steps.

1. Sunlight strikes the leaf and passes through to the cholorophyll in the food-making cells, where it is trapped.
2. Water is carried to the food-making cells by the vein.
3. The sun's energy is used to change water into two gases, hydrogen and oxygen (ok'sə jən). The oxygen gas, a waste product, moves out of the leaf through the stomata.
4. Carbon dioxide gas enters the leaf through the stomata and moves to the food-making cells.

5. The hydrogen gas joins with carbon dioxide gas to make food, a type of sugar. The sugar is carried by the vein to the rest of the plant.

A way to show what happens during photosynthesis is:

water + carbon dioxide + energy $\longrightarrow$ sugar + oxygen
(from sunlight)

Most plants make more sugar than they need. This sugar is stored in the cells of the plant. Think about the fruits and vegetables you eat. Which of them taste sweet? These sweet-tasting plants contain much stored sugar.

Some of the extra sugar made by the plant is changed to starch. Starch is also stored in the cells of the plant. A white potato is an underground stem that contains large amounts of stored starch.

Sweet-tasting fruits and vegetables

White potatoes

SUGAR TRANSPORT

— USING THE ENERGY IN FOOD —

How do plants use the energy stored in food?

Living things need energy to carry out the life processes. They get energy from food. But the energy in food is stored energy. It must be released before it can be used by living things. **Respiration** (res pə rā'shən) is the process by which living things use oxygen to release energy in food. This process takes place in the cells of all living things.

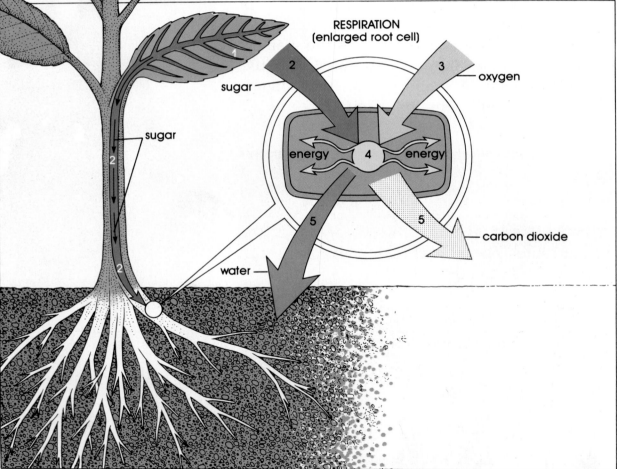

RESPIRATION
(enlarged root cell)

sugar

oxygen

energy   energy

sugar

carbon dioxide

water

16

Before cells can carry out respiration they must first have food. How do plants get the food needed for respiration? How do cells change sugar to energy? Refer to the drawing as you read the steps.

1. Sugar is made in the leaf.
2. It is carried by the veins in the leaf to the stem. Food-carrying tubes in the stem transport sugar to all parts of the stem and down to the roots.
3. The enlarged plant cell in the drawing shows oxygen entering the cell. The oxygen combines with sugar in the cell.
4. When oxygen and sugar combine, energy is released. The energy is used by the cell to carry out life processes.
5. Carbon dioxide and water are given off as waste products.

A way to show what happens during respiration is:

sugar + oxygen $\longrightarrow$ energy + carbon dioxide + water

The process of respiration is the opposite of the process of photosynthesis. Look at the chart. Compare the two processes.

COMPARISON OF PHOTOSYNTHESIS AND RESPIRATION

Photosynthesis	Respiration
Takes place only in cells with chlorophyll	Takes place in all cells
Food (sugar) is made	Food (sugar) is broken down
Sun's energy is stored in sugar	Energy stored in sugar is released
Carbon dioxide is taken in	Carbon dioxide is produced and given off
Water is taken in	Water is produced and given off
Oxygen is given off	Oxygen is used

PRODUCING NEW PLANTS

How do flowers produce seeds?

Some of the energy released by plants during respiration is used for reproduction (rē prə-duk′shən). **Reproduction** is the process by which living things produce new living things of the same kind. Many green plants grow flowers. A flower is the reproductive part of a flowering plant.

Many flowers have three main parts. The drawing shows the parts of a typical flower. The main parts of the flower are the petals, the stamen (stā′mən), and the pistil. You will see the role that each part plays in reproduction.

Lily

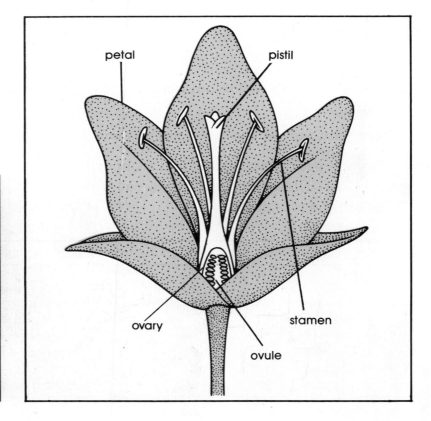

petal

pistil

ovary

ovule

stamen

The **petals** are the leaflike outer parts of a flower. They protect the inner reproductive parts. As you can see, petals are often brightly colored. Some petals have a sweet odor.

The other two parts of the flower are involved directly in reproduction. The **stamen** is the male reproductive part of a flower. The stamen is a long stalk with a sac at the top. How many stamens are shown in the drawing?

Stamens produce pollen (pol′ən) grains. A **pollen grain** is a tiny body that contains the male reproductive cell. Millions of pollen grains form in the sac at the top of the stamen. If you rub the sac, colored dust will get on your skin. This dust is made up of pollen grains. The pictures show how different kinds of pollen grains look under a microscope.

The **pistil** is the female reproductive part. The bottom part of the pistil contains the ovary (ō′vər ē). The **ovary** is the part of the plant that contains ovules (ō′vyülz). An **ovule** is a small round body that contains the female reproductive cells. Identify the pistil in the drawing. Find the ovules inside the ovary.

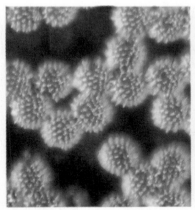

Sunflower pollen

Daylily pollen

What are the parts of a typical flower?

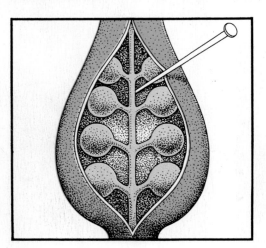

Materials 2 different kinds of flowers / hand lens / microscope slide / microscope / straight pin / sheet of paper

Procedure

A. Look at and compare two flowers. Identify the petals of each flower. Smell them.
  1. What color are the petals of each flower?
  2. Do the petals of either flower have an odor?

B. Identify the stamens and the pistil of each flower. Use a hand lens to help you see the parts.

C. Choose one flower and look at its inner parts. Carefully tear off any leafy parts around the petals. Then tear off the petals.

D. Gently remove one stamen and look at the top part with a hand lens. The powdery material is made up of many pollen grains. Shake some of the pollen grains onto a microscope slide. Look at the slide under a microscope.
  3. Draw some pollen grains.

E. Remove the rest of the stamens. Place the pistil on a sheet of paper. Use a straight pin to pick apart the base of the pistil. The ovules are inside this base. Use a hand lens to look at the ovules.
  4. Draw what you see.

Conclusion
1. What parts do the two flowers have in common?
2. What are some differences between the flowers?

Using science ideas
Suppose you wanted to know how many seeds the flower you looked at could produce. How could you find out?

For reproduction to take place, pollen grains must reach the top of the pistil. **Pollination** (pol ə-nā′shən) is the process by which pollen grains move from the stamen to the pistil. There are two main ways in which flowers are pollinated. One way is by insects. Another way is by the wind.

Most flowers are pollinated by insects. Some insects, such as the honeybee, are attracted to flowers that have a sweet odor and colorful petals. Honeybees feed on a sweet liquid produced by the flower. As the honeybee feeds, it brushes against pollen grains on the stamen. The pollen sticks to the bee. As it moves, the bee carries the pollen to the pistil.

Other flowers are pollinated when the wind blows. The wind carries pollen grains from the stamen to the pistil. Plants that do not have a sweet odor and colorful petals are often pollinated in this way. Grasses and trees, such as those shown, are pollinated by the wind.

Black birch tree

Grass (wheat)

21

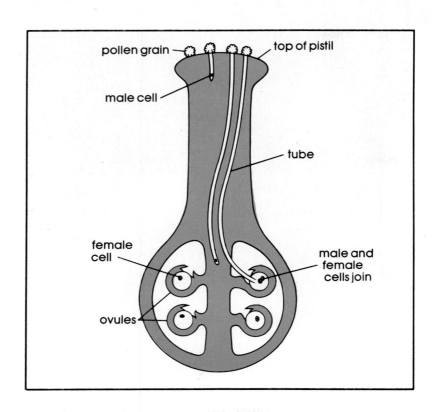

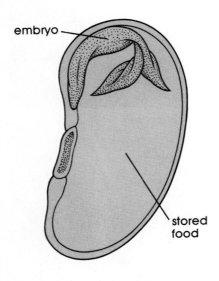

Bean seed cross section

The drawing shows what happens when a pollen grain lands on the top of the pistil. The top of the pistil is sticky. So the pollen grain sticks to it. The pollen grain begins to grow a tube. The tube grows down through the pistil until it reaches an ovule. When it reaches an ovule, the male cell from the pollen grain combines with a female cell. The joining of male and female reproductive cells is called **fertilization** (fėr tə lə zā′shən).

The fertilized ovule becomes a **seed** containing a tiny young plant and stored food. The tiny young plant is called an **embryo** (em′brē ō). When conditions are right, the embryo begins to grow. The growth of a plant embryo from a seed is called **germination** (jėr mə nā′shən). As the embryo grows, it uses the food stored in the seed.

Germinating squash seeds

Once it reaches a certain size, the young plant will make its own food by photosynthesis. The picture shows seeds in different stages of germination.

IDEAS TO REMEMBER

► The activities of living things that keep them alive are called life processes.
► The cell is the basic unit of living things.
► Photosynthesis is the process by which cells containing chlorophyll use water, carbon dioxide, and light energy to make food.
► Roots, stems, and leaves help supply food-making leaf cells with materials needed for photosynthesis.
► Respiration is the process by which living things use oxygen to release the energy in food.
► Reproduction is the process by which living things produce new living things of the same kind.
► A flower is the reproductive part of a plant.
► Seeds form from the fertilized ovule inside the pistil of a flower.

Reviewing the Chapter

SCIENCE WORDS

A. Write the letter of the term that best matches the definition. Not all the terms will be used.

1. Fertilized ovule containing tiny young plant and food
2. Green material needed by a plant to make food
3. Openings in a leaf through which air enters leaf
4. Part of a single cell that grows from a root into soil
5. Small green body in plant cells
6. Basic unit of living things
7. Tiny young plant in a seed
8. Thin tube in a leaf

a. chloroplast
b. embryo
c. vein
d. cell
e. seed
f. stamen
g. stomata
h. ovule
i. root hair
j. chlorophyll

B. Use all the terms below to complete the sentences.

fertilization   photosynthesis   reproduction   germination
life processes   pollination   respiration

The activities that keep living things alive are called __1__. Green plants make food by a process called __2__. They use oxygen to release energy in food through the process of __3__. Like all living things, green plants produce new living things of the same kind by __4__. In a flower, pollen grains are moved from the stamen to the pistil during __5__. The joining of male and female reproductive cells occurs during __6__. The growth of a plant embryo from a seed is __7__.

UNDERSTANDING IDEAS

A. Write the correct term for each number in the diagrams.

pollen grain ~~ovule~~ ~~stored food~~ ~~pistil~~ ~~embryo~~
~~stamen~~ seed ~~petal~~

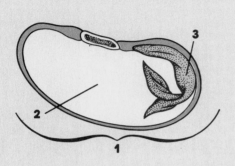 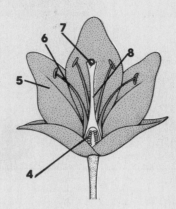

B. Write the terms that are *not* needed for photosynthesis to occur. Use the remaining terms to describe this process.

water   carbon dioxide   petal   food   stamen
chlorophyll

C. Write the terms that are *not* needed for respiration to occur. Use the remaining terms to describe this process.

light energy   sugar   carbon dioxide   seed   pistil
oxygen

USING IDEAS

1. Plant reproduction can occur without using seeds. Cut a piece of stem from a Swedish ivy or tradescantia plant. Put the stem in a jar of water. Check the jar every few days for two weeks. What happens?

Chapter 2

Animals Without a Backbone

The spider on this page is a great hunter. Did you know it can jump great distances? It can jump 40 times the length of its body. Can you see its four large eyes? It can see its insect victim from very far away.

In this chapter you will learn about all kinds of animals. Some of the animals are small, like the spider. Others are much larger than the spider. Some of these animals live in and near your home. Others live in oceans or on mountaintops.

You will find out about flying animals, floating animals, and creeping animals. You will learn about how they look and where they live. This chapter will show you how they are different and how they are alike.

— CLASSIFYING LIVING THINGS —

How do scientists classify animals?

For a few minutes make a list of all the animals you can. How many animals did you think of? There are many different kinds of animals.

Did you think of a dog, a cat, and a horse? You probably did. The chances are you did not include a sponge, a clam, or an earthworm. But these are animals, too.

Think of a way to divide up your list of animals into groups. For example, you could group all large animals together and all small animals together. You could group all fast animals and all slow animals together. Putting animals into groups is one way to sort them out. Putting animals into groups makes them easier to study.

Scientists who study animals classify (klas'ə fī), or group, them. To **classify** is to arrange in

Gannet

28

Garden spider

Zebras, wildebeests, and springboks

groups by features that are alike. Scientists classify animals by structure (struk′chər). The structure of an animal is the kind of body parts it has and the way these parts are arranged. One structure scientists look for in classifying animals is the backbone. The backbone is made up of many small bones called **vertebrae** (vêr′tə brā). Vertebrae are linked together to form the backbone.

Some animals have a backbone and some do not. Scientists have classified all animals into two large groups. One group is made up of animals with a backbone. An animal with a backbone is called a **vertebrate** (vėr′tə brĭt). The other group is made up of animals without a backbone. An animal without a backbone is called an **invertebrate** (in vėr′tə brĭt). In this chapter you will learn about invertebrates. Which animals in these pictures have a backbone? Which do not have a backbone?

Chimpanzee mother with baby

Purple sea urchin

29

SPONGES

What is a sponge, and how does it look?

What do you think of when you hear the word *sponge*? You may think of a pink or blue pad used to clean the dishes. That kind of sponge is made by people. A sponge is also an animal. A **sponge** is an invertebrate that has many cells. Almost all sponges live in oceans. A few live in freshwater streams and lakes. The orange sponge in the picture lives in the Atlantic Ocean off the northeast coast of the United States.

Sponges do not have many of the parts we usually think of as animal parts. Most animals move about, but adult sponges stay in one place. They are found attached to rocks or other objects at the bottom of the ocean. In fact, for many years scientists thought sponges were plants. Why do you think they did?

The structure of a sponge is simple. Its body is full of small holes called **pores**. The pores are connected to one another by narrow canals.

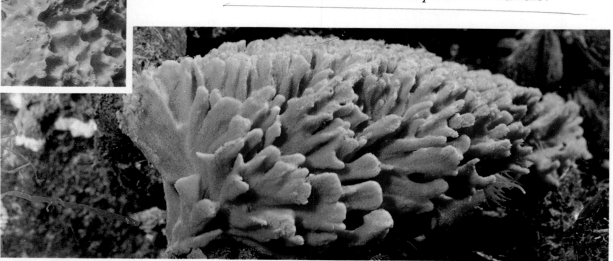

Orange sponge and close-up of pores

Special cells line the canals inside the sponge. Each cell has a threadlike part that whips back and forth. The movements of these threads send water through the body of the sponge. The water that passes through the sponge contains food and oxygen. Cells inside the sponge break down the food. The oxygen is used to release the energy in the food.

Sponges have many different shapes. Some are shaped like cups, some like fans, and others like vases. The shape of a sponge depends on its skeleton. The skeleton is the structure that supports the body of an animal.

The skeleton of some sponges is made up of hard material. But other sponges are made up of soft material. This soft skeleton is sometimes used in the home as a cleaning sponge or bath sponge. It is usually a light brown or yellowish color. It is not the same as the pink or blue sponge made by people. Are any sponges in your home from the soft skeleton of the animal?

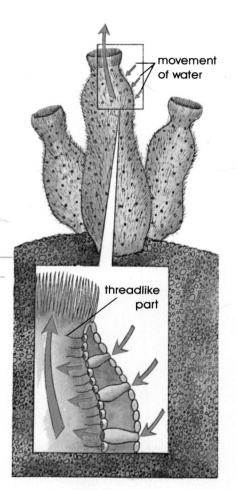

movement of water

threadlike part

Finding out

How much water can a sponge hold? Get an animal sponge, a container of water, and a measuring cup. Soak the sponge in the water for about 5 minutes. Remove the sponge from the water. Squeeze the water into the measuring cup. Measure the volume of water that was in the sponge. Record this volume of water. How much water did the sponge hold? Why is a cleaning sponge made similar to an animal sponge?

– ANIMALS WITH STINGING CELLS –

What are animals with stinging cells, and how do they look?

The hydra, jellyfish, and sea anemone (ə nem'ə-nē) are also invertebrates. Like sponges, they do not have a backbone. Hydras live in freshwater ponds and streams. Most jellyfish and sea anemones live in oceans.

These animals are more complex than sponges. Their body is shaped like a hollow sac. The sac is open at one end. The hydra uses the opening in two ways. It is used for taking in food and for getting rid of wastes. The opening is surrounded by one or more rings of tentacles (ten'tə kəlz). A **tentacle** is a long, armlike part. The picture shows a hydra with six tentacles around the opening.

Hydras and jellyfish use their tentacles to catch small animals for food. Sea anemones catch food in the same way. The tentacles contain many stinging cells. A **stinging cell** is a special structure used to help capture food. How does a stinging cell help capture food? When a small animal

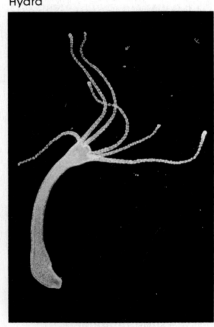

Hydra

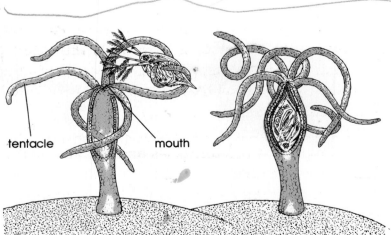

tentacle   mouth

HYDRA

comes close, the stinging cells explode. The explosion pushes tiny poisonous threads into the victim. These threads prevent the animal from moving. They may even kill it. The animal is then pushed into the mouth by the tentacles and swallowed. The drawing at the bottom of page 32 shows how the hydra captures and eats a tiny animal called a daphnia.

Sea anemone

Jellyfish

Portuguese man-of-war

Have you ever walked along a beach? Perhaps you have seen a clear blob floating in the water. This blob was a jellyfish. Jellyfish may have also washed up on the beach. If you stepped on a jellyfish, it could have given you a painful sting.

The Portuguese man-of-war is an animal similar to the jellyfish. It has tentacles and stinging cells. This is one animal that can be dangerous to people. A swimmer can be tangled in the tentacles. The stinging cells can cause a painful injury to the swimmer.

WORMS

What are the three main groups of worms?

Scientists classify worms into three main groups. These groups are the flatworms, the roundworms, and the segmented (seg'mən təd) worms. The structure of worms is more complex than that of sponges. It is more complex than the structure of the animals with stinging cells.

The first group of worms is the flatworms. The flatworm is the simplest type of worm. Some live in streams and ponds. What is the shape of a flatworm's body?

A common flatworm found in fresh water is the **planarian** (plə nār'ē ən). There are nerve cells in the head of the planarian. These cells act like a simple brain. Above this "brain" are two sense organs. An **organ** is a body part that does a certain job. These two sense organs are called eyespots. Eyespots can sense light. Can you find the eyespots on these planarians?

Planarians have a very unusual ability. They

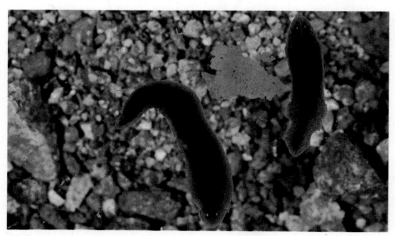

Planarians

can **regenerate** (ri jen′ə rāt), or regrow, body parts that are missing. For example, if their tail is cut off, planarians grow a new tail. If their head is cut off, a new head will grow. They can also regenerate part of their body. If a cut is made down the center of the head, two heads will grow. Look at the drawings of what these amazing animals can do!

Most flatworms are parasites. A **parasite** (par′ə sīt) is an animal or plant that depends on and harms another animal or plant. The animal or plant on which a parasite depends is the **host.** A parasite often depends on its host for food.

The tapeworm is an example of a flatworm that is a parasite. Tapeworms live in the digestive system of animals. A digestive (də jes′tiv) system is a group of body parts that breaks down food. A tapeworm does not have its own digestive system. The host animal does the eating and the digesting. The tapeworm takes in digested food through an opening in its body. It uses the host's food. The host loses weight and becomes weak. Some tapeworms may grow as long as 9 m.

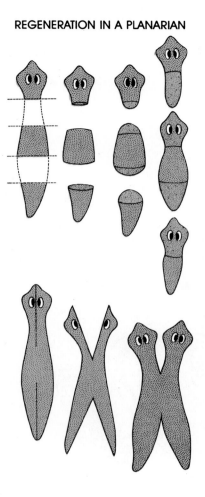

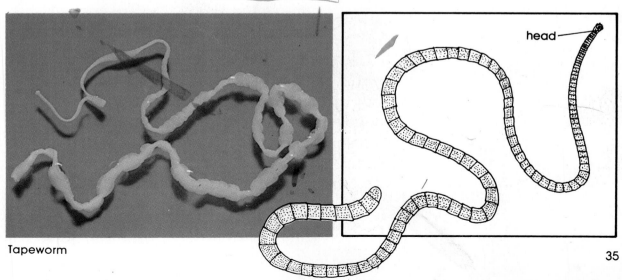

Tapeworm

35

The second group of worms is the roundworms. A **roundworm** is a worm that has a long tube-shaped body with a digestive system. The digestive system is made up of a tube that has an opening at each end. Food is taken in through the mouth opening. Wastes leave through the other opening. The drawing shows the two openings in the roundworm's body. Most roundworms live in soil, where they eat dead plant and animal matter. Other roundworms are parasites that live in host animals. Dogs must be treated to get rid of roundworms.

ROUNDWORM

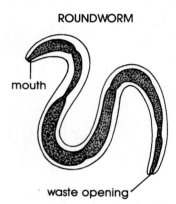

mouth

waste opening

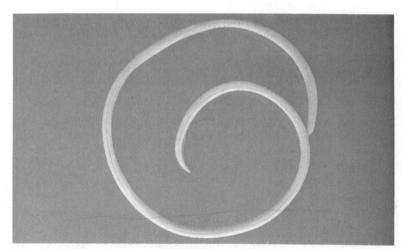

Roundworm

The third group of worms is the segmented worms. A **segmented worm** is a worm whose body is divided into segments, or sections. The segments look like a series of little rings. These segments are clearly shown in the picture of the worm on the next page.

Segmented worms are much more complex than flatworms or roundworms. A series of hearts pump blood through the worm's body. The blood

36

ANIMALS WITH SPINY SKIN

What are echinoderms, and how do they look?

If you have ever been to the seashore, you may have seen some echinoderms (i kĭ'nə dėrmz). An **echinoderm** is a spiny-skinned invertebrate that lives in the ocean. A spine is a sharp, pointy structure. The body of an echinoderm is hard and covered with spines. Some of these animals have short spines. Others have long spines. The pictures show some well-known echinoderms.

A common echinoderm is the starfish. Most starfish have five arms that come out from the center part of the animal. On the underside of each arm are two rows of tiny tube feet. A **tube foot** is a hollow structure with a sucker at the end. Most echinoderms have tube feet. The picture shows a closeup of the tube feet on a starfish.

The starfish uses its tube feet to pull itself over the ocean floor. Tube feet also help the starfish

Sea cucumber

Sand dollars

Starfish

Close-up of tube feet

39

get food. When a starfish finds a clam, it begins a kind of tug-of-war. The clam protects itself by tightly closing its two shells together. The starfish attaches its tube feet to both shells and begins pulling. It tries to pry the shells apart. Sometimes the tug-of-war goes on for a long time. But the starfish almost always wins.

Tube feet pulling open shellfish

Starfish attacking shellfish

Regenerating body parts

The starfish eats both oysters and clams. So people who gather this seafood do not like starfish. In the past, these people tried to get rid of starfish by cutting them into pieces. They threw the pieces back into the ocean. Instead of solving their problems, they made them worse. Some of the starfish pieces grew into whole new starfish. Why did this happen? The starfish is an animal with a very unusual ability. Like the planarian, it can regenerate, or regrow, body parts that are missing. When the pieces of starfish were thrown into the water, the number of starfish really got larger. Each piece grew into a whole new starfish.

— ANIMALS WITH A SOFT BODY —
What are mollusks, and how do they look?

The clam and the octopus belong to a group of animals called the mollusks (mol′əsks). A **mollusk** is an invertebrate with a soft body. Some mollusks have two outer shells. Others live inside a one-piece shell or have no shell at all. Many mollusks live in the ocean. Others live in fresh water or on land.

The body of a mollusk is more complex than the body of an echinoderm. For example, the mollusk has the beginning of a true eye. The picture shows the eyes on the body of a scallop. Mollusks also have a more complex system for pumping blood. Blood is pumped through blood vessels into spaces in the animal's body.

Scallop with tiny blue eyes

Foot of scallop

Oyster

Clams, oysters, and scallops are two-shelled mollusks. The shells are held together by muscles. The muscles open and close the shells like a hinge. The two-shelled mollusks have a part called a foot. This foot, made of a strong muscle, is used for digging. It is also used for pulling the animal along the ocean floor. Notice the foot of the scallop in the picture.

Snails and slugs are other common mollusks. Both have a large muscular foot. The foot gives off a layer of slime. Snails and slugs glide along on this layer of slime. The main difference between a slug and a snail is the shell. Usually slugs do not

Land snail on leaf

Slug

have a shell, while snails have a shell. The snail's shell protects it from enemies. When in danger, the snail can hide inside its shell. Some other mollusks in this group are limpets and periwinkles (per′ə wing kəlz). These two mollusks are shown in the pictures.

Periwinkles

There are two other common mollusks that have no shell. These mollusks are the squid and the octopus. Both have long tentacles. The tentacles are lined with suckers. These suckers help them to catch other animals for food. The squid and the octopus have an unusual way to protect

Limpet

Octopus and close-up of suckers

Squid

themselves. They give off a cloud of dark liquid when they are in danger. This dark liquid, called ink, keeps them from being seen while they escape from their enemy.

Mollusks such as clams, oysters, and scallops are a source of food for many people. In some countries certain land snails are gathered and cooked for food. The abalone (ab ə lō′nē) is an ocean snail that is gathered by divers. Its foot is so large that it is cut up and served as abalone steaks. Squid and octopus are also favorite foods of many people.

Do you know?

There are invertebrates that produce pearls. Some oysters that live in tropical waters make pearls that are very valuable. Large, perfectly shaped pearls are as valuable as some of the most expensive diamonds. A pearl forms inside the shell of an oyster when a grain of sand or other particle enters the shell. Cells inside the oyster's shell produce a material called nacre (nā′kər) that forms around the particle. Nacre is also called mother-of-pearl. The particle becomes coated by many thin layers of nacre. After several years, the particle is completely covered. A bright, shiny pearl has been formed.

— ANIMALS WITH JOINTED LEGS —
What are the four main groups of arthropods?

The arthropods (är'thrə podz) make up the largest group of animals. Some people think there may be as many as 10 million types. An **arthropod** is an invertebrate that has a segmented body and jointed legs. The body has two or three segments. The number of jointed legs is used to divide the arthropods into groups. Can you find the three body segments on the pictures of the ant?

Segmented body of ant

SEGMENTS OF ANT

All arthropods have a hard outer covering. In some arthropods the covering is harder than in others. This hard outer covering is called the **exoskeleton** (ek sō skel'ə tən). It is like a skeleton on the outside of the animal's body. It protects the soft parts of the body. Arthropods also have well-developed sense organs and a head with special mouth parts.

Millipede

Centipede

There are four main groups of arthropods. The first group includes millipedes and centipedes. A millipede looks very much like a worm with many legs. The word *millipede* means "thousand legs." (*Milli-* means "thousand" and *-pede* means "foot.") Each segment of a millipede has two pairs of legs. The millipede is a harmless animal that eats plants. When in danger, it may curl up into a ball.

A centipede is also wormlike but has fewer legs than a millipede. The word *centipede* means "hundred legs." (*Centi-* means "hundred" and *-pede* means "foot.") Unlike a millipede the centipede eats other animals. It uses a pair of poison claws near its mouth to capture its food. With these claws the centipede can inject poison into another animal.

The second group of arthropods includes shrimps, lobsters, and crayfish. Animals in this

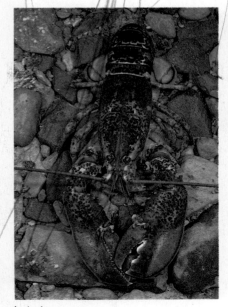

Lobster

Shrimp

group are also called **crustaceans** (krus tā'shənz). Almost all the arthropods in this group live in water. Shrimps and lobsters live in the ocean. Crayfish live in fresh water. Crustaceans have five pairs of legs. Their exoskeleton is divided into two main parts. These arthropods move by muscles attached to their exoskeleton.

Spider in web

The third group of arthropods includes animals such as spiders, ticks, and mites. These animals have four pairs of legs. They also have two main body parts. Most spiders are harmless. In fact, many are useful because they kill insects that are problems for people. You probably have seen spider webs. Why do you think spiders make webs?

Spider wrapping insect

47

A few spiders, such as the black widow, are poisonous. Ticks and mites are parasites that live by sucking blood from other animals. Ticks are also very annoying to pets, such as dogs and cats.

Black widow

Tick on skin

The fourth and largest group of arthropods is made up of insects. There are more different kinds of insects than all other animals and plants. An insect is an arthropod that has three pairs of legs and a body that is divided into three parts. The three parts of the body are the head, the abdomen (ab′də mən), and the thorax (thôr′aks). The **abdomen** is the rear part of an insect's body. The **thorax** is the middle part of an insect's body. Wings and legs are joined to the thorax. The drawing shows the three main parts of an insect's body.

PARTS OF AN INSECT

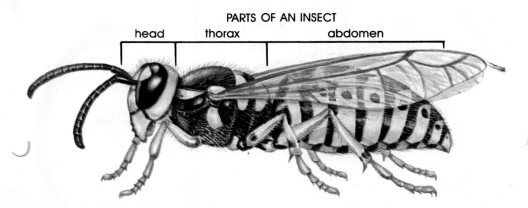
head   thorax   abdomen

Compound eyes of insect

Close-up of compound eye

Insects have very unusual sense organs. Most adult insects have compound eyes. The compound eye has thousands of lenses, as you can see in the picture. It lets the insect see motion. For example, bees can see flowers moving in a slight breeze. But they cannot see the details of the flower.

An insect's head has two feelers, or antennae (an ten'ē). The **antennae** help the insect smell and feel. Sometimes the antennae are used for tasting and hearing.

Antennae

49

Can you create an insect?

Materials egg carton / 8 pipe cleaners / several small buttons / scraps of fabric / 8 Styrofoam balls, 4 each of 2 different sizes / glue / construction paper / felt-tip pens / twist-ties / scissors / clay

Procedure

A. Use your imagination! Create your own insect. The insect does not have to look like any known insect. But it must have all the body parts needed by an insect.
  1. How many body parts will your insect have?
  2. How many legs will your insect have?

B. You may use any of the materials supplied. You may bend and twist the pipe cleaners and the twist-ties. You may glue parts of the body together.
  3. What are the names of the three parts of your insect's body?
  4. To what parts of the insect's body are the legs attached?

C. Try giving your insect special mouth parts. Decide whether you want your insect to chew, suck, or pierce with its mouth parts.
  5. Is your insect beginning to look like any insect you have seen? Which one?

D. Be sure you add antennae to your insect's head.
  6. How does an insect use its antennae?

Conclusion

1. Insects have four common characteristics. What are they?

2. List all the parts of your insect. Next to each write what it does.

Using science ideas

Describe the type of surroundings where your insect might live.

Insects have special mouth parts. These parts are formed for chewing, sucking, or piercing. The kind of mouth parts an insect has depends on the food it eats. For example, beetles and grasshoppers eat leaves. Their mouths have parts that cut and chew. Butterflies and moths have mouth parts that suck up juices from flowers. Mosquitoes have mouth parts for piercing the skin and sucking blood.

TYPES OF MOUTH PARTS

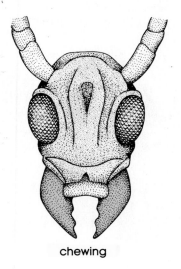
chewing

sucking

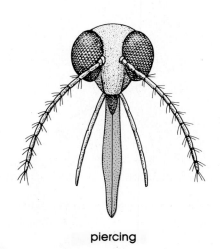
piercing

Chewing mouth parts

Sucking mouth parts

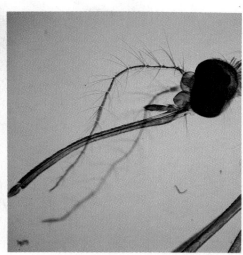
Piercing mouth parts

Dragonfly molting

An insect's body is covered with an exoskeleton. The exoskeleton does not grow as the insect grows. When the covering gets too small, the insect molts (mōlts). To **molt** is to shed the hard outer covering. The exoskeleton splits down the middle. The insect then works its way out. Once the old covering is shed, the insect forms a new exoskeleton.

Insects are both harmful and helpful. Some insects feed on other insects that destroy crops. The ladybug is an example of this type of helpful insect. Many insects are also an important source of food for fish, birds, frogs, and other animals.

Many insects are pests. An insect called the boll weevil (bōl wē′vəl) damages the cotton crop. Termites, which live on wood, can destroy homes made mainly of wood. Some insects can carry disease to animals and people. A mosquito carries the serious disease called malaria. Insects are both helpful and harmful.

Boll weevils

IDEAS TO REMEMBER

▶ Scientists classify animals in groups by features that are alike.

▶ An animal with a backbone is called a vertebrate. An animal without a backbone is called an invertebrate.

▶ A sponge is an invertebrate with a simple body full of pores. The pores are connected to one another by narrow canals.

▶ Hydra, jellyfish, and sea anemone are invertebrates with stinging cells and tentacles.

▶ Scientists classify worms into three groups—flatworms, roundworms, and segmented worms.

▶ An echinoderm is a spiny-skinned invertebrate that lives in ocean waters.

▶ A mollusk is an invertebrate with a soft body. Some mollusks have two outer shells; some live inside a one-piece shell; others have no shell at all.

▶ An arthropod is an invertebrate that has a segmented body, jointed legs, and a hard outer covering.

Reviewing the Chapter

SCIENCE WORDS

A. Copy the sentences below. Use science terms from the chapter to complete each sentence.

1. Scientists _____ animals by their structure.
2. Shrimps, lobsters, and clams are examples of _____.
3. Another name for spiny-skinned animal is _____.
4. To shed the hard outer covering is to _____.
5. The animal or plant on which a parasite lives is the _____.

B. Write the letter of the term that best matches the definition. Not all the terms will be used.

1. Animal with a segmented body and jointed legs
2. Segmented worm
3. Wormlike animal with many legs
4. Invertebrate with a body full of holes
5. Animal or plant that depends on and harms another animal or plant
6. Middle part of an insect's body
7. Hard outer covering
8. Hollow structure with a sucker at the end
9. Insect's feelers
10. Flatworm that has two eye-spots

a. stinging cell
b. planarian
c. tube foot
d. earthworm
e. exoskeleton
f. arthropod
g. sponge
h. tentacle
i. antennae
j. parasite
k. centipede
l. thorax

UNDERSTANDING IDEAS

A. Write the correct term for each number in the diagram.

antenna   thorax   jointed leg
abdomen   mouth part   head

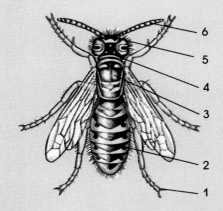

B. Make a chart like the one shown. Write the correct information under each heading. Then choose two of the groups. Explain how to tell animals in one group apart from animals in the other group.

Group	Special body part	Example
Sponges Animals with stinging cells Segmented worms Animals with spiny skin Animals with hard shells Animals with jointed legs		

USING IDEAS

1. Collect or draw pictures of each of the groups of invertebrates you have studied in this chapter. Make a chart of these pictures.

Chapter 3

Animals With a Backbone

Can you imagine a baby that has a mass of over 7,000 kg and is over 7 m long? This is the mass and length of a baby blue whale when it is born. Its mother may have a mass of over 110,000 kg!

The blue whale belongs to a group of animals called the vertebrates. Vertebrates are animals with a backbone. There are five main groups of vertebrates. Fish, frogs, snakes, birds, and dogs are examples of animals from each main group. In this chapter you will learn about the animals from each of the groups. You will see how the animals are different and how they are alike.

Blue whale

FISH

What are the main characteristics of fish?

Fish are vertebrates that live in water. They are cold-blooded animals. A **cold-blooded animal** is an animal whose body temperature changes with the temperature of the water or air around it. When the air or water around such an animal is cold, the animal becomes cold. A cold-blooded animal becomes warm when the air or water around it is warm.

The skeleton (skel'ə tən) of a fish is simpler than that of other vertebrates. Most fish have skeletons made of bone. The shark and the sting-ray have skeletons made of cartilage (kär'tə lij). So some scientists believe that sharks and sting-rays are not true fish. **Cartilage** is a soft, bonelike material that bends. You can feel cartilage in the tip of your nose.

Most fish are covered with scales. A scale is a flat bony structure. Scales cover the body of a fish and protect it. Fish also have fins. A **fin** is a struc-

Trout

Shark

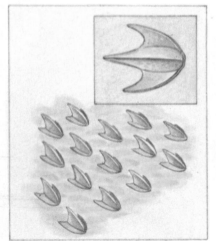
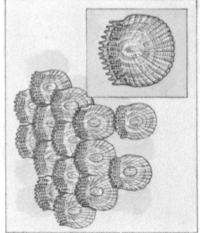
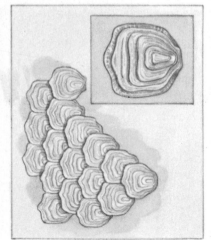

TYPES OF FISH SCALES

ture on a fish that helps it move through the water. The drawing shows the different fins on a fish. How many fins can you count on this fish?

Almost all living things need oxygen. Animals that live on land get oxygen from the air. You may wonder how fish get oxygen under water. There is oxygen dissolved in the water. Fish take in the oxygen found in water through their gills. **Gills** are thin, feathery structures that are filled with blood. Fish use gills for breathing. To breathe, a fish takes water into its mouth. The

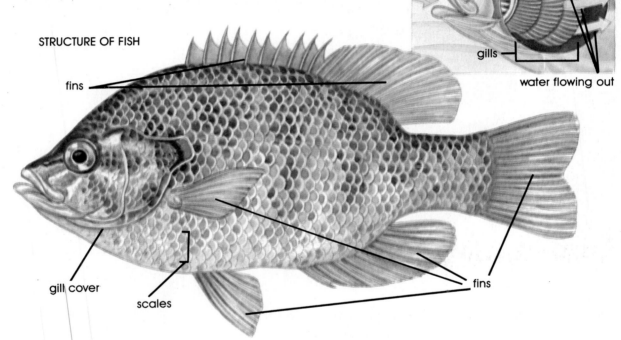

HOW GILLS WORK

gill cover cut away

water flowing in

gills

water flowing out

STRUCTURE OF FISH

fins

gill cover

scales

fins

water then flows over the gills. Oxygen from the water goes into the blood in the gills. The blood in the gills picks up a waste material from the rest of the fish's body. This waste material is carbon dioxide. The carbon dioxide passes through the gills and then out of the body into the water. This is how the fish breathes under water.

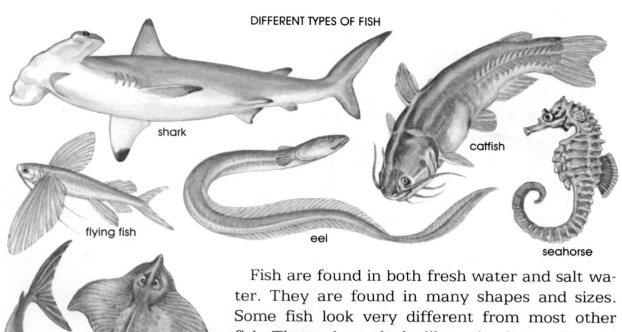

shark

catfish

flying fish

eel

seahorse

skate

swordfish

Fish are found in both fresh water and salt water. They are found in many shapes and sizes. Some fish look very different from most other fish. The seahorse looks like a tiny horse. The eel has a long slender body and small scales.

Fish are a major source of food for people. For thousands of years fish have been gathered from streams, rivers, and oceans. Each year about 66 billion kg of fish are caught. This is enough to feed each person on earth about 17 kg of fish a year.

Finding out

What does a fish scale tell about the age of a fish?
Each year a fish adds another ring to its scales. You can tell the age of a fish by counting the rings in its scales. You will need a hand lens and some fish scales. Look at the fish scales with a hand lens. Count the number of rings on one scale. How many rings are there? How old is the fish? Do all the scales you looked at have the same number of rings? Try looking at the scales of other fish.

AMPHIBIANS

What are the main characteristics of amphibians?

An **amphibian** (am fib'ē ən) is a cold-blooded vertebrate that lives part of its life in water and part on land. Frogs, toads, and salamanders are some common amphibians. The outside of an amphibian's body is usually moist and slimy. Amphibians do not have scales.

Bullfrog

Southern toad

Most adult amphibians live on land. They return to water to lay their eggs. A few amphibians spend almost their entire life in water. These include bullfrogs and some salamanders, such as mud puppies.

SALAMANDER

Gills of mud puppy

Most adult amphibians breathe through lungs. **Lungs** are organs through which animals get oxygen from air. The mud puppy does not have lungs. It has gills outside its body through which it can breathe under water. Amphibians with lungs cannot live completely in water. They must come to the surface to breathe air. Amphibians can also get oxygen through their skin.

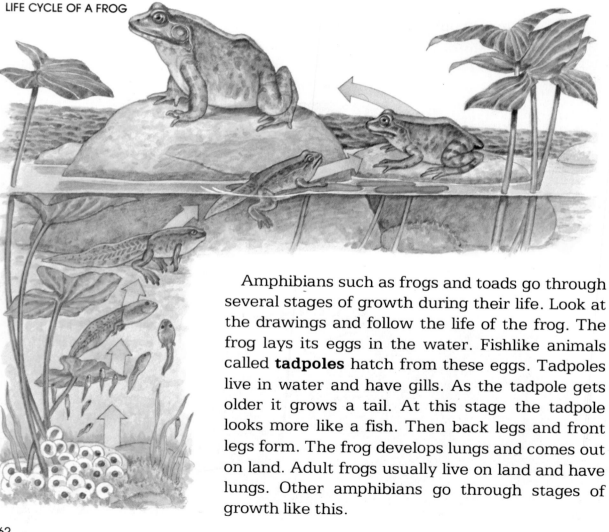
LIFE CYCLE OF A FROG

Amphibians such as frogs and toads go through several stages of growth during their life. Look at the drawings and follow the life of the frog. The frog lays its eggs in the water. Fishlike animals called **tadpoles** hatch from these eggs. Tadpoles live in water and have gills. As the tadpole gets older it grows a tail. At this stage the tadpole looks more like a fish. Then back legs and front legs form. The frog develops lungs and comes out on land. Adult frogs usually live on land and have lungs. Other amphibians go through stages of growth like this.

REPTILES

What are the main characteristics of reptiles?

A **reptile** (rep'tīl) is a cold-blooded vertebrate that has lungs and dry skin. Almost all reptiles have scales. Most reptiles live on land and lay eggs. Some give birth to live young. The eggs of reptiles are laid on land. These eggs have a tough covering that prevents the eggs from drying out on land.

There are four main groups of reptiles. These are the alligators and crocodiles, the snakes, the lizards, and the turtles.

Pine snakes hatching from eggs

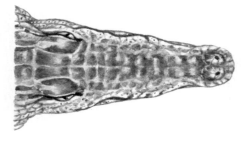

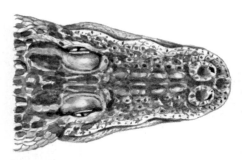

Alligators and crocodiles make up one group of reptiles. They are large four-legged reptiles. They look alike, but their color and the shape of their snout help to tell them apart. Crocodiles are green and gray, while alligators are gray and black. Crocodiles have a more slender and pointed snout than do alligators. The two drawings show how the crocodile and the alligator are different. Can you tell them apart?

Snakes make up the largest group of reptiles. They do not have legs, and their bodies are covered with thin scales. Snakes can be large or they can be small. The anaconda, from South America, can be more than 9 m long. The thread snake is only about 12 cm long.

Anaconda

Snake eating mouse and snake's curved teeth

Snakes have an interesting way of eating. They swallow their food whole. The picture shows a snake with a whole mouse in its mouth. Most of the things snakes eat are larger than their mouth. When a snake eats an animal larger than its mouth, the snake's lower jaw separates from the upper jaw. This allows the snake's mouth to open very wide. Also, the snake's teeth are curved backward. This makes it hard for an animal to escape from the snake's jaws.

Another group of reptiles is the lizards. There are many different kinds of lizards. Many live in deserts and other hot, dry areas. Lizards have claws on their toes, as shown in the picture. The body of a lizard is covered with scales.

Lizard and clawed foot

Chameleon

The chameleon (kə mē′lē ən) is one of the most interesting lizards. Chameleons live in trees and catch insects for food. They can change color. These lizards can change from brown to green to gray. The chameleon in the picture is changing color. These changes help these animals to blend in with their surroundings. How can this be helpful?

Turtles make up the last group of reptiles. The body of a turtle is protected by a shell. When in danger, a turtle pulls its legs and head into its shell. How does this help it to survive? The turtles in the picture are box turtles. They can close their shells very tightly. Some turtles live on land. Others spend most of their time in water.

Box turtles

BIRDS

What are the main characteristics of birds?

Birds are warm-blooded animals that are covered with feathers. A **warm-blooded animal** is an animal whose body temperature stays the same even when the temperature of the air or water around it changes. Birds are vertebrates with lungs. Like reptiles, birds lay eggs. Their eggs are in a hard shell. Wings and feathers make birds different from other vertebrates. Most birds use their wings to fly. Some birds, such as penguins, have feathers and wings but cannot fly. Birds can be found living on land, in trees, and on water. What birds can be found on water?

Penguins

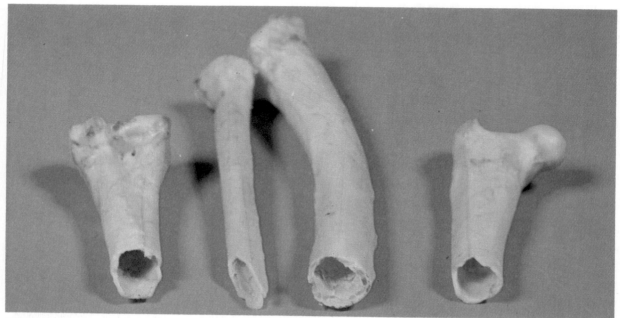
Bird bones

The bones and feathers of birds are made in a special way to help birds fly. The bones are hollow and light. The feathers have a hollow central shaft. This shaft makes feathers strong but light. Some large birds may have as many as 25,000 feathers. All birds lose and replace their feathers during a year. This regular loss of feathers is called molting.

The major use of feathers is to help birds to fly. Feathers are also needed to keep birds warm. Some birds fluff their feathers when they are cold. This fluffing forms more air spaces between the feathers and helps to keep the birds warm. Ducks and geese have small fluffy feathers called **down** near their skin. Down traps air and helps to keep the birds warm. Perhaps you have a jacket or blanket filled with down. These small feathers help to keep your body warm.

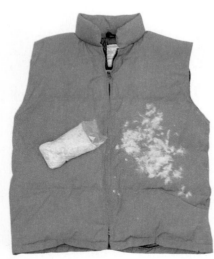
Down feathers

Oyster catcher

Snowy egret and young

Because birds are very active animals, they need a great deal of energy. So they eat a lot of food. Some birds spend most of their life hunting for food. The diet of birds is varied. Some birds eat nuts, while others eat seeds. Birds such as the one shown above eat oysters. Birds living near the water sometimes eat fish that they spear with their beaks. Still others, such as ducks and the flamingo below, eat tiny water plants and animals.

Flamingo

Nests of weaverbirds

Nest of plover

Birds show a great variety in nests and nest building. The nests of some birds are built by the male bird. Others are built by the female bird. Still others are built by both male and female. Nests are of all shapes and sizes. Some nests, such as those of the weaverbirds, are extremely large. As many as 600 birds may work together to build huge nests. Nests can be made of twigs, leaves, or feathers. They can also be made of mud or other substances that birds find. Nests can hang from tree branches or rest on the ground. Some nests are even built under piles of rotting leaves.

Some birds can be harmful to people. For example, pigeons can carry diseases that harm people's lungs. Pigeons are also pests because they damage buildings.

70

What is the structure of a bird's feather and a bird's bone?

Materials bird feather / scissors / hand lens / chicken bone / pliers / beef bone

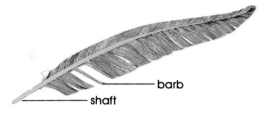

barb

shaft

Procedure

A. Look at the drawing of the bird feather on this page. Point out the central shaft and the side branches. Each side branch is called a barb.

B. Look at a bird feather. Find the central shaft. Use scissors to cut through the central shaft.
  1. Is the central shaft hollow or solid?

C. Find the barbs on the feather. Gently pull some of the barbs apart. Then put them together by pulling them through your fingers.
  2. Why do you think the barbs can be locked together?

D. Look at the feather with a hand lens. Draw the feather as you see it through a hand lens.

E. Look at a chicken bone. Break it in half with pliers.
  3. Describe what you see inside the chicken bone.

F. Compare the chicken bone with the beef bone.
  4. What are the differences between the chicken bone and the beef bone?

Conclusion

1. Describe a few important features of a feather and a chicken bone. What features of a bird's feathers and bones help it to fly?
2. Why is a beef bone not suitable for flight?

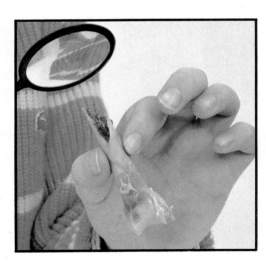

MAMMALS

What are the main characteristics of mammals?

The most complex group of vertebrates is the mammals. A mammal is a warm-blooded vertebrate that is usually covered with fur or hair. Mammals are different from other vertebrates in two main ways. First, the body of a mammal is all or partly covered with fur or hair. A very hairy mammal is the gorilla. A mammal with just a small amount of hair is the elephant.

A second way mammals differ from other vertebrates is that all mammals produce milk for their young. The picture shows springer spaniel puppies getting milk from their mother.

Springer spaniel and pups

Mammals differ from each other in many ways. Most mammals live on land. A few mammals, such as whales and dolphins, live in water. There are great differences in the size of mammals. The blue whale is the largest mammal. It can grow to be as long as 32 m and have a mass of over

110,000 kg. The common shrew is one of the smallest mammals. It is only about 10 cm long and has a mass of less than 3 g. These tiny mammals are insect eaters.

Shrew

Do you know?

Suppose you find an animal that looks like this: It has a duck's bill and webbed feet. It has a tail like a beaver and fur on its body. It feeds its young milk. Strangely, it also lays eggs. How would you classify this animal? Is it a bird? Is it a reptile? Is it a mammal? This strange animal is an egg-laying mammal. It is called a duck-billed platypus (plat' ə pəs). The platypus lives in and around Australia.

The young of most mammals develop inside the mother's body. Some mammals produce a large number of young at one time. For example, mice may give birth to as many as eight to ten young. Large mammals, such as elephants, usually have only one baby. The time needed for the young to grow inside the mother's body is not always the same. It varies from one kind of mammal to another. Large mammals take longer to grow than small mammals. A small mammal such as a hamster grows in 16 days. A large mammal such as a giraffe takes about 442 days. Dogs take about 63 days to grow in the mother's body. Whales grow in about 450 days.

Elephant and baby

IDEAS TO REMEMBER

▶ Vertebrates are animals with a backbone.

▶ There are five major groups of vertebrates. These are fish, amphibians, reptiles, birds, and mammals.

▶ A fish is a cold-blooded vertebrate with fins. It uses gills to breathe under water. Most fish have scales.

▶ An amphibian is a cold-blooded vertebrate that lives part of its life in water and part on land.

▶ A reptile is a cold-blooded vertebrate that has lungs and dry skin. Most reptiles have scales and live on land.

▶ A bird is a warm-blooded vertebrate that has feathers and wings.

▶ A mammal is a warm-blooded vertebrate that is usually covered with fur or hair. It feeds its young milk.

Reviewing the Chapter

SCIENCE WORDS

A. Write the letter of the term that best matches the definition. Not all the terms will be used.

1. Soft, bonelike material in a shark's skeleton
2. Thin, feathery structures filled with blood and used in breathing
3. Type of animal whose body temperature stays the same even when surrounding temperature changes
4. Cold-blooded vertebrate with lungs and dry skin
5. Small fluffy feathers near the skin
6. Structures that help fish move through water
7. Animal with a backbone
8. Warm-blooded vertebrate covered with fur or hair

a. warm-blooded
b. cartilage
c. down
d. cold-blooded
e. reptile
f. mammal
g. vertebrate
h. fins
i. gills

B. Identify each of the following.

1. It is a cold-blooded vertebrate. Its body is covered with scales. It can change color for protection. What is it?
2. It is a cold-blooded vertebrate. It hatches from an egg. It is fishlike. It will change into a frog. What is it?

UNDERSTANDING IDEAS

A. The pictures show the stages in the life cycle of a frog. Write the numbers of the pictures to show the correct order. Then describe what is happening in each stage.

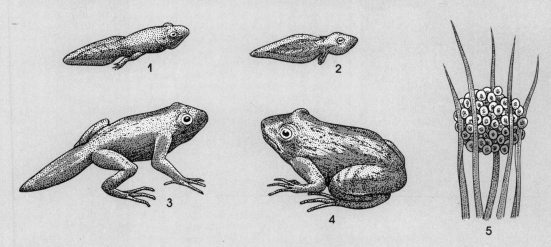

B. Each of the body parts belongs to one of the animals shown. Match the body part to the correct animal.

1. Gills inside the body
2. Pouch for developing young
3. Scaly skin and feet with claws
4. Gills outside the body
5. Teeth that curve backward
6. Skeleton made of cartilage

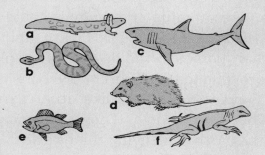

NG IDEAS

eep a diary for a week. List all the vertebrates that you during this time. You may include live animals as well as those you might see on television or in films.

Chapter 4

Living Communities

The picture shows a place in a desert in Arizona. A desert is a hot, dry place. It does not seem like a place where plants and animals could live. Yet snakes, lizards, insects, birds, rats, and rabbits make their homes in the desert. What plants do you see growing in the desert?

In many ways the desert is like other parts of the earth. There are living and nonliving things in all parts of the earth. The living things affect each other and are also affected by the nonliving things around them. And the living things affect the nonliving things. In this chapter you will learn about the ways in which living and nonliving things affect each other. You will also learn about different ways in which the living and nonliving parts of our world can change.

— THE LIVING AND NONLIVING — WORLD

What is an ecosystem?

All living things are surrounded by other living things. They are also surrounded by nonliving things. These living and nonliving things affect each other. Everything that surrounds and affects a living thing is called its **environment** (en vī′rən-mənt). What are some living things in your home environment? What are some nonliving things? In what ways do these living and nonliving things affect each other? The study of how living and nonliving things affect each other is called **ecology** (ē kol′ə jē). Scientists who study this subject are called ecologists.

Look at the picture of the fish tank. What living and nonliving things do you see? The living and nonliving things in the tank affect, or interact with, each other. Both the fish and the plants need water to survive. The plants give off oxygen, which goes into the water. The fish, which

need oxygen to live, take the oxygen from the water. As they breathe, the fish give off carbon dioxide. The plants use the carbon dioxide to make food. Without the fish, the plants would die. And without the plants, the fish would die.

The fish tank is an example of an ecosystem (ē′kə sis təm). An **ecosystem** is a group of living things and their nonliving environment. An ecosystem includes all the ways the living things in a group interact with each other. It also includes the way living things interact with their nonliving environment.

An ecosystem can be as small as a single fish and a single plant in a fishbowl. Or an ecosystem can be as large as a forest, a desert, or an ocean. Look at the picture of the city park. The park is an ecosystem that may contain several smaller ecosystems. For example, under a rock you may find a small ecosystem that has many kinds of living things. A single tree in the park may be another ecosystem. The tree may be the home of squirrels, birds, and insects. Nongreen plants as well as green plants may also live on the tree.

Ecosystem under a rock

City park

– LIVING THINGS IN ECOSYSTEMS –
What are communities and populations?

You have learned that an ecosystem is made up of living and nonliving things. The living things in an ecosystem are known as a community (kə-myü'nə tē). A **community** is all the plants and animals that live and interact with each other in a place.

Communities are often named for the kind of place in which they live. There are forest, marsh, and pond communities. What are some other kinds of communities?

Communities are made up of populations (pop-yə lā'shənz). A **population** is a group of the same kind of living thing in a community. For example, all the pine trees in this forest make up one population. It is a population of pine trees. Which picture shows a population of grass plants? What other populations are shown?

84

Every living thing in a community has a special place in which it is usually found. The special place in a community in which a plant or animal lives is called its **habitat** (hab′ə tat). You can think of an ecosystem as the neighborhood that a living thing is part of. The habitat can be thought of as its address in that neighborhood.

Some forest habitats

Elf owl in nest in saguaro cactus

Within a community there are many habitats. In a forest the soil is the habitat of ants and earthworms. A rotten tree stump is the habitat of termites. Squirrels live in the trees. Mosses grow on the forest floor, in the shade of trees. Ants and earthworms, termites, squirrels, and mosses each have their own habitat. But these living things are all part of the same community.

The populations and habitats in a desert are different from those in a forest. Look at the picture. The cactus plant is the habitat of the elf owl. The habitats of many other desert animals are burrows under the ground.

Mouse in city building

Mouse in country field

The habitat of a plant or animal supplies it with many of the things that it needs to survive. Some living things are able to live in more than one habitat. Others can live in only one habitat. For example, flies can live in many habitats. They move to different places to get food. Mice can also live in more than one habitat. They are found in city buildings as well as in country fields.

Some animals are very limited in their habitat. Trout can only live in cool streams. The koala (kō-ä'lə) of Australia eats only one kind of plant. It eats the leaves of the eucalyptus (yü kə lip'təs) tree. So the koala can only live where this kind of tree grows. Food also limits the habitat of the panda. It only eats bamboo. How many different hàbitats could you live in?

Koala eating eucalyptus leaf

Panda eating bamboo

Many plants and animals share the same habitat. Earthworms share the soil with many plants. Termites share a rotten tree stump with ants and other insects. Birds share their tree habitat with squirrels. Although they share the same habitat, the way these animals live may be very different from each other. The role that each living thing plays in a habitat is called its **niche** (nich).

Female cardinal

Red squirrel

Some squirrels and birds share the same habitat. Yet these animals each have a different niche. Squirrels gather nuts and stay close to their habitat. Some birds are insect eaters. They travel great distances from their habitat to get food. Both animals share the same habitat. But they do not have a great effect on each other.

Sometimes the niche of one population does affect other populations. A creek is the habitat of a population of beavers. The beavers build dams across the creek. The dams they build create ponds. The ponds become the habitat of fish and plants. The beavers also cut down many trees. How does this affect the tree population?

Beaver cutting down tree and building dam

CHANGES IN POPULATIONS
What factors affect the size of a population?

Ecologists study communities of living things. They try to find out what living things are present. They also want to know the size of each population. They try to learn whether the populations are changing in size. Ecologists want to know if populations are getting larger, getting smaller, or staying the same.

Ecologist studying a bird population

When an animal population changes in size, it often means there is a change in the birth rate or the death rate. The birth rate is the number of animals that are born in a period of time. What is the death rate? Many factors can cause a change in the birth rate or the death rate.

Young male white-tailed deer eating

Why might the birth rate of a population go up? Suppose a deer population has a large supply of food and water. Deer eat plants. If the deer are healthy, many will live long enough to produce young deer. So the birth rate will go up.

As the birth rate goes up, the deer population will get larger. After a while, the kinds of plants that deer eat will be scarce. Some deer may move away in search of food. What will this do to the size of the deer population? The deer that stay will still have little food. Some deer will get sick and die. Other deer may become very weak. They may be unable to run from other animals that hunt them for food.

Buck and does, members of a white-tailed deer population

The size of a population may also change because of a sudden change in the amount of food that can be found. Suppose a fire or a disease destroys the deer's food source. Then the death rate of the deer population would go up. As the death rate goes up, population size goes down.

— CHANGES IN COMMUNITIES —
What is succession and what causes it?

You learned that a sudden major change, such as a fire, can affect the size of populations. Sudden changes can also affect whole communities.

On May 18, 1980, a volcano in Washington erupted. The volcano, Mount St. Helens, exploded with great force. The force was equal to almost 10 million metric tons of dynamite. One picture shows how the area looked before the blast. The other shows the same area 4 months

Mount St. Helens before the eruption

Mount St. Helens 4 months after the eruption

Trees blown down by eruption

after the blast. Millions of trees were blown down. Many plants were burned or covered with layers of ash as much as 180 m deep. Scientists believe that thousands of bear, deer, and other animals lost their lives. Few living things in the area survived.

A fire destroyed many square kilometers of the forest below. Trees, shrubs, grasses, and other plants were burned in the fire. Many animals were also killed. Among these were snakes, lizards, rabbits, and baby birds. Some animals were able to escape the fire, and so they lived. But many of the animals that lived lost their food supply and their habitat.

Colorado forest destroyed by fire

People also cause changes in communities. The picture shows a major change in a redwood forest. People are cutting down the trees to use the wood. What changes might result from clearing the trees in this forest? In what ways are these changes like the changes from a forest fire? What are some living things that will lose their habitat?

People clearing a redwood forest

Finding out

What changes have occurred in your environment? Interview some adults who have lived in your neighborhood for a long time. Find out what the area was like many years ago. What changes have there been? Find out whether each change was brought about by people or was a natural change.

Ask about the kinds of plants and animals that lived in the neighborhood. Find out how these living things were affected by each change. Be sure to ask about the effect that the changes might have had on people.

What happens after a sudden major change destroys an ecosystem? The same community does not come back right away. It may take 100 or more years for it to return. During this time there are many changes in the kinds of living things in an ecosystem. The series of changes in the communities of an ecosystem is called **succession** (sək sesh'ən).

These drawings show succession in a forest after a fire.

1. Before the fire a forest of beech and maple trees is the habitat of many living things.
2. A fire burns the trees and other plants.
3. Several years after the fire the area has become a field. There are grasses and other low plants. Insects, birds, groundhogs, and other animals live in the field.
4. In a few years shrubs and young trees grow.
5. The beech and maple trees reappear after 100 years. What animals live in the forest?

Ecologists have found that there are different stages in the succession of any ecosystem. The first stage of succession is called the **pioneer** (pī ə-nir') **stage.** What is the number of the drawing that shows the pioneer stage in the succession of the forest? This picture shows the beginning of the pioneer stage after the Mount St. Helens blast. New plants are growing out of the ash.

The last stage in the process of succession is called the **climax** (klī'maks) **stage.** Which drawing shows the climax stage? The climax stage in a community is usually stable. This means that it rarely changes. What might cause it to change?

Pioneer stage, Mount St. Helens

Many times succession does not result from a sudden change. Succession is more often a natural process in an ecosystem. These drawings show succession in a pond community.

1. Many kinds of plants and animals live in and around the pond. Each year some animals and many plants die and sink to the bottom.
2. After many years the remains of once-living things form soil and the pond fills in.
3. As the pond fills in, a marsh develops. The marsh plants grow and die.
4. In time the marsh dries up and a field develops. Grasses and shrubs grow in the field. A few years later trees appear.
5. Finally a forest community develops. What is this last stage of succession called?

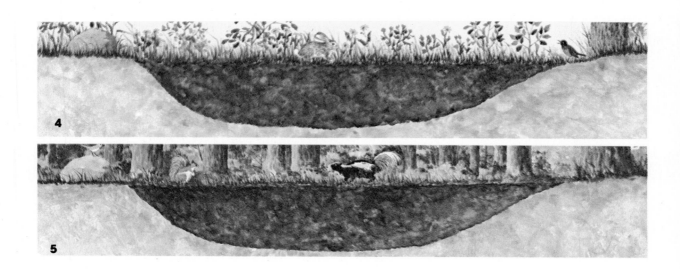

IDEAS TO REMEMBER

▶ The environment is everything that surrounds and affects a living thing.

▶ An ecosystem is a group of living things, their nonliving environment, and the interactions between them.

▶ A community is all the plants and animals that live and interact with each other in a place.

▶ A population is a group of the same kind of living thing in a community.

▶ A habitat is the special place in a community in which a plant or animal lives.

▶ The role that each living thing plays in its habitat is called its niche.

▶ Many factors affect the size of populations.

▶ Succession is the series of changes in the communities of an ecosystem.

Reviewing the Chapter

SCIENCE WORDS

A. Copy the sentences below. Use science terms from the chapter to complete each sentence.

1. A group of living things and their environment is a/an _____ .

2. The series of changes in the communities of an ecosystem is called _____ .

3. All the plants and animals that live and interact with each other in a place is called a/an _____ .

4. The special place in a community in which a plant or animal lives is called its _____ .

5. The study of how living and nonliving things affect each other is called _____ .

6. Everything that surrounds and affects a living thing is called its _____ .

7. The last stage of succession is called the _____ stage.

8. A group of the same kind of living thing in a community is called a/an _____ .

9. The role that each living thing plays in a habitat is called its _____ .

10. The first stage of succession is called the _____ stage.

B. Identify each of the following.

1. It is an animal that hunts other animals for food. What is it?

2. It is an animal. It is hunted by other animals for food. What is it?

UNDERSTANDING IDEAS

A. A *cause* makes things happen. An *effect* is what happens. For each pair of sentences, write which is the cause and which is the effect.

1. **a.** A population of predators increases in size.
   b. A population of prey increases in size.
2. **a.** A marsh develops.
   b. Many plants and animals die and sink to the bottom of a shallow pond.
3. **a.** A population of predators increases in size.
   b. A population of prey decreases in size.
4. **a.** Many members of a deer population starve to death.
   b. A fire burns all the plants in a forest.

B. Write the number of the drawings to show the right order. Then describe what is happening at each stage.

1   2   3

USING IDEAS

1. Collect old magazines and cut out pictures that show different communities. List as many plant and animal populations as you can see in each.

Science in Careers

Many people who have pets know that working with animals can be both rewarding and fun. Some people who like animals choose careers in which they take care of animals.

A *veterinarian* (vet ər ə när′ē ən) is an animal doctor. Veterinarians treat animals that are ill or injured. They also give checkups to animals.

Veterinarian

Animal keepers take care of animals in places such as zoos and circuses. Animal keepers see that the animals are properly fed and sheltered. They also check that the animal cages are kept clean and in good repair.

If you have an interest in plants, you may want to prepare for a career as a *botanist* (bot′ə nist). Botanists are scientists who study plants. Many botanists are teachers or researchers.

Botanist

Flowers are used to add beauty indoors and outdoors. They can help people express feelings. A *floral designer* is someone who arranges flowers into designs for other people. Classes in flower arranging are offered in many adult education programs. Some people who become floral designers are trained on the job.

People in Science

Libbie Hyman (1888–1969)

Few people have done more for the study of invertebrates than the zoologist (zō ol'ə jist) Libbie Hyman. Between 1940 and 1967, Hyman published six books about the biology of invertebrates. These books earned her the respect of the scientific world. Her books gave detailed information about invertebrates. They also showed the importance of studying and then describing living things. Before her books were written, scientists made guesses about the body structure of many invertebrates.

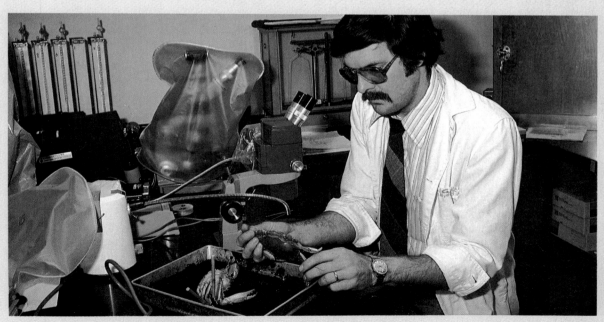

Zoologist studying a blue crab

Developing Skills

WORD SKILLS

At the back of this book is a section called the Glossary and another section called the Index. A glossary lists the important terms in a book and their definitions. An index lists the main topics covered in a book and the pages on which they can be found. Subtopics and their page numbers are listed under some of the main topics.

Use the Glossary and Index of this book to answer these questions.

1. In what order are the terms listed in the Glossary and Index?

2. Besides definitions, what other information is in the Glossary?

3. Find the term *vein* in the Glossary, and write the definitions. Now find this term in a dictionary, and write the definitions. How does a glossary differ from a dictionary?

4. In the Index, what subtopics are listed under the main topic *Energy*?

5. Which topics and subtopics would help you locate information on electricity? Write the topics, the subtopics, and their page numbers.

READING A CIRCLE GRAPH

Look at the circle graphs on the next page. A circle graph is a good way to show how something is divided. The large circle graph shows how animals are divided, or classified, into major animal groups. It gives the number of different kinds of animals in each group. The smaller circle graph shows the major groups of vertebrates and gives the number of kinds in each.

Use the circle graphs to answer these questions.

1. Which is the largest major group of animals? Which is the smallest major group?

2. How many kinds of echinoderms are there? How many kinds of arthropods are there?

3. Which is the smallest group of vertebrates? The largest?

4. How many more kinds of fish are there than kinds of reptiles?

NUMBER OF KINDS OF ANIMALS IN MAJOR ANIMAL GROUPS

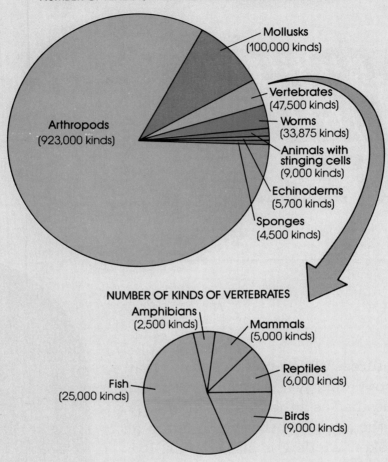

Mollusks
(100,000 kinds)

Vertebrates
(47,500 kinds)

Worms
(33,875 kinds)

Animals with
stinging cells
(9,000 kinds)

Echinoderms
(5,700 kinds)

Sponges
(4,500 kinds)

Arthropods
(923,000 kinds)

NUMBER OF KINDS OF VERTEBRATES

Amphibians
(2,500 kinds)

Mammals
(5,000 kinds)

Reptiles
(6,000 kinds)

Fish
(25,000 kinds)

Birds
(9,000 kinds)

MAKING A CIRCLE GRAPH

Make a circle graph that shows how you spend your time during a typical weekday. Your circle graph should represent a 24-hour period, from the time you get up one morning until the time you get up the next morning. Include the time you spend sleeping, eating meals, working at school, doing homework, and doing chores at home. Your circle graph should also show the time you spend playing, reading, watching television, practicing playing an instrument, and doing other activities that are part of your weekday.

UNIT TWO

Discovering Matter and Energy

Study the pictures. Which pictures show matter? Which show energy? Anything you can name can be classified as either matter or energy. The diamonds, the sign, and the windmill are all matter. The broken window is also matter. It is matter that has changed. But where is the energy? The light from the glowing sign is one form of energy. It is the only form of energy you can see. The light comes from another form of energy—electricity. The windmill blades are turning because of the energy of moving air.

In this unit you will study what matter is made of and some ways that matter can change. You will also learn about energy in the form of electricity. And you will find out about the many sources of energy people use.

Chapter 5

Building Blocks of Matter

Have you ever wondered what things are made of? Look at all the many things in the picture. What is an orange made of? An apple? A strand of hair? A piece of glass? A brick? Air?

For thousands of years people have asked such questions. The answers have taken a long time to find. Scientists working all over the world at different times have found some of the answers.

In this chapter you will learn how scientists study the world around them. You will find out about the smallest particles that things are made of. You will learn about some common materials that are formed of these particles. You will also read about the special names scientists use to talk about these materials.

STUDYING MATTER

How do scientists study the world around them?

Scientists study the world around them. They have found that all things are alike in some ways. All things are made up of matter. **Matter** is anything that has mass and takes up space. **Mass** is a measure of the amount of matter in an object. An elephant has more mass than a mouse. An iceberg has more mass than an ice cube. Scientists are curious about what makes up matter.

How do scientists study matter? They use their senses. The senses of sight, smell, hearing, taste, and touch help scientists learn about matter. Sometimes scientists use special devices to study matter. They use devices to see very small things

Collecting water samples

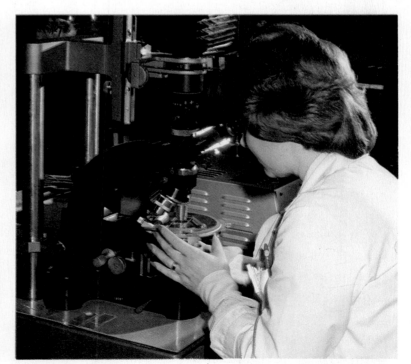

Using a microscope

Using a telescope

or things that are very far away. They use microscopes to see very small objects. They use telescopes to study the stars. All the scientists in the pictures are gathering information about matter.

Scientists have learned that all matter is made of small particles. They have never seen these particles with the unaided eye. From the results of tests, scientists believe that the particles exist.

Scientists make guesses about many things they cannot test directly. They make guesses about what the inside of the earth is like. They make guesses about what the stars are made of. So far, scientists have not been able to drill into the center of the earth. They have not yet traveled to a star. But they have made guesses about the matter in these places.

The guesses that scientists make are based on many careful studies. These studies give scientists clues about things that they cannot see or test directly. **Indirect evidence** (in də rekt′ ev′ə dəns) is a set of clues that scientists use to make guesses about things they cannot see or test directly.

The picture shows two closed boxes. An umbrella is inside one box. A fish bowl is inside the other box. Guess which box holds the umbrella. You probably guessed box *A.* What clues did you base your guess on? These clues are indirect evidence of what is inside each box.

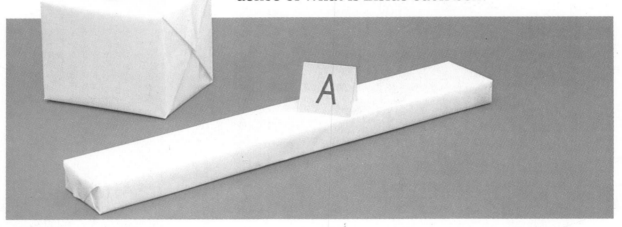

Collecting indirect evidence

The girl in the picture cannot see what is in the box. By shaking the box, she is trying to find out what is inside. By holding the box in her hands, she is learning about its mass.

As you have read, scientists use indirect evidence to find out about the world around them. They gather facts, or data, about things they cannot observe directly. Scientists use indirect evidence to learn about distant objects. They also use indirect evidence to study very small objects.

114

What can you learn from indirect evidence?

Materials sealed box with unknown object / metric ruler / balance and masses / magnet

Procedure
A. Lift and shake the box. Use the balance to measure the object's mass. Move the magnet along the outside of the box. Measure the box.

 1. What happens when you lift and shake the box?

B. Gather all the information you can. Make a chart like the one below. List each thing you did and what you learned.

Result of shaking	Effect of magnet	Mass	Size of box

C. Study your chart.
 2. From your information, what do you guess is in the box?

D. Open the box and look inside. Compare your guess with what actually is in the box.
 3. In what ways was your guess correct?
 4. In what ways was it wrong?

Conclusion
You have just collected indirect evidence. What can you learn from indirect evidence?

Using science ideas
List some other ways you can learn about the contents of a sealed box.

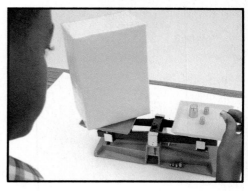

THE ATOM

What is matter made of?

Scientists have problems studying matter they cannot see. They use indirect evidence to make guesses about what matter is made of. They have found that all matter is made up of small particles. Each particle is called an atom (at'əm). An **atom** is the basic unit of all matter. Atoms are very small. Suppose a million of the smallest atoms were stacked on top of one another. The stack would not be as thick as this page.

Scientists must use indirect evidence to learn about atoms. Can you explain why? They use their indirect evidence to make models of atoms.

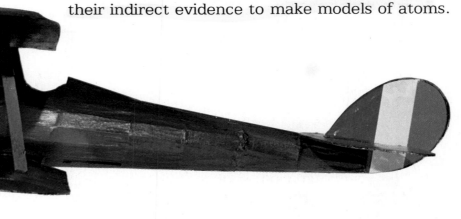

Model airplane

A model is a way to describe how something looks or acts. A model can be made of wood or clay. Or a model can be a picture. A model can even be words that describe an idea.

Have you ever made a model of a ship, a plane, a house, or a car? The picture shows a model of an airplane. This model is much smaller than the real thing. But models of atoms are much larger than real atoms.

For many years scientists have been making models of the atom. What do the models show? Scientists think the atom has a central part called a **nucleus** (nü'klē əs). The nucleus of an atom contains two kinds of particles, **protons** (prō'tonz) and **neutrons** (nü'tronz). Protons and neutrons are tightly packed·together in the nucleus. Tiny particles called **electrons** (i lek'tronz) travel around the nucleus. The drawing shows a model of a hydrogen atom.

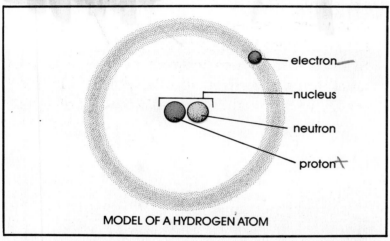

electron

nucleus

neutron

proton

MODEL OF A HYDROGEN ATOM

An atom is almost all empty space. Suppose you were to make a model of a hydrogen atom. The nucleus of the atom would be the size of an orange. The electrons would be in the space outside the orange. Then your model of the atom would be very large. It would be about 22 football fields across!

The electrons in your model would be very small. They would each be smaller than the head of a pin. The electrons would be moving quickly all around the orange. This shows that in a real atom there is mostly empty space between the nucleus and the electrons.

ELEMENTS

What is an easy way to write the names of elements?

Some kinds of matter cannot be broken down into simpler kinds of matter. Suppose a silver bar is broken down into the smallest particle that is still silver. The smallest particle of the silver bar would be a silver atom. A silver atom cannot be broken down into a simpler kind of matter and still be silver.

Silver bar

Silver is an element (el′ə mənt). An **element** is matter that is made up of only one kind of atom. It is a basic kind of matter. The smallest particle of an element is an atom.

Scientists have discovered 106 different elements. The atoms of these elements are different from one another. One way in which they differ is in the number of protons. Different atoms have different numbers of protons. For example, an atom of silver has 47 protons. An atom of gold has 79 protons. Of the 106 elements, 92 of these oc-

cur naturally on the earth. The other 14 elements have been made by scientists using special machines. The picture shows objects made mainly of only one element. Can you name the elements that make up the objects in the picture?

Each of the elements has its own symbol. A **symbol** is a short way to write the name of an element. The symbol stands for the name of the element. Why do scientists use symbols? They find it easier and quicker to write the symbol than to write the whole name of the element. Scientists all over the world use the same symbols.

Made mainly of one element

Do you know?

Some of the elements were named in an interesting way. The element tungsten was discovered in Sweden and in Spain at the same time. In Sweden it was found in a heavy yellow rock. The element was named *tungsten.* The name comes from two Swedish words. *Tung* means ''heavy'' and *sten* means ''stone.'' The Spanish scientists called the same element *wolfram.* It was found in a mineral called wolframite.

Today in most parts of the world the element is called wolfram. In the United States it is called tungsten. But it is known by the symbol *W.* The picture shows a bulb with a tungsten filament.

How can you group the elements? One way scientists group the elements is to put all metals in one group and all nonmetals into a second group. Most metals are good conductors of electricity and are shiny. Most nonmetals are poor conductors of electricity and are not shiny. Many nonmetals are gases. Which of the objects shown here is made mainly of a metal? Which is made mainly of a nonmetal? Which of the elements in the following list are metals? Which are nonmetals?
aluminum   carbon   helium   lead   nickel   oxygen

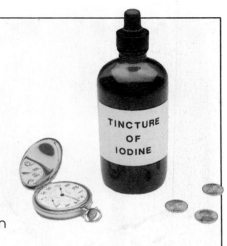

Helium-filled balloons

The table on page 121 lists some elements and their symbols. It describes how the elements look. Look at the list of symbols. You will see that sometimes the symbol for an element is the first letter of its name. For example, the symbol for carbon is *C.* Sometimes the symbol is two letters. For example, the symbol for calcium is *Ca.* A two-letter symbol is sometimes used because the names of some elements begin with the same letter. So the symbol *Ca* stands for calcium and the symbol *Co* stands for cobalt.

Look at the symbol for iron. It is *Fe.* The word for iron in Latin is *ferrum* (fer′əm). So the symbol for iron comes from that word. Find the symbol for silver. It is *Ag.* The word for silver in Latin is *argentum* (är jen′təm). The symbol for silver comes from that word. The symbols for some other elements also come from their names in Latin and other languages. Find mercury in the table. It is an unusual metal. Is mercury a solid, a liquid, or a gas at room temperature?

Diamond—a form of carbon

SOME COMMON ELEMENTS

Element	Symbol	Description
Calcium	Ca	Silver-white metal
Carbon	C	Black solid or colorless crystal
Chlorine	Cl	Greenish-yellow poisonous gas
Cobalt	Co	Silver-white metal
Gold	Au	Heavy yellow metal
Helium	He	Light gas with no color, taste, or odor
Hydrogen	H	Gas with no color, taste, or odor
Iron	Fe	Gray-white metal
Mercury	Hg	Heavy silver-colored metal; liquid at room temperature
Nitrogen	N	Gas with no color, taste, or odor
Oxygen	O	Gas with no color, taste, or odor
Silver	Ag	Shiny white metal
Sodium	Na	Soft silvery metal
Sulfur	S	Powdery yellow solid

Thermometer

- MOLECULES AND COMPOUNDS -
What happens when atoms combine?

You have learned that the smallest particle of matter is the atom. Atoms do not usually exist alone on earth. They combine, sometimes in pairs, sometimes in threes. Sometimes hundreds of atoms combine. New substances form when atoms of different elements combine. These new substances are called **compounds** (kom'poundz). The simplest particle of many compounds is a **molecule** (mol'ə kyül). Most molecules are made of two or more atoms.

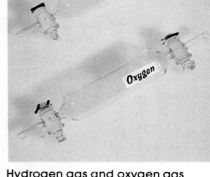

Hydrogen gas and oxygen gas

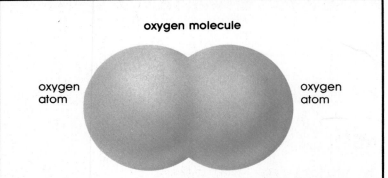

oxygen molecule

oxygen atom

oxygen atom

Sometimes two atoms of the *same* element combine to form a molecule. Think about these examples. Two atoms of the element oxygen join to form a molecule of oxygen. In the same way, two atoms of the element hydrogen join to form a molecule of hydrogen. Look at the drawing above. It shows a molecule of oxygen. You can see that two oxygen atoms have joined to form this molecule. The oxygen and hydrogen molecules are not compounds. Compounds are formed only when atoms of *different* elements join.

Can you form a compound?

Materials   2 test tubes / steel wool pad / magnet / water / 2 test-tube clamps / ring stand / 600-ml beaker / wax pencil / hand lens

Procedure

A. Test a steel wool pad with a magnet.
   1. Is the steel wool attracted to the magnet?

B. Wet the steel wool pad with water. Fill the lower 2 cm of a test tube with a piece of the steel wool pad as shown. Use a pencil to push the pad into the tube. Use a wax pencil to make a mark 2 cm from the open end of each test tube.

C. Half fill a beaker with water. Set up the two test tubes with the beaker and a ring stand. One test tube will be empty. Make sure the wax pencil mark is even with the surface of the water.
   2. Predict what will happen in each test tube.

D. Observe the test tubes for 5 days. Note any changes that occur inside the test tubes each day.
   3. How has the steel wool pad changed?
   4. How has the water level changed?

E. After 5 days remove the steel wool pad and look at it with a hand lens. Test it with a magnet.
   5. Describe how the steel wool pad looks.
   6. Is the steel wool attracted to the magnet?

Conclusion

A new compound has been formed. It is called iron oxide. Iron oxide is made from iron and oxygen. The oxygen came from the air.
   1. Where did the iron come from?
   2. Why do you think the water level changed?

Using science ideas

There are many things around you that are made of iron. Name some ways that you can prevent iron objects from changing to iron oxide.

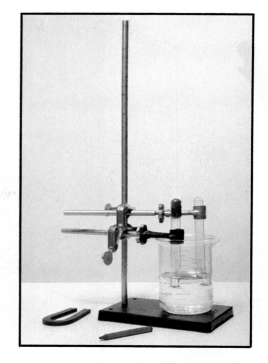

You have learned that the atoms in a compound are from different elements. Table salt, for example, is made of the elements sodium and chlorine. Sugar is another compound. It is made of atoms of the elements carbon, hydrogen, and oxygen. A compound may be very different from the atoms it is made of. Sugar is a white crystal that tastes sweet. It is formed of the elements carbon, hydrogen, and oxygen. Are these three elements very different from sugar?

Salt and salt crystals

Sugar and sugar crystals

Look at the table of the compounds on page 125. The table lists four common compounds. It shows the elements they are made of and describes these elements. Find the description of the elements that make up sugar. You will find that the elements making up sugar are different from the compound sugar.

Find the elements that make up table salt. Do the elements sodium and chlorine look like table salt? No. Sodium is a silvery metal. Chlorine is a greenish-yellow poisonous gas. Table salt is a white crystal used to season food. Notice that the compound salt is different from the elements that make it up.

FOUR COMMON COMPOUNDS

Compound	Description of compound	Elements in compound; symbol for elements	Description of elements
Table salt	Salty-tasting white crystal used to season food	Sodium (Na)	Soft silvery metal
		Chlorine (Cl)	Greenish-yellow poisonous gas
Water	Liquid found over three fourths of the earth's surface	Hydrogen (H)	Gas with no color, taste, or odor
		Oxygen (O)	Gas with no color, taste, or odor
Sugar	Sweet-tasting white crystal used to sweeten food	Carbon (C)	Black solid found in coal, charcoal, and diamonds
		Hydrogen (H)	Gas with no color, taste, or odor
		Oxygen (O)	Gas with no color, taste, or odor
Ammonia	Strong-smelling gas that dissolves in water	Nitrogen (N)	Gas with no color, taste, or odor
		Hydrogen (H)	Gas with no color, taste, or odor

Enlarged salt crystals   Water droplets   Enlarged sugar crystals   Ammonia in water

Water for recreation

Here is another example. Water is a compound formed from elements that are different from water. On the earth water can be found as a liquid, as a solid, and as a gas. We drink it and we bathe in it. It makes up about two thirds of our body.

Water is made up of the elements hydrogen and oxygen. Hydrogen is a gas that has no color, taste, or odor. Oxygen is also a gas. It, too, has no color, taste, or odor. It makes up about one fifth of the air. The elements that make up water are very different from the compound water.

Remember that scientists use symbols for the names of elements. It is easier to write the symbol for an element than to spell out its name. Scientists also use these symbols to write the names of compounds. Water is written H_2O. H_2O stands for one molecule of water. The symbol for hydrogen (H) is joined with the symbol for oxygen (O).

The small number 2 after the H means there are two atoms of hydrogen in a molecule of water. Notice that there is no number after the O. This means there is only one atom of oxygen in a molecule of water.

Do you know?

The chemical symbols used by scientists today were not always used. Over the centuries the symbols for the elements have changed. In the sixteenth century the symbol for gold was a picture of the sun. The symbol for mercury was a staff carried by the god Mercury. Lead was represented by a farm tool carried by the god Saturn.

In 1814 all this changed. A chemist in Sweden decided to use letter symbols for the elements. These symbols were based on the ancient names of the elements. *Au,* used for gold, stands for *aurum* (ôr'əm). *Hg,* used for mercury, stands for *hydrargyrum* (hī drär'jər əm). *Pb,* used for lead, stands for *plumbum.* These same letter symbols are still used today by chemists all over the world.

gold	☼	☉	Ⓖ	Au
mercury		☿		Hg
lead		♄	Ⓛ	Pb

H_2O is the formula (fôr′myə lə) for water. A **formula** is a group of symbols and numbers that stands for a compound. The symbols in a formula

oxygen
atom

hydrogen
atom

hydrogen
atom

water molecule

show the kinds of atoms in a compound. The numbers in a formula show the number of atoms in the smallest particle of a compound.

Every compound can be written with a formula. The formula for one type of sugar is $C_{12}H_{22}O_{11}$. What does this formula show you? It shows you that one molecule of sugar contains atoms of carbon, hydrogen, and oxygen. It also shows you there are 12 atoms of carbon, 22 atoms of hydrogen, and 11 atoms of oxygen. You can see that a formula shows a lot about a compound.

IDEAS TO REMEMBER

▶ Matter is anything that has mass and takes up space.

▶ Indirect evidence gives clues that scientists use to make guesses about things they cannot see or test directly.

▶ An atom is the basic unit of all matter. An atom is the smallest particle of an element.

▶ The central part of an atom is the nucleus, which contains protons and neutrons. Electrons travel around the nucleus.

▶ An element is matter that is made up of only one kind of atom.

▶ A symbol is a short way to write the name of an element.

▶ A molecule is the simplest particle of many compounds.

▶ A compound is matter formed when two or more atoms of different elements are combined. Scientists use formulas to write the names of compounds.

Reviewing the Chapter

SCIENCE WORDS

A. Copy the sentences below. Use science terms from the chapter to complete the sentences.

1. Scientists call a group of symbols and numbers that stands for a compound a/an _____.
2. The central part of the atom is called the _____.
3. Matter made of only one kind of atom is a/an _____.
4. A measure of the amount of matter in an object is its _____.
5. A substance formed when atoms of different elements combine is a/an _____.
6. A tiny particle that travels around the nucleus of an atom is a/an _____.
7. Anything that has mass and takes up space is _____.
8. A set of clues that scientists use to make guesses about things they cannot see or test directly is _____.

B. Unscramble each group of letters to find a science term from the chapter. Write a sentence using each term.

ulelomec   notrop   tunnero   myblos

C. Identify each of the following.

1. It is a very tiny particle. It is part of an atom. It travels around the nucleus. What is it?
2. It is made of numbers. It is made of symbols. It stands for a compound. What is it?

UNDERSTANDING IDEAS

A. The drawing shows a water molecule. Write the correct term for each number in the drawing. What is the formula for this compound?

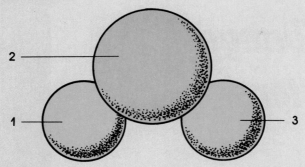

B. Make a chart like the one shown below. Write the correct information in the empty boxes.

Element	Symbol
Carbon	
Mercury	
	Fe
	Ag
Sodium	
	Au

USING IDEAS

1. You can use indirect evidence to play a game. You will need at least four players. Collect objects from around your home or school. Put each object into a paper bag. Each player is given a bag and looks at the object. He or she gives clues to the other players about what is in the bag. The winner is the person whose object is guessed with the fewest clues.

Chapter 6

Physical Changes in Matter

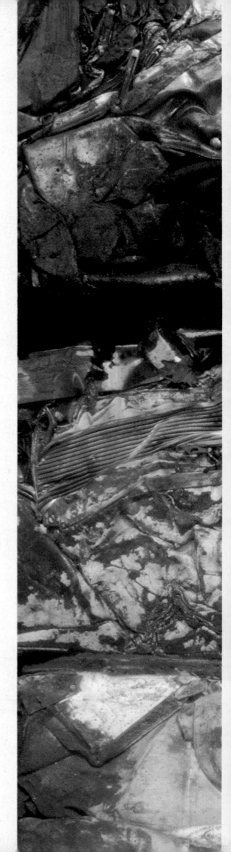

Matter changes in different ways. Do you know what the objects stacked around the flower were? They were cars. The cars were changed to solid cubes when they were crushed, or compacted, into this shape.

In what ways has the matter that makes up the cars changed? What has happened to the metal body and glass windows of the cars? The metal and glass have changed shape. They have also changed in size. These are two ways in which matter can change.

In this chapter you will learn about some of the ways in which matter can change. You will also learn how matter can be identified.

PHYSICAL PROPERTIES
What are physical properties of matter?

The children in the picture are playing a game. The girl is blindfolded and then asked to smell two different kinds of food. She must identify which is a piece of onion and which is a piece of orange. The girl is using odor as a way of identifying matter.

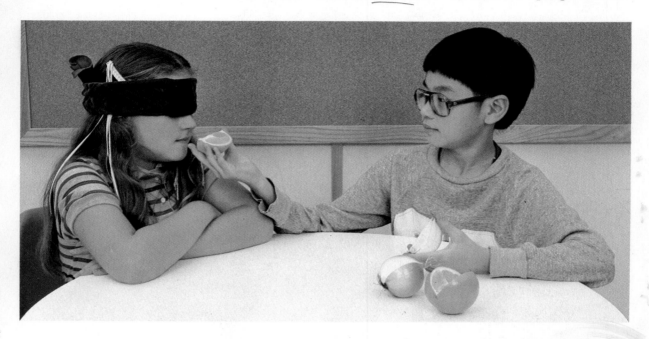

These pictures show two elements—gold and carbon. How can you tell the piece of gold from the piece of carbon? One way to tell is by observing how each one looks. The color of gold is different from the color of carbon. Based on color, which piece is gold and which is carbon?

Odor and color are physical properties of matter. A **physical property** is one that can be used to identify matter. Two other physical properties are shape and hardness.

Density is also a physical property of matter. It is the mass in a certain volume of matter. For example, the piece of wood has a certain volume. Its mass is 8 g. The piece of iron has the same volume as the wood. The mass of the iron is 136 g. So the density of the iron is greater than the density of the wood. How many times greater?

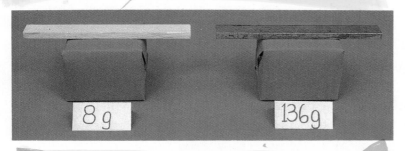

You can use the property of density to help you identify matter. In the pictures below, the glasses labeled *A* and *B* each contain a colorless liquid. One liquid is water and the other is alcohol. Water has a greater density than alcohol. Look at the picture on the right. An ice cube has been put into each liquid. The ice floats in the denser liquid and sinks in the less dense liquid. Which glass contains alcohol, *A* or *B*? How do you know?

PHYSICAL CHANGES
What kinds of physical changes can occur in matter?

Matter can change in different ways. The pictures show a glass cup before and after it was dropped. Breaking the glass cup changes its size and shape. This kind of change is a physical change. A **physical change** is a change in the size, shape, or state of matter. New materials are not formed when there is a physical change. The same kind of matter is present both before and after a physical change. The pieces of the cup are no longer in the shape of a cup. But you can see that the pieces are still glass.

Changes in size and shape are common physical changes. When you write with chalk, tiny bits of chalk are rubbed from the stick of chalk onto the chalkboard. However, the bits of chalk are still chalk. The atoms and molecules in the chalk are

Writing with chalk is an example of a physical change in matter

136

not changed. They simply have been spread out across the chalkboard.

In each case, a physical change has taken place. The size and shape of matter have been changed. But the atoms and molecules in the matter have not been changed. The same kind of matter is present before and after each change.

Matter can exist in three forms, or states. The three states of matter are solid, liquid, and gas. Many kinds of matter can change from one state to another. A change in state is another kind of physical change.

Water is one of the few kinds of matter that commonly exists in all three states. Rain is liquid water. Ice cubes and icebergs are solid water. Water as a gas is invisible. It is called water vapor. Although you cannot see it, there is always water vapor in the air. How many states of water can you see in the picture? How many do you think there are?

How do the three states of matter differ? Remember that all matter is made of tiny particles. Different states of matter differ in how far apart these particles are. There is an attraction between the particles in matter. The strength of this attraction varies with the amount of space between particles. Also, the way in which particles in each state of matter move is different. The drawing shows how particles in a solid, a liquid, and a gas might look.

Particles in solid matter are packed very close together. This causes the attraction between these particles to be strong. The particles move back and forth in a very small space. Because the particles have a strong attraction for each other, they do not move around very much. For this reason, solids have a definite shape. It is also why solids have a definite volume. A cube of sugar and a brick are solids. What are some other solids?

Particles in liquid matter are not as close together as those in a solid. So the attraction between particles in a liquid is weaker than in a

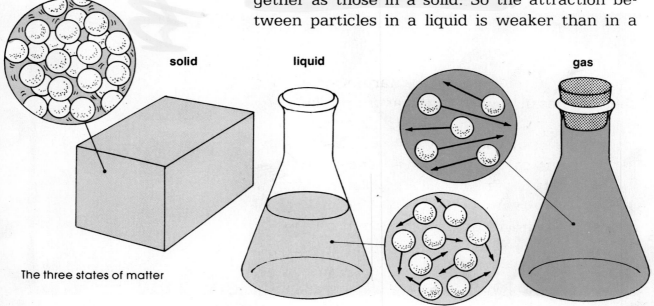

solid **liquid** **gas**

The three states of matter

solid. The weaker attraction allows particles in a liquid to slip and slide over and around one another. Because of the way the particles move, liquids have no definite shape. Liquids take the shape of the container they are in. As the particles in liquids move, the spaces between them do not change. So liquids have a definite volume.

The picture shows containers of different sizes and shapes. The same volume of water is in each one. What property of liquids does this show?

Particles in gases are spread farther apart than the particles in liquids. So the attraction between them is very weak. This very weak attraction allows particles in a gas to move freely. Because the attraction is so weak and the spaces so great, gases have no definite shape or volume. Suppose a gas is put in a closed box or jar. The particles of the gas will spread out until they fill the box or jar.

Changes in state are common physical changes. Energy is involved when matter changes from one state to another. Energy must be added to

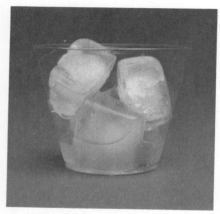
Melting ice

Boiling water

change a solid to a liquid. Energy must also be added to change a liquid to a gas. The energy that is added is usually in the form of heat. Heat energy causes the particles in solids and liquids to move faster. This increases the spaces between the particles and weakens the attraction. So a solid changes to a liquid and a liquid to a gas.

A glass of ice cubes left out on a hot summer day will melt. Melting is the change of state from a solid to a liquid. When heat is added to a solid, what happens to the particles in the solid? How does this explain why the solid melts? The temperature at which a solid changes to a liquid is called the **melting point.**

Cooking food often involves boiling liquids. When something boils, it changes from a liquid to a gas. As heat energy is added, some particles in the liquid have enough energy to escape from the liquid. The escaped particles are now particles in a gas. The temperature at which a liquid changes to a gas is called the **boiling point.**

Finding out

How fast and how far can particles in a gas move?
Get a bottle of perfume and some absorbent cotton. Have a partner stand about 5 m away. Have your partner open the bottle of perfume and pour a small amount of it onto the cotton. Note the time. When you can smell the perfume, note the time again. How long did it take for you to smell the perfume?

How far did the perfume particles travel to reach you? What conditions in the room might have affected how quickly the perfume particles reached you?

Most substances have a definite melting point and boiling point. Melting point and boiling point are physical properties of matter. The melting point of water is 0°C. Its boiling point is 100°C.

Some changes of state involve taking energy away. To change a gas to a liquid or a liquid to a solid, energy must be removed. The energy that is removed is usually heat energy. When heat energy is removed, the particles in matter move more slowly. So the spaces between the particles become smaller. What happens to the attraction between particles? How does this cause a liquid to change to a solid? How is the liquid orange juice changed to a solid?

Melting, boiling, and other changes in state may not seem like physical changes, but they are. Molecules in liquid water are not changed when the water changes to a gas or a solid. Liquid iron is made up of the same kinds of atoms that make up solid iron. Physical changes do not change the particles that make up matter.

Liquid orange juice

Solid orange juice

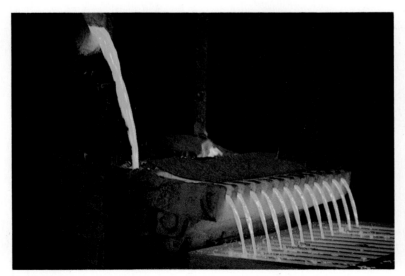

Liquid iron

Solid iron

MIXTURES

What are the properties of a mixture?

The children in the picture below are making a salad. They are mixing some lettuce, carrots, green peppers, and other vegetables. A salad is a mixture (miks′chər) of different vegetables. A **mixture** is a material formed by the physical combining of two or more different materials. Mixed nuts are another example of a mixture.

The materials in a mixture are not combined as they are in a compound. In a compound, substances have combined to form a new substance. But the materials that are in a mixture do not change to something else. Lettuce remains lettuce when it is mixed with carrots. The materials in a mixture can be physically separated. How could you separate the pieces of vegetable in the salad mixture?

A mixture of nuts

142

How can substances in a mixture be separated?

Materials spoon / table salt / sand / dark-colored paper / hand lens / 2 jars / filter paper / funnel / paper towel / glass or plastic dish

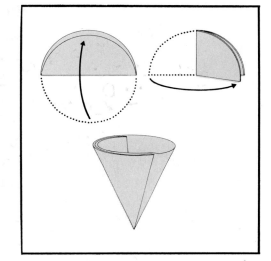

Procedure
A. Put a spoonful of table salt and a spoonful of sand on a sheet of dark paper. Use a hand lens to look at the sand and the salt. Draw some particles of each.
   1. How are the particles different?

B. Mix the sand and the salt together. Put water into a jar so the jar is half full. Add the salt-sand mixture to the water in the jar. Stir the mixture with the spoon.
   2. What happens?

C. Fold a piece of filter paper as shown. Put the filter paper into a clean funnel. Put the funnel in another jar so it rests on the mouth of the jar.

D. Slowly pour all the salt-sand-water mixture into the funnel. Now take the filter paper out, open it, and place it on a paper towel. Allow the material on the filter paper to dry.

E. Pour a small amount of the liquid from the jar into a dish. Allow the liquid in the dish to evaporate.
   3. What material do you think will be left in the dish after the water evaporates?

F. Use a hand lens to look at the dried materials on the filter paper and in the dish.
   4. What material is left on the filter paper?
   5. What material is left in the dish?

Conclusion
1. When you made the salt-sand-water mixture, what kind of change in matter occurred?
2. Describe how the materials in the mixture were separated.

The pieces or particles in a mixture can be of different sizes. The pieces of vegetable in the salad are large. Suppose you mix sand and salt together. The particles are small, but they can be seen. They can also be separated from each other by physical means.

Mixtures are found everywhere. Almost all foods are mixtures. Nearly all the water on the earth is a mixture. If you have ever tasted ocean water, you know it is salty. Ocean water is a mixture of water and different kinds of salts. What mixtures are shown at the left?

Do you know?

One special type of mixture is called an alloy (al'oi). Most alloys are mixtures of two or more metals. Most alloys are harder and stronger than each of the metals they are made from. For example, when iron is mixed with carbon and certain other elements, steel is formed. Steel is stronger and better able to resist rust than iron alone.

Some scientists think that alloys can be made cheaper and better in space. They are testing this idea by making certain alloys during missions of the Space Shuttle. Some day most of the alloys we use on the earth may be made in factories in space.

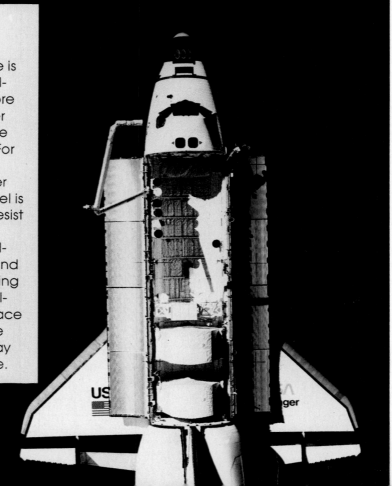

TWO KINDS OF MIXTURES

How are a solution and a suspension different?

You have learned that the particles in some mixtures are large enough to be seen. You can see the grains that make up a mixture of sand and salt. In other mixtures the particles that are mixed together are individual molecules. You cannot see the particles in a mixture of sugar and water. The particles of sugar and water are individual molecules.

A mixture of sugar and water is a special kind of mixture. It is called a solution (sə lü'shən). A **solution** is a mixture that forms when one substance dissolves in another. In a solution the particles of the substances are evenly mixed. Most solutions are a solid dissolved in a liquid. These solutions are clear, even if they are colored.

What happens when sugar mixes with water? The sugar particles seem to disappear in the water. Of course the sugar has not disappeared. It has dissolved in the water. This means that the

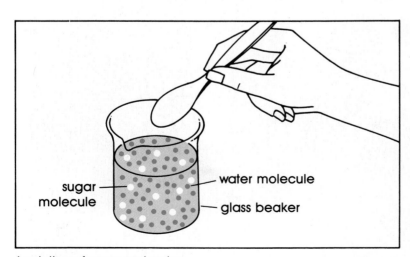

A solution of sugar and water

sugar molecules are evenly mixed with the water molecules. You cannot see the tiny sugar molecules. But if the water evaporates, the sugar molecules form solid sugar again.

A solution has two parts. The **solute** (sol′yüt) is the substance in a solution that dissolves. In a sugar-and-water solution, sugar is the solute. Water is the solvent. The **solvent** (sol′vənt) is the substance in a solution that does the dissolving.

Several things affect how fast a solute dissolves in a solvent. Stirring makes a solute dissolve faster. Temperature also affects how fast a solute dissolves. Most solutes dissolve faster in a warm solvent than in a cold one. The picture shows powdered tea in hot water and in cold water. The same amount of tea was put into each glass at the same time. Why is there a difference in the amount of tea dissolved in each glass?

The size of the solute particles also affects how fast the solute dissolves. Small solute particles dissolve faster than large solute particles. For example, small grains of sugar will dissolve faster than a whole sugar cube.

— ANOTHER KIND OF CHANGE —
What is a chemical change?

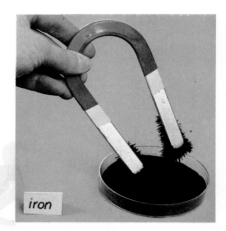

iron

You have learned about many different physical changes in matter. But matter can change in another way. When a piece of wood burns, it changes into new substances. Burning wood is an example of a chemical change. A **chemical change** is a change in matter in which one or more different kinds of matter form.

The physical properties of matter change when there is a chemical change. You can see that iron is a dark-gray metal. Iron is attracted by a magnet. Sulfur is a yellow powder that is not attracted by a magnet. When iron and sulfur are mixed together, they can easily be separated. Neither substance has changed. But when iron and sulfur are heated together, a chemical change takes place. A new substance is formed. This substance is iron sulfide. It is brown-black in color. And it is not attracted to a magnet.

sulfur

iron sulfide

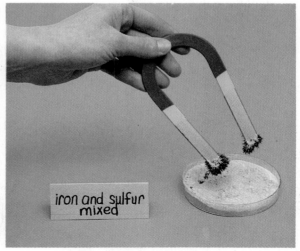

iron and sulfur mixed

Some chemical changes take place slowly. The rust on the body of this car formed from a slow chemical change. Oxygen from the air joined with iron to form the compound iron oxide. Iron oxide is commonly called rust. How does paint help stop rust from forming?

Rusting—a slow chemical change

Other chemical changes take place more quickly. When vinegar is poured on baking soda, a rapid chemical change takes place. There are new substances formed. One new substance is carbon dioxide gas.

A rapid chemical change

IDEAS TO REMEMBER

▶ A physical property is one that can be used to identify matter. Color, odor, shape, hardness, and density are physical properties.

▶ A physical change is a change in the size, shape, or state of matter.

▶ The three states of matter—solid, liquid, and gas—differ in how particles move, in how far apart particles are, and in the strength of attraction between particles.

▶ Melting point and boiling point are physical properties.

▶ A mixture is a material formed by the physical combining of two or more different materials.

▶ A solution is a mixture that forms when one substance dissolves in another. A suspension is a mixture in which particles of a substance do not dissolve in another substance.

▶ A chemical change is a change in matter in which one or more different kinds of matter form.

Reviewing the Chapter

SCIENCE WORDS

A. Copy the sentences below. Use science terms from the chapter to complete the sentences.

1. The temperature at which a solid changes to a liquid is the _____.
2. The same kind of matter is present both before and after a/an _____ in matter.
3. Density is a/an _____ that can be used to identify matter.
4. A substance changes from a liquid to a gas when that substance reaches its _____.
5. When iron and sulfur are heated together, a/an _____ takes place and a new substance is formed.

B. Write the letter of the term that best matches the definition. Not all the terms will be used.

1. Mixture in which particles of a substance do not dissolve in another substance
2. Substance in a solution that dissolves
3. Mixture that forms when one substance dissolves in another
4. Substance in a solution that does the dissolving
5. Material formed by the physical combining of two or more different materials

    a. solute
    b. particle
    c. mixture
    d. solution
    e. liquid
    f. suspension
    g. solvent

UNDERSTANDING IDEAS

A. Write whether each drawing shows a physical change or a chemical change. Describe each change.

B. Identify each of the following as matter that is solid, liquid, or gas.

1. It is the state of matter in which particles slip and slide over and around one another. Matter in this state has no definite shape, but it does have a definite volume.
2. It is the state of matter in which particles move freely and are spread far apart. Matter in this state has no definite shape or volume.
3. It is the state of matter in which particles move back and forth in a very small space. Matter in this state has a definite shape and a definite volume.

USING IDEAS

1. For a 1-week period, identify all the physical changes that occur in your home.

Chapter 7

Understanding Electricity

You live in a world that depends on electricity. Look around. You may have many things in your home that run on electricity. A television, a stereo, and a radio use electricity. The lights in your house, the clock on the wall, and the toaster in the kitchen all need electricity. You may have toys and games that run on electricity. Your home may be heated by electricity. Your food may be cooked in an electric oven.

The boy in the picture is looking at the many electrical devices on display. Can you imagine your life without electricity?

In this chapter you will learn what electricity is. You will learn how it is produced, used, and measured. You will also learn about some of the dangers of electricity and how it can be used safely.

ELECTRICITY
What is electricity?

You depend a great deal on electricity. But what *is* electricity? You cannot see it. You can only see what it does. For a long time scientists have been interested in what electricity is and does.

What is known about electricity? Scientists know that everything is either matter or energy. Matter has mass and takes up space. Since electricity does not have mass or take up space, it must be energy.

Train running on electricity

You know that electricity can do work. What kind of work is being done in the picture?

To understand electrical energy, you must understand matter. Remember that all matter is made of atoms. Knowing the structure of the atom will help solve the mystery of electricity.

You have learned that the atom has a central part called a nucleus. There are particles in the nucleus. Some of these particles have a positive charge. They are called protons. Moving around the nucleus are other particles, called electrons. The electrons in an atom have a negative charge. If the number of protons and the number of electrons in an atom are the same, their charges balance one another. When this happens, the atom has no charge. An atom with no charge is neutral (nü′trəl). Under normal conditions the atoms in most matter are neutral. As the drawing shows, the number of electrons and protons is balanced.

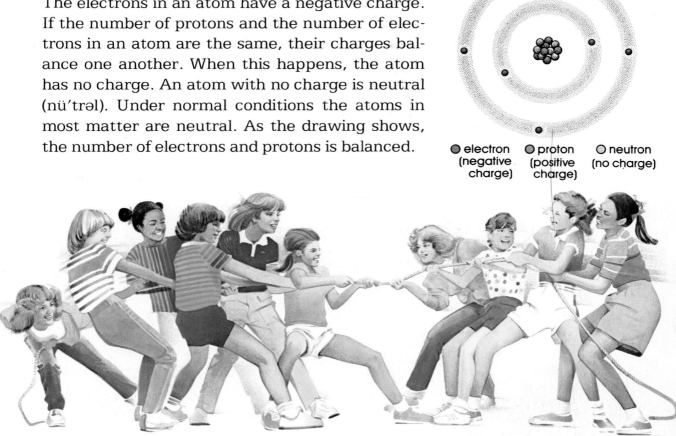

NEUTRAL ATOM

● electron (negative charge) ● proton (positive charge) ○ neutron (no charge)

Look at the drawing of the children playing tug-of-war. You can see that the teams are not balanced. One team has six children and the other has four. To balance the teams, some children will have to move. They can move in only one direction. Some children will have to move from the side with the larger number to the side with the smaller number. How many children will have to move to balance the teams?

In some ways electricity is like this game of tug-of-war. Suppose the number of protons and the number of electrons in an atom are not the same. This happens when an atom gains or loses electrons. If an atom has more electrons than protons, the atom has a negative charge. An atom with more protons than electrons has a positive charge.

Look at the drawings of the atoms. As you can see, atoms can gain or lose electrons. Atom **A** is losing an electron. Atom **B** is gaining an electron. This movement of electrons produces electricity. Which atom has a positive charge? Which atom has a negative charge?

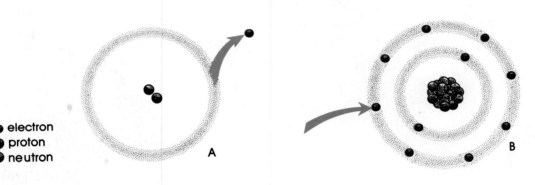

● electron
● proton
● neutron

A

B

Finding out

Does clear tape have an electric charge? You will need a roll of clear tape. Remove two strips of tape from the roll. Each strip should be about 8 cm long. Make sure that you touch only one end of the tape. Slowly move the two sticky sides of the tape toward each other. Then slowly move the two smooth sides toward each other. Watch what happens. Do the pieces of tape have an electric charge? How can you tell?

KINDS OF ELECTRICITY

What are two kinds of electricity?

It is a cold, dry day in winter. You walk across a wool carpet and reach out to turn a doorknob. You feel a shock. What happened? When you moved across the carpet, you gained electrons. Your shoes rubbed electrons off the carpet. The electrons built up on your body and stayed there. This buildup of electrons gave your body an electric charge. An electric charge that does not move is called **static** (stat'ik) **electricity.**

collection of electrons

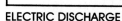

ELECTRIC DISCHARGE

When you touched the doorknob, electrons moved from you to the doorknob. Why did this happen? Electrons move from a place where there are many electrons to a place where there are fewer electrons. Your body had more electrons than the doorknob. When you touched the doorknob, the extra electrons moved from your

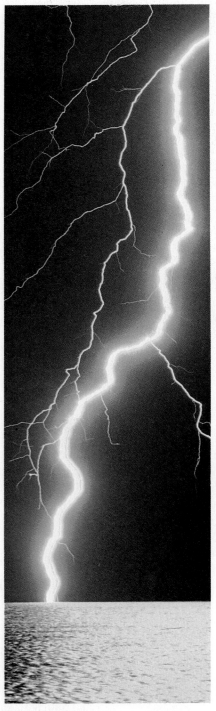

Electric discharge

body to the doorknob. This movement of the extra electrons is called an **electric discharge** (dis'-chärj). After the electric discharge, you became neutral again.

Lightning is another example of a discharge of static electricity. Lightning is often caused by a buildup of electrons on a cloud. The cloud has more electrons than the ground. When the difference between the charge on the cloud and the charge on the ground is great enough, an electric discharge occurs. You can see this discharge as lightning.

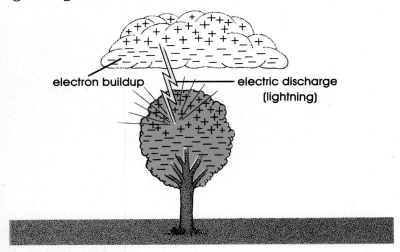

electron buildup   electric discharge (lightning)

WHY LIGHTNING STRIKES

Electrons move when they jump from a finger to a doorknob. They also move when lightning strikes the earth. This movement of electrons is called **current electricity.** Current electricity is more useful than static electricity. What are some ways that current electricity is used?

The electricity that jumped to the doorknob had to move through some form of matter. It moved through air. Electricity can move through

other forms of matter, such as metal. Matter through which an electric current moves easily is called a **conductor** (kən duk'tər). Most metals are good conductors. Some metals are better conductors than others. Gold, silver, and copper are all good conductors. Copper is low-priced and easy to obtain. So it is often used as a conductor.

Not all kinds of matter are good conductors. Current cannot move easily through wood, rubber, glass, or plastic. Matter that is not a good conductor is called an **insulator** (in'sə lā tər). Rubber is often used as an insulator around copper wire. The rubber helps to keep electricity in the wire. An insulator helps to prevent electric shock.

TYPES OF INSULATED WIRE

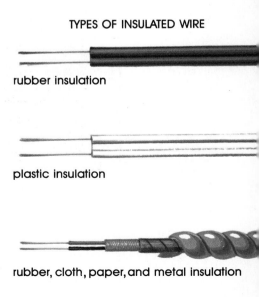

rubber insulation

plastic insulation

rubber, cloth, paper, and metal insulation

Which materials are conductors?

Materials 6-volt battery / light bulb and socket / 3 test leads / copper penny / cardboard strip / toothpick /aluminum foil / paper clip / rubber band

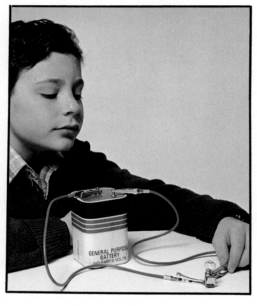

Procedure

A. You are going to test different materials to see if they are conductors or insulators. Make a chart like the one shown below.

Material tested	Conductor	Insulator
copper penny		
toothpick		
cardboard strip		
aluminum foil		
paper clip		
rubber band		

B. Connect the battery, test leads, and light bulb as shown.

C. Remove one of the test leads from the bulb. Clip it to a copper penny. Use another test lead to clip the penny to the bulb as shown.

    1. What happens to the bulb?

    2. Is the penny a conductor or an insulator?

D. Repeat step **C** for each of the other materials. Fill in your chart.

Conclusion

1. Which materials are conductors of electricity?

2. How are all the conductors alike?

3. Which materials are insulators? How do you know?

Using science ideas

Look around your home for tools that are used to repair electric devices. The handles of some of the tools will be covered with rubber. Explain why.

ELECTRIC CIRCUITS

What are two kinds of electric circuits?

Electricity must flow through a path to be useful. The path through which an electric current flows is a **circuit** (sër'kit). A circuit lets electrons flow from a place where there are many electrons to a place where there are few. The flow of electrons in a circuit is similar to the flow of water in a pipe. Like water, electrons need a path to follow. The pipe gives water a path to follow. The circuit gives electrons a path to follow. The drawing shows a light bulb in an electric circuit. Electricity flowing through the wire lights the bulb.

An electric circuit must be complete for electricity to flow through it. A circuit that is complete is called a closed circuit. If there is a break in the circuit, electricity will not flow through it. A circuit that is broken, or incomplete, is called an open circuit. The opening and closing of a circuit is controlled by a device called a switch.

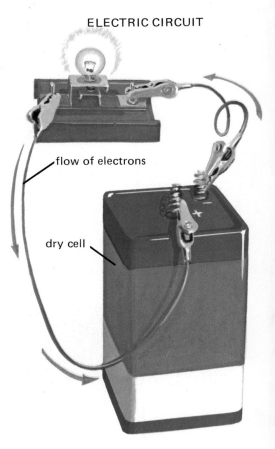

ELECTRIC CIRCUIT

flow of electrons

dry cell

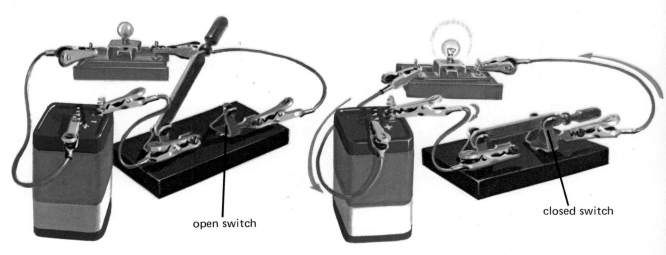

open switch

closed switch

OPEN CIRCUIT

CLOSED CIRCUIT

163

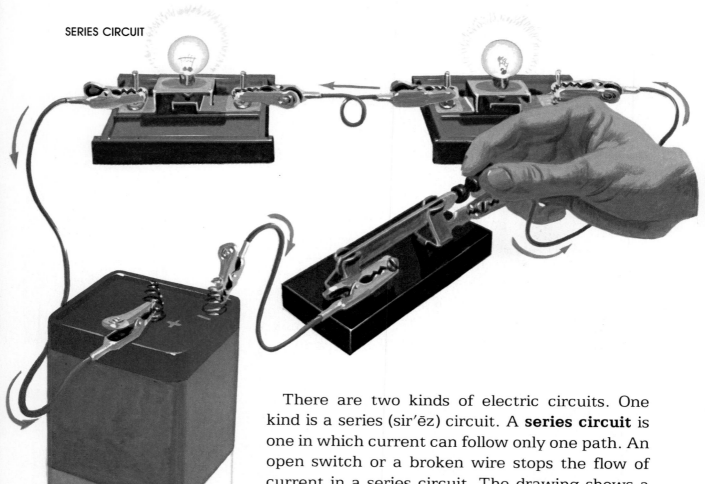

SERIES CIRCUIT

There are two kinds of electric circuits. One kind is a series (sir'ēz) circuit. A **series circuit** is one in which current can follow only one path. An open switch or a broken wire stops the flow of current in a series circuit. The drawing shows a simple series circuit. It has an energy source, a copper wire, a switch, and two light bulbs. What happens to the flow of current when the switch is open? What happens when the switch is closed? Suppose one more light bulb is added to the circuit. The current must flow through it also. If one of the bulbs burns out, the path is broken. The current no longer has a path to move through.

The other kind of electric circuit is a parallel (par'ə lel) circuit. A **parallel circuit** is one in which current can follow more than one path. Look at the parallel circuit with two bulbs shown in the drawing. The current does not have to flow through the green bulb to reach the red bulb. Compare it with the drawing of the series circuit. How many paths can you trace in the parallel circuit?

Most circuits used in homes are parallel circuits. If you turn off one light in your home, the other lights will stay on. The parallel circuit provides another path for the current to follow. It is like taking a detour on a road. Traffic can flow from one point to another, but it goes along a different route. What would happen if the lights in your home were not wired in a parallel circuit?

PARALLEL CIRCUIT

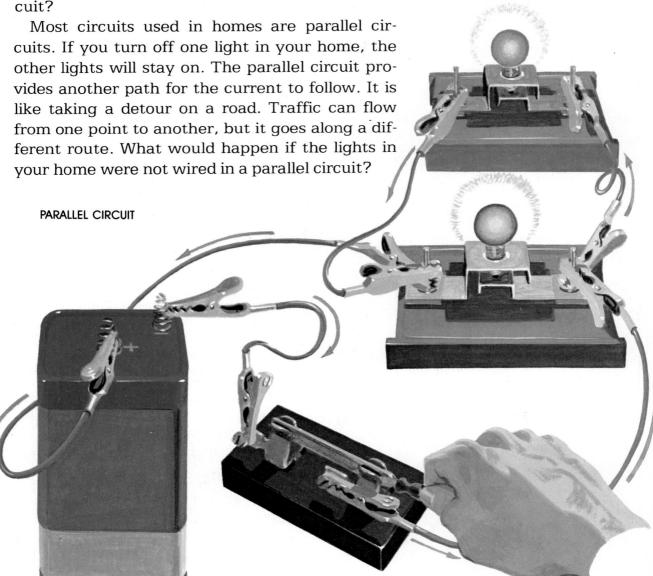

Are bulbs brighter in a series circuit or a parallel circuit?

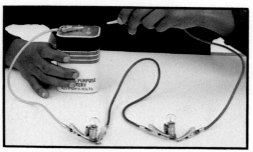

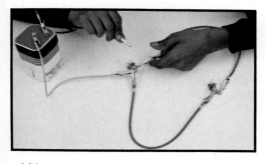

Materials 6-volt battery / 2 light bulbs and sockets / 5 test leads / insulated copper wire

Procedure

A. Connect one light bulb in a circuit, as shown in the top picture.

  1. Observe the brightness of the bulb.
  2. What would happen if you added one more bulb?

B. Add one more bulb to the circuit, as shown in the middle picture. You have connected the bulbs in a series circuit. Observe the brightness of the two bulbs.

  3. Are the two bulbs brighter than the one bulb?
  4. Why is there a difference?

C. Connect two bulbs in the circuit, as shown in the bottom picture. This is a parallel circuit. Observe the brightness of the bulbs.

  5. Are the bulbs as bright as the bulbs in step **B**?
  6. Are the bulbs as bright as the bulb in step **A**?

Conclusion

1. Which circuit has the brighter bulbs?
2. Explain in your own words the difference between a series circuit and a parallel circuit.

Using science ideas

1. Draw a series circuit that has five bulbs. Suppose one bulb burned out. What would happen to the other bulbs?
2. Draw a parallel circuit that has five bulbs. Suppose one bulb burned out. What would happen to the other bulbs?

PRODUCING ELECTRICITY
How can a magnet be used to produce electricity?

Have you ever used a magnet to pick up pins or paper clips? Did you know that a magnet can also be used to produce electricity? This property of magnets was known in 1831. A scientist named Michael Faraday found that a magnet can be used to produce electricity.

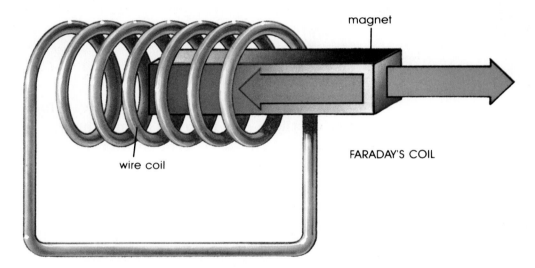

magnet

wire coil

FARADAY'S COIL

The drawing shows, in a simple way, what Faraday did. He moved a strong magnet back and forth through a coil of wire. Electrons moved along the wire! How did this happen? Electrons were not moving along the wire before the magnet was passed through it.

You may know that a magnet has lines of force around it. These lines of force cause some metal objects to move toward the magnet. They can also make electrons move inside a wire. Moving electrons produce an electric current.

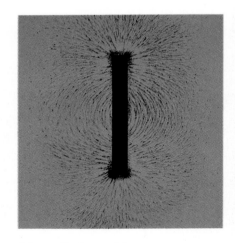

Magnetic lines of force

Generator

Faraday's discovery was used to make a machine that is still in use today. This machine is a **generator** (jen'ə rā tər). A generator changes energy of motion into electrical energy. When coils of wire cut through a strong magnetic field, electrons move through the wire. To keep the electrons moving, either the wire or the magnet must be kept moving.

To produce electricity, a generator needs energy from an outside source. Most of this energy comes from the burning of fuels, such as coal, oil, and gas.

The drawing shows how electrical energy is produced by a generator. Look at the drawing as you read each step.

1. Gas is burned to heat water to produce steam.
2. The steam turns the blades of a turbine (tër'bin). A **turbine** is a device that is made up of a wheel and blades.

3. The turbine is attached to a generator, which is shown as a magnet inside a coil of wire. As the turbine moves, it turns the magnet. This produces an electric current inside the coil of wire.
4. The current produced in the coil of wire lights the bulb.

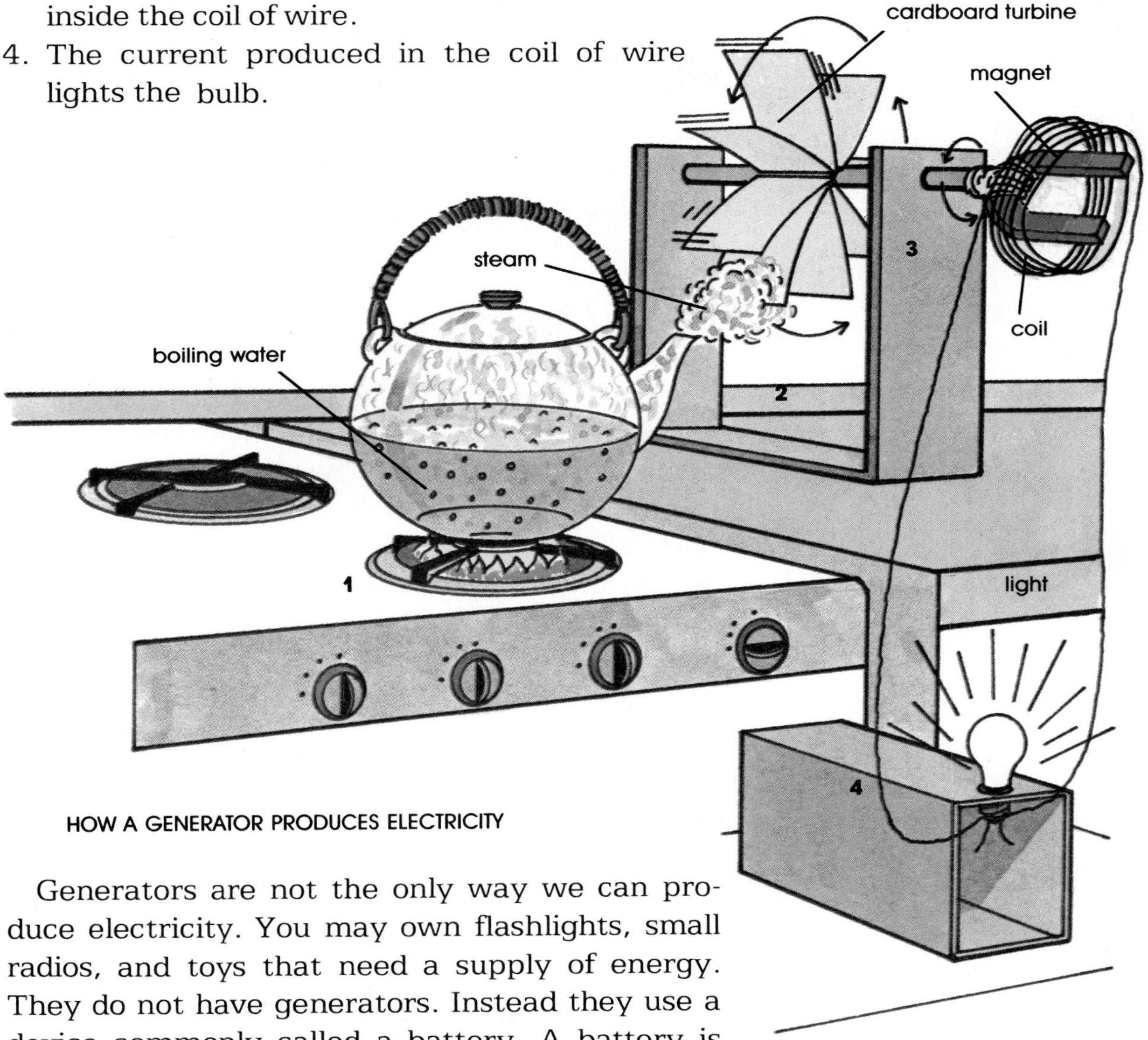

cardboard turbine

magnet

steam

boiling water

coil

2

3

1

light

4

HOW A GENERATOR PRODUCES ELECTRICITY

Generators are not the only way we can produce electricity. You may own flashlights, small radios, and toys that need a supply of energy. They do not have generators. Instead they use a device commonly called a battery. A battery is really two or more electric cells joined together. An **electric cell** is a device that changes chemical energy to electrical energy.

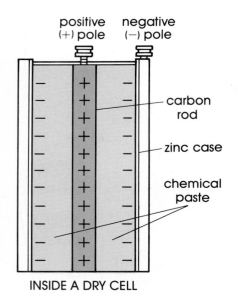

positive (+) pole   negative (−) pole

carbon rod

zinc case

chemical paste

INSIDE A DRY CELL

One type of electric cell is called a dry cell. A **dry cell** uses a chemical paste, carbon rod, and zinc case to produce a flow of electrons. Chemical reactions occur inside the dry cell. One reaction causes the walls of the zinc case to become negatively charged. Another reaction causes the carbon rod to become positively charged. The zinc case is called the negative pole. The carbon rod is called the positive pole. If the dry cell is connected to a circuit, electrons flow from the negative pole to the positive. This movement of electrons forms an electric current.

A true battery is made of two or more cells. Most car batteries are made of six cells. A car battery does not use a chemical paste to make electricity. Instead it uses acid and water, which react with metal plates. The chemical reaction of the metal and acid produces a flow of electrons. Such a battery is called a **wet cell battery.** The car battery, below, is a wet cell battery.

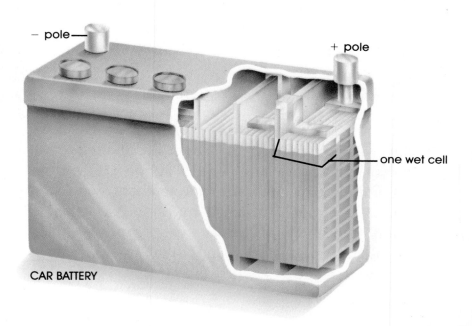

− pole

+ pole

one wet cell

CAR BATTERY

USING ELECTRICITY

How is electricity used?

Every day you use electricity in many ways. You may wake up to the sound of an electric alarm clock. You may eat breakfast cooked on an electric stove. You use electricity at home and in school. It is also used in stores and factories. Look at the drawing of the house. How many uses of electricity can you find?

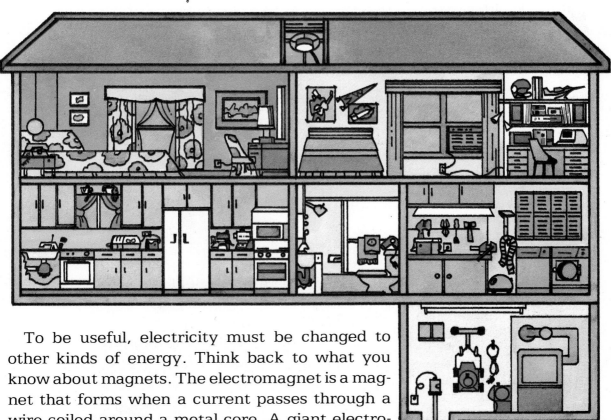

To be useful, electricity must be changed to other kinds of energy. Think back to what you know about magnets. The electromagnet is a magnet that forms when a current passes through a wire coiled around a metal core. A giant electromagnet can be used to lift heavy metal objects in a scrapyard. This is an example of how electricity can be changed to another kind of energy.

Electrical energy can also be changed to mechanical (mə kan'ə kəl) energy. **Mechanical energy** is energy of moving machine parts. You can see this change in an electric motor. An **electric motor** is a machine that changes electrical energy to mechanical energy. When you plug a motor into a wall outlet, the electricity turns the motor. Mixers, fans, and power tools all have motors. Look again at the drawing of the house on page 171. Where are motors used?

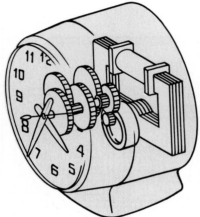

Motors in electric appliances

Electricity is also an important source of light and heat. For example, in a light bulb or a toaster, electricity is changed to light or heat energy.

Let's see how a light bulb produces light. The light bulb has a glass cover, a base, and a filament. The **filament** (fil'ə mənt) is a thin coil of wire. When a current moves through the filament it becomes hot. The hot filament glows and gives off light. The glass cover prevents air from reaching the filament. What would happen if air reached the glowing filament?

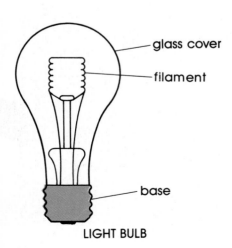

- glass cover
- filament
- base

LIGHT BULB

MEASURING ELECTRICITY

How is the flow of electricity measured?

Each day great amounts of electrical energy are used in homes, schools, and offices. How is electricity used in the picture of the office building? You use a certain amount of electricity when you watch television for an hour. You use a different amount when you read for 2 hours by the light of a lamp. Have you ever had someone tell you to turn off a light? Energy use costs money. Someone must pay for all the energy you use. But before you can pay for it, it has to be measured. The person in the picture is reading a meter that measures the amount of electricity used.

Reading an electric meter

Electricity is used to do work. The more work a device does, the more electricity it uses. Also, the faster a device works, the more electricity it uses. The amount of work that is done in a certain period of time is called **power.** Small amounts of electric power are measured in units called **watts** (wots). Large amounts of power are measured in kilowatts. A **kilowatt** (kil'ə wot) is 1,000 watts.

The World Trade Center, New York City

Most electric devices have the number of watts they use printed on them. One motor may have *50 watts* printed on it. Another motor may have *100 watts* printed on it. The 100-watt motor uses twice as much energy as the 50-watt motor in the same amount of time. Look at the light bulbs in the picture. How many watts does each bulb use? Which one uses the most power?

Electric companies measure how much electricity a customer uses in kilowatt-hours. A **kilowatt-hour** is equal to 1,000 watts of electricity used for 1 hour. A 100-watt motor can run for 10 hours before it uses a kilowatt-hour of electricity. How long can a 50-watt light bulb burn before it uses a kilowatt-hour of electricity?

Meters measure the amount of electricity used in a building. Do you know where the meter is at your house? The meter shows how many kilowatt-hours of electricity were used in your home. Each kilowatt-hour costs a certain amount of money. Look at the picture of an electric bill. How many kilowatt-hours of electricity were used during the month? How much did the electricity cost?

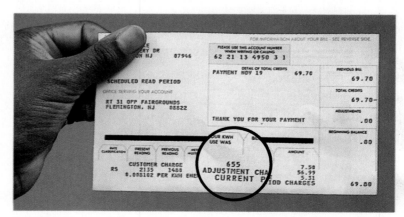

Electric bill

USING ELECTRICITY SAFELY

How can a building be made electrically safe?

Every building has safety devices to help keep electricity safe. **Fuses** (fyüz'ez) and **circuit breakers** protect buildings against fire. How do they do this? Each circuit is made to handle a certain amount of electric current. If too many appliances are plugged into a circuit, the wires may become too hot. When this happens, fuses and circuit breakers help to keep fires from starting.

Fuse box

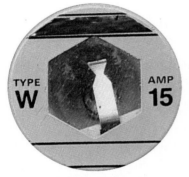 

Good fuse and blown fuse

These two safety devices are made to break the circuit if the wires become too hot. A metal strip inside a fuse melts and the fuse blows. This breaks the circuit. A special switch in a circuit breaker turns off to break the circuit.

Electricity should not be allowed to flow again until the cause of the problem is found. The number of appliances on the circuit should be checked. There may be too many. There may also be something wrong with one of the appliances.

When the circuit has been checked, the current can be turned on again. The blown fuse can be replaced with a new fuse. The switch on the circuit breaker can be turned on again.

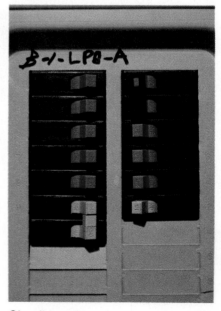

Circuit breakers

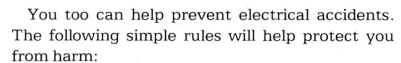

You too can help prevent electrical accidents. The following simple rules will help protect you from harm:

DON'T put anything except an electrical plug into an electrical outlet.

DON'T touch any electric appliance while you are wet.

DON'T use an electric appliance that has a frayed cord.

DON'T run an electrical cord under a carpet.

DON'T plug too many electric devices into one outlet.

DON'T touch a fallen power line.

DON'T fly a kite near power lines.

DON'T swim, play in an open field, or stand under a tree during a lightning storm.

IDEAS TO REMEMBER

▶ There are two kinds of electricity—static electricity and current electricity.

▶ Static electricity is an electric charge that does not move.

▶ Current electricity is the movement of electrons.

▶ A series circuit is one in which current can follow only one path.

▶ A parallel circuit is one in which current can follow more than one path.

▶ A generator is a machine that changes mechanical energy into electrical energy.

▶ An electric cell is a device that changes chemical energy to electrical energy.

▶ An electric motor is a machine that changes electrical energy to mechanical energy.

▶ The amount of electricity used is measured in kilowatt-hours.

▶ Fuses and circuit breakers are safety devices in electric circuits.

Reviewing the Chapter

SCIENCE WORDS

A. Identify each of the following.
1. It protects your home from fire. It is made of glass and metal. It is small enough to hold in your hand. What is it?
2. It is coiled and it glows. Electric current passes through it. It is inside a glass case. What is it?
3. It contains a chemical paste. A carbon rod passes through the middle of it. Electricity is produced inside it. What is it?

B. Write the letter of the term that best matches the definition. Not all the terms will be used.
1. Unit for measuring small amounts of electric power
2. Circuit in which current can follow only one path
3. Matter through which an electric current moves easily
4. Device that changes chemical energy to electrical energy
5. Atom that has no charge
6. Path through which an electric current flows
7. Circuit in which current can follow more than one path
8. Machine that changes energy of motion into electrical energy

a. circuit
b. generator
c. parallel circuit
d. static electricity
e. neutral
f. watt
g. current electricity
h. series circuit
i. electric cell
j. conductor
k. turbine
l. insulator

UNDERSTANDING IDEAS

A. Write the correct term for each number in the drawings.

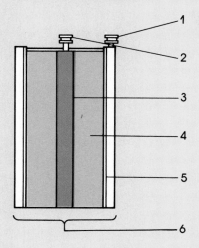

B. Look at the drawing of the house on page 171. List all the electrical appliances shown.

C. Explain how electrical energy is produced by a generator. Describe how you could make a model of a generator.

D. Name five safety rules that should be followed when using electricity.

USING IDEAS

1. Look at the next electric bill you get at your house. How many kilowatt-hours did you use? How much do you have to pay for each kilowatt-hour?

2. Do a survey of electrical safety in your home. Look for things that do not follow the safety rules found on page 176. Discuss with your family how the hazards can be corrected.

Chapter 8

Sources of Energy

Think about how you used energy today. You used energy to get dressed. This energy came from the food you ate. Perhaps you rode to school in a bus or a car. Where do buses and cars get energy to move?

The "solar power tower" in the picture is a modern device that uses the sun as a source of energy. The many mirrors focus sunlight onto the tower. The sunlight is used to produce electricity.

The sun is one source of energy that people use. The earth has other energy sources. Some of these sources are plentiful but hard to collect. Others are scarce. In this chapter you will learn about these energy sources and some of the problems involved in using them.

— ENERGY FROM FOSSIL FUELS —
What are three fossil fuels and their uses?

All machines need energy to do work. Some machines get their energy from muscle power. A bicycle is a machine that runs on muscle power. But most machines that are used today do not run on muscle power. They use another source of energy. This major energy source is fossil fuels. A **fossil fuel** is a fuel that forms from the remains of dead plants and animals. Coal, oil, and natural gas are fossil fuels.

Millions of years ago the earth was warm and wet. Much of the earth's surface was swampy. The drawing below shows what these swamps may have looked like. Many green plants grew and died in these swamps. Each plant had energy stored in it. Year after year, more plants died and piled up. The land sank beneath the weight of the

Swamp plants from which coal formed

182

plants. Seas began to form. Streams emptying into the seas carried sand and other material. The weight of all this matter pushed down hard on the dead plants. Over the years, heat and pressure caused the dead plants to change into coal.

In other places, the earth of the past was covered with shallow seas. Tiny living things in these seas died and fell to the bottom. After many years, they became covered with sand, mud, and other material. Heat and pressure changed the remains of these living things to oil and natural gas.

Coal, oil, and gas are taken from the earth. Coal and gas do not have to be changed for use as fuels. Oil that is taken from the earth is called **crude oil**. Before crude oil can be used, it must be changed. Crude oil is changed to useful products in a **refinery** (ri fī′nər ē). These products include fuels such as gasoline, diesel (dē′zəl) fuel, and home heating oil.

Oil well

gasoline

diesel fuel

home heating oil

Oil refinery

183

Fossil fuels have many uses. The most important use is as a source of energy. But before their energy can be used, fossil fuels must be burned. This process is called combustion (kəm bus′chən). In **combustion**, oxygen from the air combines with a fuel, producing heat and light.

Most of our electricity comes from the heat of burning fossil fuels. Look at the drawing. It shows coal being burned to heat water. When the water boils, it changes to steam. The steam is forced against a fan-shaped turbine. The force of the steam turns the blades of the turbine. The turbine is attached to a generator. The turbine turns the generator, which produces electricity. Power lines carry the electricity to other places.

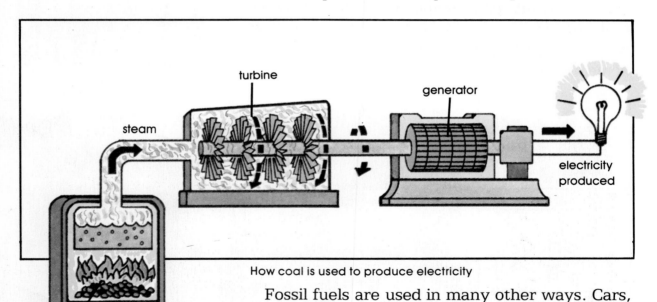

turbine

generator

steam

electricity produced

heat from combustion of coal

How coal is used to produce electricity

Fossil fuels are used in many other ways. Cars, trucks, planes, and trains all burn fossil fuels. The heat from burning fossil fuels is changed to the energy of motion by engines. Factories burn fossil fuels to make their products. The table on the next page lists main energy uses of fossil fuels.

ENERGY USES OF FOSSIL FUELS	
Fossil fuel	**Main energy uses**
Coal	Electricity production Manufacturing, such as making steel Home heating
Crude oil	Gasoline for automobiles Diesel fuel for cars, trucks, and trains Jet fuel Kerosene for home heating Oil for home heating
Natural gas	Home heating Cooking Bottled gas for campers and outdoor grills

Supplies of fossil fuels are limited. Once they are used, they are gone forever. They cannot be replaced. The world will someday run out of this major energy source. So people must make wise use of fossil fuels.

Finding out

Are you wasting energy? You can locate heat energy leaks at home and at school. Get a pencil, a piece of plastic wrap, and some transparent tape. Tape the piece of plastic wrap along one side of the pencil. The plastic wrap should hang down about 15 cm from the pencil. You have made an energy-leak finder.

Test your classroom or a room at home for energy leaks. Hold the energy-leak finder in a place where you think air might be leaking to the outside. Check around windows and doors. If there is a leak, the plastic wrap will move. Find out what could be done to prevent this waste of energy.

ENERGY FROM ATOMS
How is energy obtained from an atom?

The second major source of energy being used in the world is nuclear (nü′klē ər) energy. What is nuclear energy? You have learned that the atom is a small particle from which all matter is made. You have also learned that there is a nucleus in the. center of every atom. The energy stored in the nucleus of an atom is called **nuclear energy**. This energy has to be released before it can be used.

There are two ways to release the energy that is stored in an atom. The most common process used is called fission (fish′ən). In **nuclear fission** the nucleus of an atom is split, releasing energy. The atom that is most often used in fission is the uranium (yù rā′nē əm) atom.

Nuclear power plant

The other process used to release the energy that is stored in the atom is called fusion (fyü′zhən). Fusion is the opposite of fission. In **nuclear fusion** the nuclei (nü′klē ī) of atoms are combined, releasing energy. (The word *nuclei* means "more than one nucleus.") In both fission and fusion large amounts of energy are released.

The most important use of nuclear energy today is to produce electricity. Fission is the process used to produce energy for electricity. Fission takes place in a special structure called a **nuclear reactor**. The large amounts of heat energy that result from fission are controlled in the reactor. In nuclear power plants the heat from fission is used to change water to steam. Look at the drawing below. Just as in coal-burning power plants, the steam is used to turn a turbine. The turbine is attached to a generator that produces electricity.

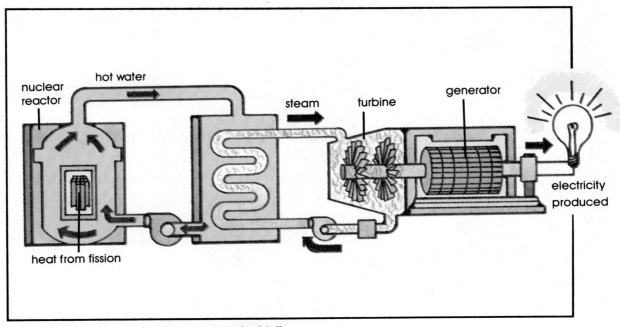

How nuclear energy is used to produce electricity

Fusion is not used today to produce useful energy. This is because scientists have not yet learned to control the great amount of energy released from fusion. Scientists are using the nuclear test reactor shown to help them learn to control fusion.

Nuclear test reactor

Although fusion cannot be controlled, almost all the energy on the earth comes from fusion. This is because the sun is the source of most of the earth's energy. And the sun produces energy from fusion.

Nuclear energy is one way to meet the world's energy needs. Some people think its benefits outweigh its problems. People who favor using nuclear energy say it helps save fossil fuels. Electricity can be produced by using a lot less

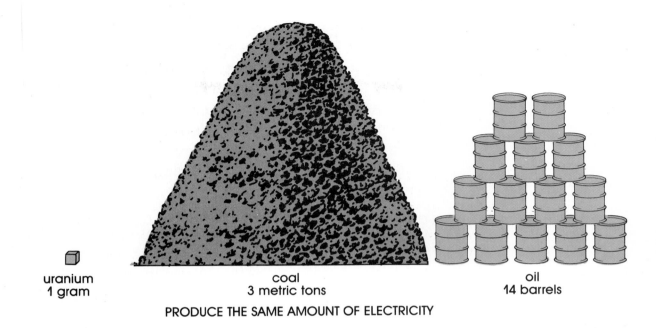

uranium
1 gram

coal
3 metric tons

oil
14 barrels

PRODUCE THE SAME AMOUNT OF ELECTRICITY

uranium than by using either coal or oil. In fact, just 1 gram of uranium produces as much energy as 3 metric tons of coal or 14 barrels of oil.

Supporters of nuclear energy also say that it is clean energy. It does not release harmful smoke into the air, as happens when coal is burned. Why do nuclear power plants not give off smoke?

But other people point to the problems in using nuclear energy. The fuel used inside these power plants gives off radiation (rā dē ā'shən). Radiation is the release of energy and particles from atoms. It can harm living things. Some people fear that radiation inside power plants might leak to the outside.

Another problem is where to put the wastes from nuclear reactors. Some of these wastes give off harmful radiation for hundreds of years. So getting rid of them in a safe way is important. Scientists are looking for ways to do this.

189

ENERGY FROM THE SUN

How is solar energy used, and what are some problems with its use?

Almost all the energy on the earth comes from solar (sō'lər) energy. **Solar energy** is energy from the sun. Today solar energy is used mostly as a source of heat. Office buildings and houses are heated with solar energy.

One way to use solar energy is to "trap" it. Have you ever gotten into a closed car that had been parked in direct sunlight? If so, you know that a lot of heat was trapped in the car. The air in the car may have been much warmer than the air outside.

How does the air in the car become warmed? Solar energy passes through the glass windows. When it strikes the material inside the car, the solar energy changes to heat. This warms the air inside the car. Because the car is sealed, very little heat escapes to the outside. So the air in the car becomes warmer and warmer. This buildup of heat is called the **greenhouse effect**.

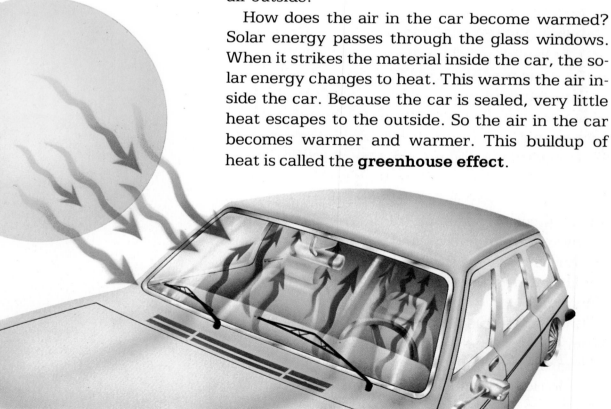

Look at the picture of the greenhouse. Why are the walls and roof made of glass? The greenhouse effect is used to heat some houses and other buildings. This kind of heating is called passive solar heating.

There are other ways to use solar energy. One method makes use of large solar collectors. A **solar collector** is a device that collects sunlight and changes it to heat energy. You can see solar collectors on the roof of this apartment building.

Inside the solar collectors there are rows of black tubes carrying water or air. Sunlight strikes the tubes and heats the water or air inside them. The tubes carry the heated water or air to pipes that run through the building. The heated water or air is pumped through the pipes. If the heat is not needed, the heated material goes to a storage area. On a cloudy day or at night, the stored heat can be used. Systems that have pumps or other moving parts use active solar heating.

Solar collectors on roof

In addition to producing heat, solar energy can also be used to produce electricity. This can be done in two ways. One way is an indirect method. Solar energy is first used to produce heat. The heat changes liquid water to steam. The steam turns a turbine that is attached to a generator.

The type of solar collector shown below uses an indirect method to produce electricity. It has mirrors that gather sunlight. Another picture of this type of collector is on pages 180–181 of this

Solar collector that uses mirrors

Solar cells on *Viking* spacecraft

chapter. The sunlight is reflected onto a small area on the tower. Inside the tower is a boiler that holds water. How can solar collectors such as this be used to produce electricity?

Another way to use solar energy to produce electricity is a direct method. A device called a **solar cell** changes solar energy into electrical energy. Solar cells are an energy source for many spacecraft and some buildings. There are solar cells covering the four arms of this spacecraft. Why would solar cells be useful in spacecraft?

Solar energy seems to be a perfect energy source. It is clean, plentiful, and free! But there are problems in using solar energy. One problem is that not all places receive enough sunlight to make solar energy useful. Also solar energy is not constant. If there are several cloudy days in a row, the stored heat or electrical energy may be used up.

Do you know?

The *Solar Challenger* is an airplane that is powered solely by the sun's energy. There are a total of 16,128 solar cells covering the upper surface of this one-person plane. You can see these solar cells in the picture. They produce electricity that runs two small motors that turn the plane's propeller. The entire plane weighs less than 98 kg.

On July 5, 1981, the *Solar Challenger* made a record-setting flight. It took off from France, flew across the English Channel, and landed more than 267 km away in England. During its Channel crossing, the craft reached an air speed of over 75 km/h, and the only fuel it used was energy from the sun! A drawing of the *Solar Challenger* appears on the back cover of this book.

Which direction receives more solar energy?

Materials 2 cardboard shoe boxes with lids / scissors / clear plastic wrap / transparent tape / 2 thermometers / compass

Procedure

A. Use scissors to cut out a rectangular hole in one side of two shoe boxes. Cover the hole in each box with a piece of clear plastic wrap. Use transparent tape to attach the plastic wrap.

B. Place a thermometer inside each box and put the lids on. Then make a chart like the one shown.

C. Take the boxes outdoors on a sunny day. Use a compass to find north and south. Place one box so that its "window" faces south. Place the other box so that its "window" faces north.

D. Open the boxes and check the temperature in each. Record this number as the starting temperature in your chart. Now close the boxes.
  1. What is the temperature inside each box?
  2. How do you think the temperature in the two boxes will change during the next 40 minutes?

E. Every 10 minutes, for the next 40 minutes, record in your chart the temperature inside each box.
  3. In which box was the final temperature greater?

F. Make a graph showing how the temperature in each box changed.

Conclusion

1. What was the difference between the starting and final temperature in each box?
2. Which lets in more solar energy, a north-facing window or a south-facing window?
3. In which direction should the windows face in a house that uses passive solar energy? Why?

Time	Temperature	
	North	South
0 min		
10 min		
20 min		
30 min		
40 min		

ENERGY FROM WATER

What are two ways that moving water is used for energy?

Moving water is an important source of energy used to produce electricity. In a **hydroelectric** (hī-drō i lek'trik) **power plant** the energy of moving water turns turbines attached to generators that produce electricity. Hydroelectric power plants, such as the one shown, are built as part of dams on rivers. Falling water flows through pipes inside the dam. The water flows over turbine blades at the bottom of the dam. The moving blades turn generators.

Hydroelectric power plant

The number of places where hydroelectric power plants can be built are limited. Also when dams are built on rivers, large land areas may be flooded. This can destroy places where many plants and animals live.

There is another way of using the energy of flowing water. Have you ever spent a day at an ocean beach? If so, you have probably seen that

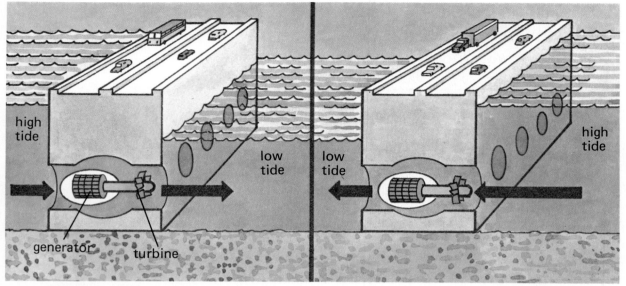

How tidal energy is used to produce electricity

Tidal power plant

the water level along the shore rises and falls. In most areas the water level rises and falls twice a day. These daily movements of the water level along the shore are called **tides.**

Tidal (tī′dəl) energy is another energy source. **Tidal energy** is the energy of rising and falling tides. It can be used to produce electricity. To see how this is done, look at the drawing. A dam is built across a narrow opening to the ocean. During high and low tides, water moves in and out of the openings in the dam. As it moves through the openings, the water flows over turbine blades inside the dam. The turbines turn generators.

Very few tidal power plants are in use today. The picture shows one that was built on a river in France. Tidal energy will probably never be a major energy source. For tidal energy to be used, there must be a large difference in the height of the water between low and high tides. But there are only a few places in the world where tides are high and low enough to produce much energy.

ENERGY FROM HEAT IN THE EARTH

How is geothermal energy used?

You have learned that almost all energy on the earth comes from solar energy. But there is also an energy source that is deep inside the earth. This kind of energy is called **geothermal** (jē ə-thėr'məl) **energy.** It is energy from natural heat trapped beneath the earth's surface. This heat melts rock inside the earth. Melted rock inside the earth is called **magma** (mag'mə). In some places the magma comes close to the earth's surface. The magma collects in areas beneath the surface called hot spots. These **hot spots** are areas of geothermal energy.

How can geothermal energy be used to produce electricity? When water in the ground comes in contact with hot spots, the water turns to steam. By drilling wells into the earth in hot spots, this

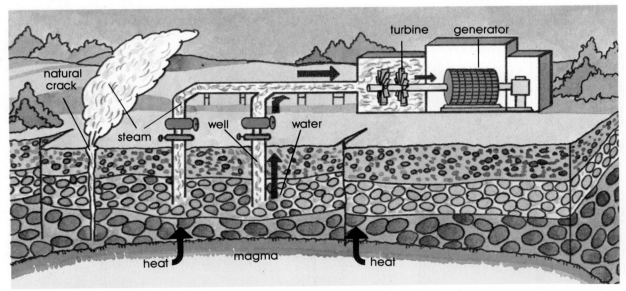

How geothermal energy is used to produce electricity

steam can be released. The released steam can be used to turn turbines that run generators.

In some places steam and hot water come to the surface without drilling. There are deep cracks in rock inside the earth through which the steam and hot water can move. When they reach the surface, the steam and hot water may gush out of the ground. This is called a geyser (gī′zər). You can see one geyser, Old Faithful, in the picture on the left.

The geothermal power plant in the picture is the largest in the world. This plant, called The Geysers, is located in California. It supplies enough electricity to run a large city. There are plans to expand The Geysers.

There are problems with geothermal energy. Many areas of geothermal energy are far from any large towns or cities. Electricity produced in these places would have to be carried great distances. This can be very costly.

A geyser

Geothermal power plant

198

ENERGY FROM THE WIND

How is energy from the wind used?

The wind has been used as a source of energy for more than a thousand years. Wind energy is the energy of moving air. Long ago people used windmills to grind wheat into flour. Today windmills are being used to make electricity.

Old windmill used for grinding wheat

Modern windmills look different from the windmills of long ago. However, they work in much the same way. The wind turns blades at the top of the windmill. The blades are connected to a generator that produces electricity. This device is often called a wind turbine.

The high cost of other sources of energy has made windmills popular in some places. But there are problems with wind energy. One problem is that there are not many places where the wind blows strong and steady. Another problem is the high cost of building and fixing windmills. So energy from the wind is not likely to do much to help the world's future energy needs.

Modern wind turbine

Can the wind make electricity where you live?

Materials nylon thread, 20 cm long / Ping-Pong ball / transparent tape / colored marking pen / protractor / cardboard strip, 10 cm x 2 cm

Procedure

A. Tape one end of a piece of nylon thread to a Ping-Pong ball. Use a marking pen to color the thread so it will be easier to see. Tape the free end of the thread to the center of a protractor as shown. Then tape a cardboard strip to one side of the protractor. This will serve as a handle. You have now made a device to measure wind speed.

B. Take your device outdoors. Hold the protractor so that the flat edge is level with the ground, as in the bottom picture. When the wind blows the ball, the thread will line up with marks on the protractor. Record the number of the highest mark that the thread reaches. Use the table below to find out what this number equals in wind speed.

    1. What is the wind speed?

Number of mark	90	85	80	75	70	65	60	55	50	45	40	35	30	25	20
Wind speed (km/h)	0	9	13	16	19	21	24	26	29	31	34	37	41	46	52

C. Take wind speed readings several times a day for 4 to 5 days. Record your findings.

    2. What is the highest speed recorded?

D. For a wind turbine to produce electricity, wind speed must be 13 km/h or over.

    3. What was the average speed of the wind?

Conclusion

1. Is there enough wind to make electricity where you live?

2. What effect would the steadiness of wind speed have on the ability of a wind turbine to produce electricity?

— ENERGY FROM LIVING THINGS —

How is energy from living things used?

You have learned that millions of years must pass before the remains of living things become fossil fuels. Today scientists are looking for ways of changing plant and animal matter directly into energy. Plant and animal matter is called **biomass** (bī′ō mas). Biomass can be used to produce energy. The process of changing biomass into usable energy is called **bioconversion** (bī ō kən-vėr′zhən).

A campfire is an example of bioconversion. Wood is the biomass that is changed to produce energy. In recent years many people in the United States have bought wood-burning stoves. They use them to heat their homes. People save money by using wood as a fuel, since oil and natural gas are so costly. What could happen if a great many people use wood-burning stoves?

Wood-burning stove used to heat home

Bioconversion power plant

There is biomass in the trash that people throw away. In the United States, the average person produces more than 1 kg of trash each day. Much of it can be burned to make heat. This heat can be used to change water to steam. The steam can run generators. Bioconversion of trash helps in two ways. It produces useful energy from low-cost fuel. And it gets rid of unwanted materials. The picture on the left shows trash that will be burned to produce electricity.

Trash containing dead plant and animal matter can be used to make energy in yet another way. By using tiny living things called bacteria (bak-tir'ē ə), trash can be changed to fuel. The bacteria use the biomass in trash as a source of food. In the process, they produce a fuel called methane (meth'ān) gas. Methane gas can be burned for heat energy.

There is another way plants can be used for energy. The girl in the picture is filling the car's

Gasohol—a gasoline-and-alcohol mixture

tank with a gasoline-and-alcohol mixture. Alcohol is added to gasoline to help stretch the supply of this fuel. The alcohol comes from a process in which corn and yeast (yēst) are mixed. Yeasts are tiny nongreen plants. They use sugar as food. As the yeasts use the sugar that is stored in corn, they produce alcohol. You can see that there are many ways in which living things and the remains of living things help supply energy.

IDEAS TO REMEMBER

▶ A fossil fuel is a fuel that forms from the remains of dead plants and animals.
▶ Fission and fusion are processes used to release the nuclear energy of atoms.
▶ Solar energy can be used to heat buildings and produce electricity.
▶ Moving water can be used to produce electrical energy in hydroelectric and tidal power plants.
▶ Geothermal energy is energy from natural heat trapped beneath the earth's surface.
▶ Modern windmills use the energy of the wind to produce electricity.
▶ Plant and animal matter can be changed into useful forms of energy through bioconversion.

Reviewing the Chapter

SCIENCE WORDS

A. Use all the terms below to complete the sentences.

nuclear fusion   fossil fuel   refinery   nuclear reactor
crude oil   nuclear energy   combustion   nuclear fission

Oil is one kind of __1__. Oil that is taken from the earth is called __2__. It is changed to useful products in a/an __3__. During __4__ oxygen from the air combines with a fuel, producing heat and light.

The energy stored in the nucleus of an atom is called __5__. Scientists are learning to control the energy released when the nuclei of atoms are combined in the process of __6__. The nucleus of an atom is split in the process of __7__. The splitting of atoms takes place in a structure called a/an __8__.

B. Write the letter of the term that best matches the definition. Not all the terms will be used.

1. Device that collects sunlight and changes it to heat energy
2. Melted rock inside the earth
3. Plant and animal matter
4. Areas of geothermal energy
5. Device that changes solar energy to electricity
6. Daily movement of the water level along the shore
7. Energy from the sun

a. biomass
b. hot spots
c. solar energy
d. tides
e. wind turbine
f. solar collector
g. hydroelectric power plant
h. magma
i. solar cell

UNDERSTANDING IDEAS

A. Write the term that best matches each picture.

tidal energy   bioconversion   energy from a fossil fuel
greenhouse effect   hydroelectric power
geothermal energy

B. List one problem in using each energy source above.

C. Describe three ways to use energy from the sun.

USING IDEAS

1. Suppose you had to design a house for you and your family to live in. Which energy source or sources would you use to provide heat and electricity? Tell where you would have the house built. Explain how its location relates to the energy source or sources you choose. Also list the benefits and problems for each energy source.

2. Use pictures from old magazines to make a poster that shows different fossil fuels and how they are used.

Science in Careers

A person who studies the properties of matter is called a *chemist*. There are many different kinds of chemists. Food chemists test foods for quality and also make chemicals that help keep foods from spoiling. Other chemists invent new materials. Much of the clothing sold today is made from new materials developed by chemists.

Today many people see the value of using solar energy. *Architects* (är′kə tekts) who specialize in designing buildings that use solar energy are much in demand. These architects plan additions to older buildings so that solar energy can be used. They also plan new homes and factories that make use of devices such as solar collectors.

Telephone cable worker

The electrical energy needed to run telephones is carried by large cables. *Telephone cable workers* put these cables in place. When the cables break, as can happen during a storm, the cable worker repairs them. Cable workers must understand how electricity works.

Architect

People in Science

Percy Julian (1899–1975)

Dr. Julian spent his life studying uses for chemicals taken from the soybean plant. In 1935 he discovered a chemical that cures a disease which causes blindness. Another discovery made by Julian greatly lowered the cost of a drug used to help people suffering from arthritis. In all, Dr. Julian owned more than 1,000 patents. These patents included one for a fire-fighting chemical that saved many lives during World War II.

Dr. Julian in his chemistry laboratory

Developing Skills

WORD SKILLS

Prefixes and suffixes are word parts that change the meanings of the base words to which they are added. A prefix is added to the beginning of a base word. A suffix is added to the end of a base word. The tables show how prefixes and suffixes are used to change the meanings of words.

Prefix	Meaning	Example
anti-	against	antisocial
di-	two	dioxide
in-	not	indirect
semi-	half, partly	semicircle

Use the tables to help you write a definition for each of the following words. If you do not know the meaning of the base word, look it up in a dictionary.

1. mechanical
2. semiconductor
3. generator
4. fissionable
5. diatomic
6. insoluble
7. electrify
8. antifreeze

Suffix	Meaning	Example
-able	that can be	obtainable
-al	of, like	musical
-fy	make, cause to be	horrify
-or	person or thing performing an act	conveyor

READING A PICTOGRAPH

A pictograph is a way to show information using pictures as symbols. The pictograph shows the amount of oil that could be saved in 1 year in different ways.

Use the pictograph to answer these questions.

1. How much oil could be saved in 1 year if all clothes were washed in cold water?
2. Which energy-saving idea saves the most oil? How much is saved?
3. Which two of the energy-saving ideas save the same amount of oil? How much is saved?
4. Which of the energy-saving ideas saves 570,000 barrels of oil?
5. If all cars carried one more person and all cars averaged 8.9 km/L of gasoline, how much oil would be saved in 1 year?
6. How much oil would be saved in 1 year if all houses had 15 cm of insulation and all thermostats were set at 16°C?

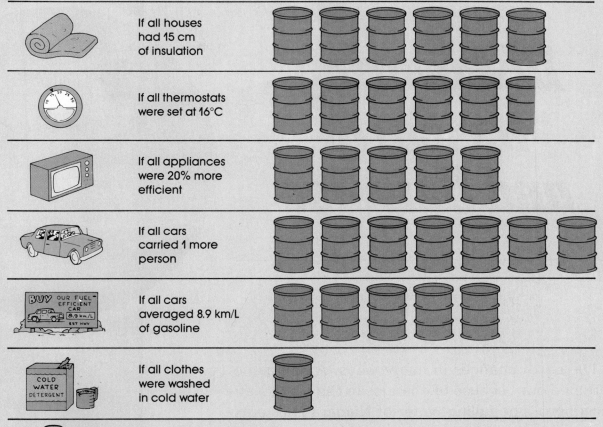

WAYS TO SAVE OIL

	If all houses had 15 cm of insulation	
	If all thermostats were set at 16°C	
	If all appliances were 20% more efficient	
	If all cars carried 1 more person	
	If all cars averaged 8.9 km/L of gasoline	
	If all clothes were washed in cold water	

Each [barrel] equals 100,000 barrels of oil per year

MAKING A PICTOGRAPH

Make a pictograph that shows the number of watts of electric power used by some electric appliances. Use a drawing of an electric outlet, such as the one shown, to represent 100 watts of electric power. Include the following data in your pictograph.

Appliance	Watts	Appliance	Watts
Blender	300	Lamp bulb	100
Microwave oven	1450	Washing machine	550
Television	145	Clothes dryer	5000
Coffee maker	1200	Hair dryer	1000
Sewing machine	75	Iron	1100
Air conditioner	900	Toaster	1000
Vacuum cleaner	600	Radio	75

UNIT THREE

Discovering the Earth and Universe

The earth changes in many ways. A ball game is rained out because of changes in the earth's atmosphere. The falling water of Niagara Falls cuts into rock below it. This changes the shape of the rock. People also change the earth. Sometimes these changes are harmful. Which picture shows a harmful change brought about by people? What has been changed? Even the many stars that are part of our universe undergo changes.

In this unit you will learn some of the reasons for changes in the weather. You will also learn about the natural forces that change the shape of the land. And you will see how people can avoid making harmful changes in the world. Finally you will explore the universe. You will learn how the stars and other bodies in space change.

Chapter 9

Changes in the Earth

Have you ever seen a place that looked like this? What caused the rocks to be shaped in these ways? This place is Bryce Canyon in Utah. The rocks in Bryce Canyon were shaped by the movement of water over millions of years.

The land that covers the earth has changed its shape many times during the history of the earth. The force of moving water, ice, and air have caused these changes. In this chapter you will learn how the earth is worn away in some places. You will also learn how it is built up in other places. You will see how water, ice, and wind move materials from place to place.

WEATHERING CHANGES THE LAND

How does physical weathering occur?

If you view the earth while flying in a plane, you can see many features of its surface. You may see high mountains and rolling hills. You may see flat land, valleys, and cliffs. The surface of the earth is always changing. It is changed by natural processes. In time, flat land may become a mountain range. Hills and mountains may slowly be worn down. The land is worn down by weathering. **Weathering** is all the processes that break rock into smaller pieces. The processes of weathering can be put into two groups.

One kind of weathering is called physical weathering. **Physical weathering** is all the processes that break apart rock without changing its chemical makeup. This weathering causes rock to change its size and shape. The rock is broken into smaller pieces. But the pieces have the same makeup as the rock they came from. The only change they have gone through is a physical one.

The effect that the freezing and melting of water has on rock is a type of physical weathering. In some mountain regions the daytime temperatures are above the freezing point of water. Water seeps into cracks in rock. At night, temperatures drop below the freezing point. So the water turns to ice.

When water freezes, it expands. As the water in a crack expands, it pushes with great force against both sides of the crack. This causes the crack to become larger. The daily freezing and melting of water causes large rocks to break up into smaller pieces. This kind of physical weathering is called **frost action.**

Ice on rock

Cliffs weathered by frost action

If you live in a place where it gets cold enough, you may see the result of frost action. During the winter large cracks can form in sidewalks. Many cracks and holes, such as the pothole on the left, also form in roads. These are caused by the freezing and melting of water.

Plants can also cause rocks to crack and break apart. Small plants and trees can grow in soil found in the cracks of rocks. As they grow, the plants push against the sides of the cracks. They cause the cracks to get larger. In time they split the rocks. The tree trunk on the left has split the large rock.

If you look carefully in your neighborhood, you may see places where plants have split some rocks and sidewalks. There may also be places, such as the one shown in the picture below, where tree roots have lifted up parts of the sidewalk.

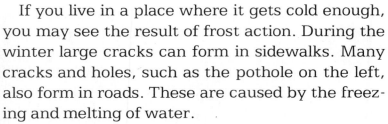

How does the freezing and melting of water weather rocks? Wash out an empty milk carton. Open the top of the carton and fill it with water. Be sure the carton is completely filled. Close the top of the carton and tape it shut with a piece of masking tape. Place the carton in a freezer overnight.

The next day remove the carton from the freezer. Describe what you see. What has happened? What do you think caused it? How could this process weather rocks?

Physical weathering can also be seen along an ocean shore. Large waves pound rocks at the shore. When waves crash against rocky cliffs, such as those on the right, cracks can form. After a while, rocks may break away and fall into the ocean. The rocks may be lifted and dropped many times by the waves. As they are moved, the rocks strike other rocks. In time the rocks may be ground into small stones and pebbles. Waves may throw the stones and pebbles back against the cliffs. This helps to weather the rocks and cliffs even more.

Have you ever picked up smooth stones from a beach? This is another example of physical weathering by ocean waves. Many of the rocks weathered by waves are smooth and round.

Wind can also weather rocks. Wind can blow small pieces of sand against rocks. This can polish and smooth the rocks. But the wind alone does not weather rocks very much.

-ANOTHER KIND OF WEATHERING-

How does chemical weathering occur?

Rock is also broken apart by chemical weathering. **Chemical weathering** is all the processes that break apart rock by changing its chemical makeup.

In some places there are large amounts of limestone and water in the ground. Chemical weathering is common in such places. As rain falls through air, it mixes with carbon dioxide gas in the air. Some of this gas dissolves in the rainwater. This changes the rainwater into carbonic (kär bon'ik) acid. This weak acid drains through rock and soil. When it reaches the limestone in the ground, it seeps into cracks in the limestone. As it does, the acid dissolves some of the limestone. This makes the cracks grow larger.

Over thousands of years the dissolving of limestone can form a system of tunnels under the ground. Large caves are often part of these tunnel systems. The picture below shows one of the largest caves that was formed in this way.

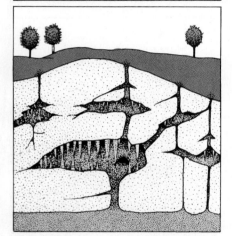

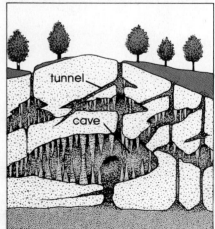

How limestone caves form

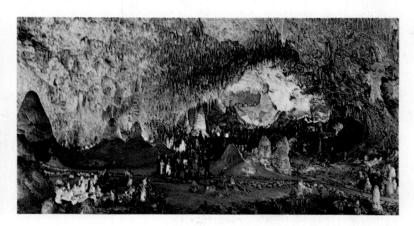

Chemical weathering also breaks up rocks that contain iron. Rainwater contains oxygen from the air. The oxygen is dissolved in the water. Iron in rocks joins with the oxygen in rainwater. Iron oxide, or rust, is the new substance that forms. Iron oxide is soft and easily breaks off rock. When it breaks off, even more of the rock's surface can be changed by falling rain. The red-orange color in the rock on the right is caused by iron oxide.

Mosses and other tiny plants, called lichens (lī′kənz), also weather rock by chemical action. These plants grow on rock and send out rootlike parts. The rootlike parts grow into tiny openings in the rock. They produce acids that dissolve some of the rock.

Rock containing iron oxide

Lichens on rock

Mosses on rock

Both physical and chemical weathering cause rock to break down. Chemical weathering happens at a fast rate in places that are wet and fairly warm. Physical weathering is greatest in wet places that are cooler. Dry places show little weathering effects, except for those caused by wind. Both kinds of weathering result in the forming of soil. Pieces of weathered rock mix with remains of living things. This forms soil.

river

─ WATER CHANGES THE LAND ─

How does water change the land?

Most weathered materials are carried to other places. The movement of weathered rock and soil from one place to another is called **erosion** (i rō'zhən). Water, ice, and wind are called the **agents of erosion.** This is because moving water, moving ice, and moving air carry away weathered materials.

The most important agent of erosion is water. The force behind water erosion is gravity. Gravity causes water to run downhill. The steeper the hill, the faster the water will flow down it. The faster the water flows, the greater the rate of erosion. The amount of water also affects the rate of erosion. The more water there is, the more erosion there will be.

Erosion may begin when raindrops hit the soil. The falling drops break up large lumps of soil. Some of the water from rain and melting snow flows over the earth's surface. This water is called **runoff.** As runoff moves downhill, it may form small streams. Small streams may come together to form a larger stream. Several larger streams may join to form a river. Rivers flow into lakes or oceans.

rain

runoff

streams

ocean

As water moves over the surface, it may erode soil and rocks. The amount of material that is moved depends partly on the amount of water. The speed of the water is an even more important factor. Fast-moving water erodes far more material than slower-moving water. If there are no plants growing in soil, moving water may erode a lot of soil.

The erosion of soil by runoff can be a problem for farmers. The top layers of soil are rich in materials that plants need. So it is important for farmers to prevent erosion of this soil. The picture below shows one way this is done. There is a lot of erosion in hilly places. So farmers plant rows of crops around the sides of hills. The rows follow the curve of the land. When it rains, the rows hold the water and soil in place.

Erosion of soil by runoff

Crops following curve of land to prevent erosion

Terraces built to prevent erosion

Another way to prevent soil erosion on hills is to build terraces. Terraces, such as those on the left, are flat areas cut into a hillside. They, too, keep water and soil from washing down the hillside. Soil erosion can also be reduced by not clearing the land of all plants. How does this help?

Soil erosion is not the only effect of moving water. As water flows in a river, it wears away the riverbed. The riverbed is the rock under the river. The moving water carries materials that act like sandpaper. They grind rock and wear it away. The weathered materials are then carried by the moving water in the river.

The downward cutting of a riverbed can create a deep valley with steep sides. Such a valley is called a **canyon.** The Colorado River has been cutting the rocks of its riverbed for millions of years. This has formed the Grand Canyon, which is over 1.5 km deep.

Two views of the Grand Canyon and Colorado River

Ocean waves can erode sand from beaches along the shore. In some places the shoreline may lose as much as 380 cubic meters of sand each day. The pictures show a lighthouse at the tip of Long Island, New York. The picture on the top was taken almost 90 years ago. Compare it with the recent picture. Notice how much land has been eroded by ocean waves.

You have learned that erosion is greatest in fast-moving water. As a river flows downstream, the water starts to slow down. This slowing down causes the river to drop some sediments (sed'ə-mənts). **Sediments** are the materials that are dropped by the agents of erosion. Sediments include sand, soil, and rocks. The dropping of sediments by the agents of erosion is called **deposition** (dep ə zish'ən).

Erosion and deposition are related. Weathered materials are picked up and carried from one place. They are dropped, or deposited, as sediment in another place. In this way the land is constantly changing. In some places it is worn down by erosion. At the same time it is built up in other places by deposition.

In the spring, snow on the ground melts and there is often a lot of rain. So spring floods are common in some places. Flooding can erode valuable soil and destroy property. But flooding of rivers can be helpful because of deposition.

Spring flood

The floodwaters that overflow the banks of a river carry a lot of material. When these floodwaters soak into the ground, sediments are depos-

Rich farmland deposited by floodwaters

ited on the land along the river. These sediments enrich the soil. So land near rivers is often good farmland.

Most rivers empty into the ocean. The place where a river empties into the ocean is called the mouth of the river. The water at the mouth of a river moves very slowly. Much of the material carried by the river is deposited at the mouth of the river. The sediments form a fan-shaped land-mass called a **delta.** Deltas are made up of sediments of weathered rock.

Mississippi River delta

The delta shown on the right is at the mouth of the Mississippi River. It is the largest delta in the United States. The picture was taken from an airplane, using special film. Other large rivers also have deltas.

The few remaining sediments that are not deposited on the delta are carried out to sea by ocean currents. Waves may carry some of these sediments and deposit them back on the shore. This forms sand beaches. Sediments may also be deposited as sandbars near the shore.

Sandbar

What factors affect the rate of erosion by water?

Materials sand-and-gravel mixture / rectangular metal baking pan / metric ruler / 2 books / plastic squeeze bottle / clock or watch with second hand

Procedure

A. Put a sand-and-gravel mixture into one half of a pan. The mixture should be about 3 cm deep.

B. Use a book to raise the same end of the pan that contains the mixture. This represents material on a hillside.

C. Fill a plastic squeeze bottle with water. Begin to drop water on the mixture at the rate of one drop every 3 seconds.
   1. What do you observe?

D. Increase the rate to two drops every 3 seconds.
   2. Compare the amount of erosion with that in step **C**.

E. Put another book under the same end of the tray.
   3. What does this do to the angle of the tray? Does it make the hill more, or less, steep?

F. Again drop two drops every 3 seconds. Compare your results with those from step **D**.

Conclusion

1. What did the water do to the sand-and-gravel mixture?
2. Did increasing the rate of water flow affect the amount of material moved? Explain.
3. Did increasing the angle of the tray affect the amount of material moved? Explain.

Using science ideas

How would a steady stream of running water affect the amount of material moved? What body of water would this be like?

ICE CHANGES THE LAND

How do glaciers change the land?

In the past, there were long periods of very cold temperatures. Ice and snow built up on the land. These periods are known as ice ages. During these ice ages, the land was covered by large, slow-moving masses of ice called **glaciers** (glā'shərz). The movement of glaciers during ice ages changed the shape of much of the land. The last ice age ended about 10,000 years ago.

During the last ice age, the temperatures over the earth changed from cold to warm and back again. This happened several times. During the cold periods, a lot of snow and ice piled up, and the glaciers grew larger. The weight of the snow and ice caused the glaciers to move southward.

As the huge ice sheets moved forward, they weathered and eroded the land over which they

Rock polished by glacier

Rock scratched by glacier

moved. They carried soil, rock, and huge boulders great distances. The materials carried by glaciers scraped and cut the land. This action smoothed, polished, and scratched rock. In some places, the tops of mountains were weathered and eroded by glaciers. This formed rounded hills.

Rocky material deposited when glacier stopped

During the warm periods, the southern edge of the glaciers melted. As they did, they left behind large hilly ridges of rocky materials. These hilly ridges can be seen today in the northern United States and in Canada. They mark the places where glaciers stopped. The picture above shows one of the ridges made of rocks deposited by a glacier.

In some places, glaciers dug out large amounts of rock and soil. Many of these dug-out areas filled in with water when the glaciers melted. These places became lakes. The lake regions of Wisconsin and Minnesota contain examples of this. The picture on the left shows a chain of small lakes that were formed by a glacier. Some large lakes were also formed. Glaciers helped form the Great Lakes.

Lakes formed by glacier

Ice sheet

In some places glaciers exist today. Ice sheets, much like the glaciers of the ice ages, are found in Greenland and the South Pole region. Smaller mountain glaciers are found in high mountains, such as the Alps and the Rocky Mountains. Mountain glaciers are sometimes called rivers of ice. Why is this a good name?

Mountain glacier

Mountain glaciers scoop out material from valleys. This widens the valleys and gives them a U shape. The drawing shows a cutaway view of a U-shaped valley formed by a mountain glacier.

Glaciers of past ice ages have had a great effect on changing the shape of the land. The amount of erosion done by today's glaciers is limited. But some scientists believe that ice sheets will return someday and spread across the earth. If this happens, glaciers will reshape the land once again.

U-shaped valley formed by glacier

How does a glacier change the land?

Materials   sand-and-gravel mixture / small paper cup / metric ruler / freezer / metal baking pan / modeling clay

Procedure

A. Place about 2 cm of a sand-and-gravel mixture in a paper cup.

B. Fill the cup with water and stir the mixture. Place the cup in a freezer. Allow the mixture to freeze overnight.

C. Line the bottom of a baking pan with a layer of modeling clay about 1 cm thick. Put a layer of sand-and-gravel mixture over the clay. This layer should also be about 1 cm thick.

D. The next day, remove the paper cup from the freezer. Peel the paper cup away from the ice. Examine the ice mixture. This represents a glacier.

E. Place the ice mixture in the pan. Press down as you slowly move the ice mixture across the tray.
  1. What happens to the sand-and-gravel mixture?
  2. What happens to the clay?

Conclusion

1. What do the particles frozen in the ice represent?

2. How do glaciers affect loose rock and soil as they move over them?

3. How do glaciers affect layers of smooth, soft rock? Which material in the pan showed this effect?

Using science ideas

What must happen to cause a glacier to deposit the material it carries?

WIND CHANGES THE LAND

How does wind change the land?

Like water and ice, wind carries materials from one place to another. When the wind blows, it lifts and carries small dry particles. Most of the particles carried by wind are sand, soil, and dust. When these particles are blown against rock, they can cause physical weathering of the rock.

As wind blows sand from one place to another, the speed of the wind may be slowed by rocks or plants. When the wind slows, it deposits the sand it carries. This causes the sand to pile up. The deposition of wind-carried sand causes piles of sand, called **sand dunes**, to form. Some sand dunes may be as much as 50 m high. Sand dunes have many shapes. The forming of sand dunes is another way the earth is changed by building up.

Sand dunes

Desert pavement

In some places in the desert, wind blows away all loose sand. Only coarse pebbles and other small rocks are left behind. Such areas are known as desert pavement. The picture on the right shows desert pavement. Once desert pavement forms, almost no wind erosion will occur. Why?

231

Do you know?

Sand dunes are moved by the wind. Some dunes travel as much as 30 m in a single year. This can create problems for people. Moving dunes have buried farms, towns, and forests.

On the southern shore of Lake Michigan, there are strong winds that blow from the west. These winds have caused a series of large sand dunes to move inland. The dunes are slowly burying trees in an Indiana forest known as Indiana Dunes.

Indiana Dunes, Indiana

Dust storm during 1930s

Sometimes wind erosion can affect a large region. During the 1930s there were several years of drought (drout) in the Great Plains of the United States. A drought is a long period without rain. Many kinds of plants died, and the land became bare. Strong winds eroded the loose dry topsoil. The land affected by this drought and erosion became known as the Dust Bowl. It was named this because of the many dust storms that occurred. Some dust storms were so bad that they blocked out all the sunlight during the day.

There are ways for farmers to help prevent wind erosion. One way is to plant rows of trees or bushes. These plants act like fences or walls.

Windbreak

They block the force of the wind. Something that blocks the force of the wind is called a **wind-break.** Where fields are not being used, farmers can plant ground cover. Ground cover are plants that hold soil in place and prevent erosion.

IDEAS TO REMEMBER

▶ Weathering is all the processes that break rock into smaller pieces.
▶ Physical weathering is all the processes that break apart rock without changing its chemical makeup.
▶ Chemical weathering is all the processes that break apart rock by changing its chemical makeup.
▶ Erosion is the movement of weathered rock and soil from one place to another.
▶ The agents of erosion are moving water, moving ice, and wind.
▶ Deposition is the dropping of sediments by the agents of erosion.

Reviewing the Chapter

SCIENCE WORDS

A. Identify each of the following.

1. It is formed when moving water cuts downward into a riverbed. It is a valley. It has steep sides. What is it?
2. It is made of sediment deposited by the waters of a river. It forms at the mouth of a river. It is a fan-shaped landmass. What is it?

B. Write the letter of the term that best matches the definition. Not all the terms will be used.

1. Movement of weathered rock and soil from one place to another
2. Dropping of sediments by moving water, moving ice, and wind
3. Processes that break apart rock by changing its chemical makeup
4. Daily freezing and melting of water that causes large rocks to break up into small pieces
5. Moving water, moving ice, and wind
6. Slow-moving mass of ice on land
7. Materials dropped by moving water, moving ice, and wind
8. Pile of sand deposited by wind
9. Trees or bushes that block the force of the wind
10. Water that comes from rain and melting snow and flows over the earth's surface

a. frost action
b. physical weathering
c. sand dune
d. canyon
e. agents of erosion
f. runoff
g. chemical weathering
h. deposition
i. delta
j. windbreak
k. sediments
l. erosion
m. glacier

UNDERSTANDING IDEAS

A. Make a chart like the one shown. Write each example under the correct heading.

Physical weathering	Chemical weathering

1. Plants growing in the crack of a rock split the rock
2. Mosses and lichens produce acids that dissolve rock
3. Ocean waves pound rock cliffs and crack them
4. Carbonic acid dissolves limestone, forming caves
5. Frost action
6. Iron oxide forms and breaks off rock

B. Identify whether each of the following resulted from erosion or deposition. Then write whether moving water, moving ice, or wind was involved.

1. Sand dune
2. Canyon
3. U-shaped valley
4. Delta
5. Hilly ridge of rocky material
6. Dust storm

USING IDEAS

1. Look in your neighborhood for examples of physical weathering, chemical weathering, erosion, and deposition. List all the examples you find and identify which process each one is. Draw pictures of the examples or, whenever possible, bring in samples.
2. Design an experiment to show one way that erosion of soil by wind or water can be prevented.

Chapter 10

Cleaning Up the Earth

Imagine that you are living 100 years ago. Would you have seen what is shown in the picture? The air today is not as clean as it was 100 years ago. This is an industrial age. Thousands of factories have been built during the past 100 years. In many areas, highways have become crowded with cars and trucks.

Each year huge amounts of wastes pour into the air, water, and soil. In this chapter you will learn about the sources of these wastes. You will learn about how the wastes affect the air, water, and land. You will also learn about what is being done to control these wastes.

NATURAL RESOURCES

Why is there a shortage of some resources?

Look around at the things you use. You use paper, pencils, and books. You walk on the land, drink the water, and breathe the air. All these things are natural resources or come from natural resources. A **natural resource** is a useful material found in or on the earth. The paper, pencils, and books you use come from trees. Trees are natural resources found on the earth. So are all other plants. Air, water, and land are also valuable natural resources. Can you name other natural resources?

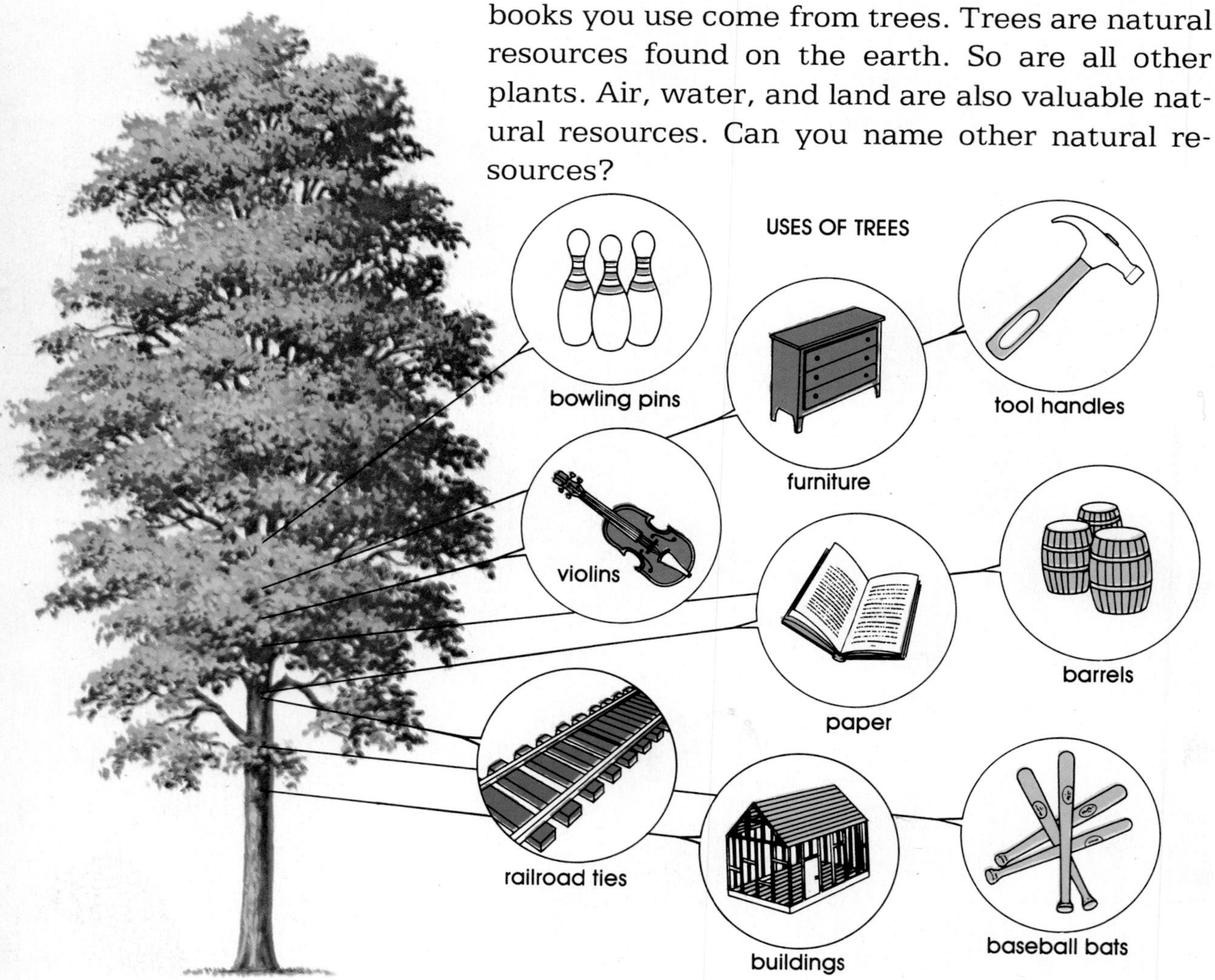

USES OF TREES

bowling pins

furniture

tool handles

violins

paper

barrels

railroad ties

buildings

baseball bats

Some resources can be replaced after they are used. For example, as trees are cut down for wood, new trees can be planted. A tree is a renewable (ri nü'ə bəl) resource. A **renewable resource** is one that can be replaced after it is used. Air, water, and land are also renewable resources.

Since some resources can be renewed, there should be no shortages. There should be a large enough supply for everyone. But the supply has become smaller because of pollution (pə lü'shən). **Pollution** is the presence of waste or other unwanted materials in a resource. The substances that cause pollution are called **pollutants** (pə-lü'tənts). Pollution of air, water, and land has reduced the useful supply of these resources.

Planting tree seedlings

Littered forest

239

AIR POLLUTION
What causes air pollution?

Pure air is made up of nitrogen, oxygen, and other harmless gases. The graph below shows the gases in air. The air you breathe often contains unwanted substances. When these substances are added to pure air, air pollution results. Most pollutants in air come from cars, trucks, homes, factories, and power plants. Some come from burning leaves and garbage. Some pollutants in nature are fumes and smoke from forest fires and volcanoes.

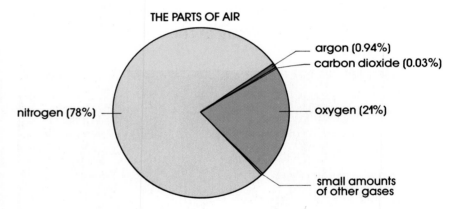

THE PARTS OF AIR

argon (0.94%)
carbon dioxide (0.03%)
nitrogen (78%)
oxygen (21%)
small amounts of other gases

Cars, trucks, homes, and factories burn fossil fuels for energy. Fossil fuels include coal, oil, and gas. Over the past 100 years, the use of fossil fuels has increased. Millions of cars and trucks are now on the roads. There are also many more factories. As a result, more fossil fuels are burned and more waste products are given off into the air.

Carbon dioxide and carbon monoxide (kär'bən mon ok'sīd) are examples of waste products given

Traffic on bridge

240

off by burning fuels. Smoke carries soot, ash, and dust into the air. These light particles may float in the air for a long time. Winds can carry them to regions far from the source of pollution.

Coal-burning power plant

In parts of the United States and Canada, there is much concern over a special kind of pollution. The major cause of this pollution is the burning of fossil fuels. Volcanoes and forest fires also add to this kind of pollution. When fuels burn and volcanoes erupt, chemical wastes enter the air. Water vapor in the air combines with these chemicals to form weak acids in the air. These weak acids fall to the ground as snow or rain. They are called **acid rain**.

Acid rain falls on the land and into lakes and streams. When it reaches lakes and streams, it increases the amount of acid in the water. This change kills fish and other living things. Acid rain also breaks down minerals in the soil. The breakdown of minerals robs plants of important materials for growth. So some plants cannot live where there is acid rain.

Statue damaged by acid rain

Acid rain even damages buildings, water systems, and statues. Scientists know the causes of acid rain. They must find a way to stop acid rain from forming.

Another kind of pollution occurs in towns and cities that have many factories, cars, and trucks. This pollution is called smog. Most **smog** is a mixture of smoke and fog. Smog occurs when calm, moist air near the ground is trapped and does not move away. The air remains in the area for several days. The longer the air stays in one place, the worse the pollution becomes. In the pictures below, you can see the effects of smog. Smog can be harmful. It can even cause death. In certain cities, smog is not as common as it once was. These cities have tried to control air pollution.

Today, people are aware that air pollution is a big problem. There are many ways that pollution can be controlled. Since cars and trucks cause

New York City in smog

New York City on a clear day

much of the pollution, people can walk, ride bicycles, or take trains and buses. They can join car pools to get to school or work. In this way, fewer cars and trucks will be on the roads.

Using trains and buses

Checking car exhaust

Today new cars must have devices that trap or burn up harmful gases in car exhaust. Most new cars are built so that they burn only unleaded gasoline. Burning gasoline that has lead in it causes harmful substances to be released. The picture shows the testing of car exhaust.

Factories are required to use special devices in their smokestacks. These devices use an electrical charge to attract particles from smoke. They also remove harmful waste gases.

An important law, the Clean Air Act, was passed in 1970. This law limits the amount of pollution allowed in the air. When the amount gets too high, factories are ordered to stop burning certain fuels. When pollution is reduced to a safe level, the factories can begin burning these fuels again. The picture shows a machine that tests for air pollutants.

Checking air pollutants in air

Are there solid particles in the air you breathe?

Materials large empty coffee can / 1 m of wire / scissors / white paper / glue / petroleum jelly / hand lens

Procedure

A. Wrap a piece of wire once around an empty coffee can. Twist the wire as shown. With the free end, form a handle.

B. Cut out a round piece of white paper a little smaller than the bottom of the can. Glue the paper to the inside bottom of the can.

C. Spread petroleum jelly over the paper.
   1. Why do you think you need to spread petroleum jelly on the paper?

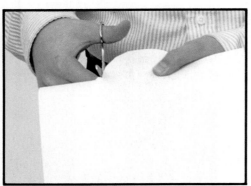

D. Hang the can outdoors in an open area. A good place would be on a clothesline or a fence.

E. After 1 or 2 weeks, take the can indoors. Remove the paper circle from the can. Examine the paper with a hand lens.
   2. Did you find anything on the jelly-covered paper? If so, draw what you found.
   3. Compare your findings with those of your classmates. Was there any difference? Make a list of what you found and what the others found.

Conclusion

Are there solid particles in the air you breathe? If so, where might they come from?

Using science ideas

Suppose you want to find the difference between pollution in the city and pollution in the country. Describe an activity you might do that would show this.

WATER POLLUTION

What causes water pollution?

Most of the water on the earth is in the oceans. Because of the salt in the oceans, this water cannot be used for drinking. It also cannot be used in industry or in farming. People must depend on fresh water for their needs. Most fresh water comes either from under the ground or from lakes, rivers, and streams. It is important to take care of the limited supply of water.

Watering crops

How much water do you use each day? Some studies show that each person in the United States uses nearly 400 L a day. Some people have guessed that industries in the United States use about 10 billion L of water a day. Large amounts are also needed to water farmland in certain parts of the country. Most of this water comes from lakes, rivers, and reservoirs.

If the freshwater supply is polluted, there is less water left for people, farms, and industries. Polluted water means there is also less water for fishing and swimming.

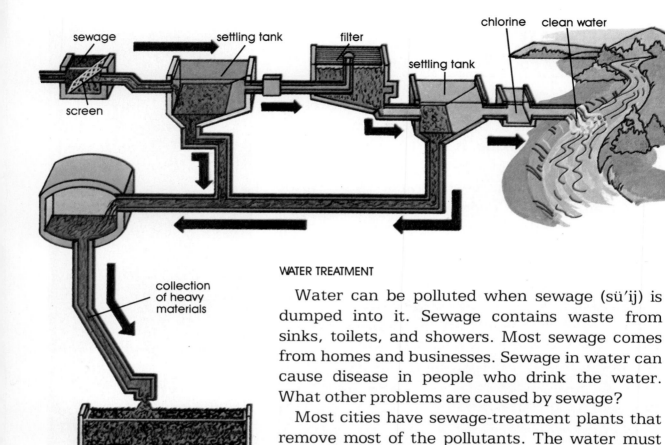

sewage

screen

settling tank

filter

chlorine   clean water

settling tank

collection
of heavy
materials

Sewage treatment plant

246

WATER TREATMENT

Water can be polluted when sewage (sü'ij) is dumped into it. Sewage contains waste from sinks, toilets, and showers. Most sewage comes from homes and businesses. Sewage in water can cause disease in people who drink the water. What other problems are caused by sewage?

Most cities have sewage-treatment plants that remove most of the pollutants. The water must pass through several steps. Follow these steps in the drawing.

First, sewage that enters these plants must pass through screens. These screens filter and remove large objects. The water then passes to a settling tank. Light materials float to the top, where they are skimmed off. Heavier materials sink and are removed. The water is pumped through a filter and then to a second settling tank. From there it is treated with the chemical chlorine (klôr'ēn). The chlorine kills certain harmful living things in the water. After the water has been treated, it is returned to lakes, streams, and rivers.

Water can be polluted by fertilizers and chemical sprays. Many farmers use chemical fertilizers (fèr'tə lī zərz) on their crops. A **fertilizer** is a substance that helps plants grow. Chemical sprays are often used to kill insects and weeds that damage crops. Chemicals from the fertilizers and sprays soak into the soil when it rains. In time water carrying these chemicals drains into streams and rivers. The streams and rivers then empty into lakes and oceans. This is how these waters become polluted.

Fertilizers entering the water increase the growth of small plants called algae. When the algae die, they pile up on the bottoms of ponds and lakes. As the dead plants decay, they may use oxygen from the water. As the oxygen supply decreases, fish and other animals that get oxygen from the water may die. This kind of pollution is shown in the drawing.

EFFECT OF FERTILIZER RUNOFF

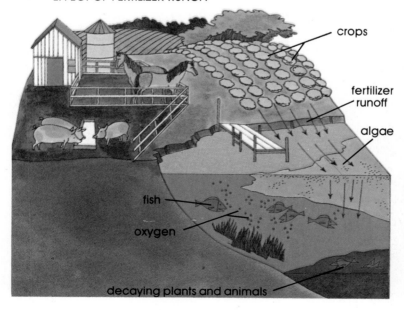

crops

fertilizer runoff

algae

fish

oxygen

decaying plants and animals

Algae covering water

247

Chemicals from insect and weed sprays can poison fish and other living things in the water. The sprays can even affect living things that live near the water. This happens through a food chain. For example, a small fish may take in the poison when it eats small plants. The small fish may be eaten by a larger fish. The larger fish may be eaten by a large bird. The poisons build up in the bird as it eats more fish. In time the bird dies from the poison.

POISON IN THE FOOD CHAIN

Runoff with poisonous materials

Pollution from fertilizers and insect sprays can be reduced by using less of these chemicals. Sometimes farmers plant shrubs and grasses near water. These plants help prevent soil erosion. In this way, soil carrying chemicals will not enter the water.

Taking water samples

Industries can also pollute water. When industries make products, they may dump liquid or solid wastes into rivers and lakes. Many of these wastes poison the water. The poison wastes make the water unsafe for drinking and swimming.

Many industries have built their own waste treatment plants. These plants remove harmful substances from water before it enters rivers, lakes, or streams.

Some industries also release hot water into streams and lakes. The dumping of heated material into water is called **thermal** (thėr′məl) **pollution.** Hot water cannot hold as much oxygen as cold water. With lower amounts of oxygen, certain plants and animals cannot live in the water.

There are ways in which industries and power plants can stop thermal pollution. Instead of re-

249

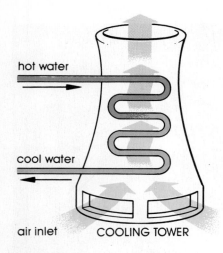

hot water

cool water

air inlet   COOLING TOWER

leasing heated materials into lakes and rivers, the heat can be released into the air. For example, some nuclear power plants have large cooling towers like the one shown. Hot water from the power plant is pumped to the cooling tower. In the tower, the hot water passes through coiled pipes. Cool air is then blown over the pipes. The air, which is now heated, is released through the top of the tower. The cooled water is returned to the power plant for reuse.

In recent years a new problem has developed. This problem is oil spills. Huge ships are used to carry oil across the oceans. Sometimes the tanks in these ships leak oil into the ocean. Another source of oil spills is offshore drilling for oil. Long stretches of beach have been damaged because of oil spills from these offshore wells. Fish and other wildlife have been killed by oil spills. The bird in the picture is being cleaned up after an oil spill. The people are tossing straw to stop the spread of oil.

Cooling tower

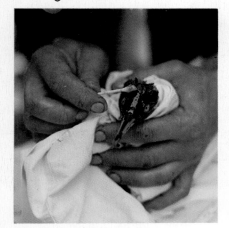

Bird rescued from oil spill

Cleanup after oil spill

Do you know?

Several years ago a disaster occurred off the coast of England. The merchant ship *Torrey Canyon,* carrying thousands of metric tons of crude oil, crashed into some rocks. Oil began to pour out of the ship.

Ships that were sent to help the *Torrey Canyon* dumped hundreds of metric tons of detergent into the water to break up the spreading oil slick. But the oil slick did not break up. Workers tried to burn the oil that floated on the water. The fire spread far across the water. But the oil kept spreading.

Soon the oil reached the nearby French coast. Chicken wire and straw were laid over the oyster beds to keep out the oil. Still, the oil kept spreading.

Several weeks passed before the oil could be controlled. By that time, 192 km of British beaches had been ruined. Thousands of oysters, mussels, birds, fish, and plants had died.

Does dilution help to reduce water pollution?

Materials graduate / 2-L plastic soft-drink bottle / clear plastic pill bottle / red or blue food coloring / white paper / water / 500-mL beaker

Procedure

A. Use a graduate to measure 10 mL of water. Pour the water into a plastic pill bottle.

B. Add 1 drop of food coloring to the water in the pill bottle. Swirl the bottle gently to mix the color evenly. Hold a sheet of white paper behind the pill bottle. Observe how deep the color of the water is.

C. Using a 500-mL beaker, pour 1,000 mL of water into a plastic soft-drink bottle. (Fill the beaker twice.)

D. Add 1 drop of food coloring to the bottle. Swirl the bottle to mix the color evenly. Hold a sheet of white paper behind the bottle. Observe how deep the color of the water is.

  1. Is the color of the water in the soft-drink bottle deeper than the color of the water in the pill bottle?

E. Imagine that the food coloring is a harmful pollutant. Imagine that the pill bottle represents a small pond and the soft-drink bottle represents a lake.

  2. Will the pollutant do more harm in the pond or in the lake? Explain your answer.

Conclusion

1. What is the difference between the effect of food coloring in the pill bottle and in the soft-drink bottle?

2. Compare the effect of the same amount of pollution on both a small and a large body of water.

LAND POLLUTION
What causes land pollution?

There are several things that threaten the soil. One of the most serious is soil erosion. If soil erosion is not controlled, valuable land can be lost forever. The plants in the picture were planted along the road to prevent erosion of the hillside.

Soil can be polluted by toxic (tok'sik) wastes. **Toxic wastes** are wastes that are poisonous. These wastes may be produced by certain industries and then buried in the soil. Even toxic wastes stored in drums can reach the soil if these drums leak. The chemicals can stay in the soil a long time. They can harm or kill living things in the soil. They can even seep into water supplies.

Government and industries are working to clean up chemical dump sites. New ways to store and get rid of chemical wastes are being studied. The picture below shows workers testing drums for leakage. They are helping to prevent further land pollution.

Plants that prevent erosion

Drums of toxic wastes

Checking leaking drums

One of the ugliest kinds of pollution is litter. It is on city streets, country roads, and in fields and forests. People throw away huge amounts of trash.

Some forms of litter are more of a problem than others. Paper, cloth, cardboard, and wood are biodegradable (bī ō di grā′də bəl) materials. **Biodegradable materials** are materials that decay, or are broken down by living things. When materials decay, they break down into simpler materials. Small organisms in the soil break down biodegradable materials as they use them for food. These materials become part of the soil.

But not all materials are biodegradable. Plastic and aluminum are not broken down by living things. Materials that are not broken down by living things are **nonbiodegradable** (non bī ō di-grā′də bəl) **materials.** These materials litter the land long after they have been thrown away.

Finding out

Which materials are biodegradable?   Collect several items that might be thrown out. You might get a cardboard cereal box, an aluminum can, and table scraps. You will also need a shallow pan and enough soil to fill the pan. Place a thin layer of soil in the pan. Then place the items you collected over this layer. Leave space between each item. Cover with more soil. Moisten the soil with water. Place the pan outdoors for a week. Take the pan inside and dig out the items you covered. Have any changed? Have any stayed the same?

Laws have been passed in many areas to help stop litter. Most states fine people who are caught littering. Some states have even stopped the sale of throw-away bottles.

Pollution of air, water, and land is a problem that affects all people. Everyone must use the air, water, and land. Everyone can help to clean up the earth.

IDEAS TO REMEMBER

► A renewable resource is one that can be replaced after it is used.
► Pollution is the presence of waste or other unwanted materials in a resource.
► The major cause of air pollution is the burning of fossil fuels by cars, trucks, homes, and factories.
► Air pollution can be controlled by the use of unleaded gas and antipollution devices on cars and smokestacks.
► Acid rain is rain with weak acids dissolved in it. It can harm or kill plants and animals in streams, lakes, and rivers.
► The major causes of water pollution are the dumping of sewage, chemicals, and heated material into water.
► The major causes of land pollution are careless dumping of litter, sewage, and harmful chemicals.
► Laws are helping to control pollution of air, water, and land.

Reviewing the Chapter

SCIENCE WORDS

A. Write the letter of the term that best matches the definition. Not all the terms will be used.

1. Mixture of smoke and fog
2. Able to decay or break down
3. Substance that improves the growth of plants
4. Poisonous
5. Substances that cause pollution
6. Wastes from sinks, toilets, and showers
7. Dumping hot substances into water
8. Presence of waste or other unwanted materials in a resource
9. Useful material found in or on the earth
10. Resource that can be replaced as it is used

a. nonbiodegradable
b. thermal pollution
c. natural resource
d. renewable
e. sewage
f. pollution
g. smog
h. toxic
i. pollutants
j. fertilizer
k. biodegradable
l. carbon dioxide

B. Identify each of the following.

1. It could be plastic. It could be aluminum. It does not decay. What is it?
2. It can take the nose off a statue. It can kill the fish in a lake. It can travel great distances. It falls from clouds. What is it?

UNDERSTANDING IDEAS

A. The drawing below shows at least six examples of pollution. Describe each of the types of pollution shown.

B. A *cause* makes things happen. An *effect* is what happens. For each pair of sentences, write which is the cause and which is the effect.

1. **a.** A picnic area is littered with nonbiodegradable materials.
   b. A family leaves aluminum cans and plastic bags at a picnic area.
2. **a.** Fertilizer runoff pollutes a stream.
   b. Algae cover the surface of a stream.
3. **a.** A city is covered with smog.
   b. Calm, moist air becomes trapped near the ground and does not move.

USING IDEAS

1. Think of three ways that you and your family pollute the air, water, and land. Suggest three ways you can help stop this pollution.

Chapter 11

Changes in the Weather

People often talk about the condition of the atmosphere in a place. You may talk about it every day. This popular topic is the weather. What is the weather like in the picture?

When people talk about weather, they usually discuss the changing conditions of the atmosphere. The atmosphere is the layer of air that surrounds the earth. In just a few hours the weather in the picture may be very different. This is because conditions in the atmosphere can change rapidly.

In this chapter you will learn what causes weather and why weather changes. You will also learn about some unusual kinds of weather.

HOW WEATHER BEGINS
What causes uneven heating of the atmosphere?

How does weather begin? It begins with energy from the sun. You have learned that energy from the sun is called solar energy. It is this energy that causes weather.

What happens to the sun's energy as it enters the atmosphere? Some of it is reflected, or bounced back, into space by clouds, dust, and air particles. A small amount is absorbed, or taken in, by the atmosphere. Absorbed solar energy changes to heat energy. So only a small amount of the atmosphere is heated directly by the sun.

About half of the sun's energy that enters the atmosphere passes through the air and strikes the earth's surface. Some of this energy is absorbed and changed to heat. This warms the earth's surface. Heat from the earth's surface then warms the air above it. You can see that the atmosphere gets most of its energy secondhand.

WHAT HAPPENS TO SOLAR ENERGY

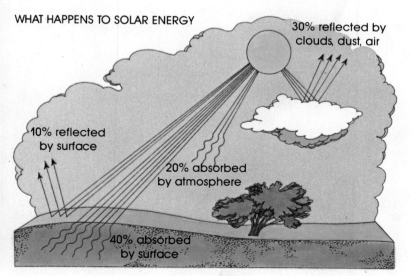

30% reflected by clouds, dust, air

10% reflected by surface

20% absorbed by atmosphere

40% absorbed by surface

Weather is caused by the uneven heating of the atmosphere. The air is heated unevenly because the earth's surface is heated unevenly. Why does this happen? There are several reasons. One reason is due to the round shape of the earth. It causes different parts of the earth to receive different amounts of solar energy.

Look at the drawing. The rays of the sun strike the equator directly. When the sun's rays strike the earth directly, the earth's surface is heated the most. Look at the areas north and south of the equator. In these places the sun's rays strike the earth's surface at a slant. When the rays strike the surface at a slant, the surface is heated less.

You can see why the earth is heated more at the equator than at the poles. Where would the atmosphere be colder, over the poles or over the equator? Why?

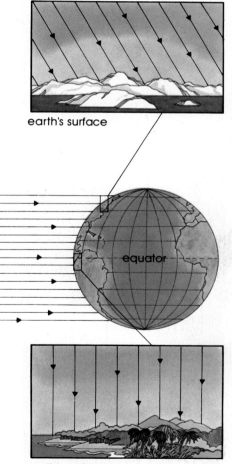

earth's surface

earth's surface

Another reason that the earth's surface is heated unevenly can be seen in pictures taken from a plane. Such pictures show places covered by white snow and dark soil. They show green fields and forests, blue water, and red deserts. These different-colored surfaces absorb different amounts of energy from the sun. The amount of solar energy that they reflect is also different.

Light-colored surfaces reflect much of the sun's energy that strikes them. Dark-colored surfaces absorb much of the sun's energy that strikes them. Which gets warmer, a light-colored surface or a dark-colored surface? What color clothing is best to wear on a hot summer day? Why?

The more solar energy a surface absorbs, the more the surface warms the air above it. Do you think that snow reflects, or absorbs, most of the solar energy that strikes it? Would dark soil absorb, or reflect, more solar energy? Would the air above dark soil be warmed more, or less, than the air above snow? You can see that differences in the color of the earth's surface cause uneven heating of the earth's atmosphere.

There is another factor that causes the earth's surface to heat unevenly. About three-fourths of the earth is covered by water. Water and land areas absorb solar energy at different rates.

Land and water heat up at different rates. During the day, the sun shines and the land heats up

faster than the water. So the air over the land becomes warmer than the air over the water. While the land heats up faster than the water, it also loses heat faster. At night, when there is no sunlight, the warm land cools quickly. So the air over the land becomes cooler. The water holds heat and stays warm at night. What would the air over the water be like at night?

Very little heat from the earth's surface and atmosphere escapes into space. This is because clouds, dust, and air particles trap the heat. This is an example of the greenhouse effect. In Chapter 8 you learned how the greenhouse effect can be used to heat buildings. On a large scale, the greenhouse effect keeps the earth warm.

How do materials differ in the way they heat and cool?

Material	Starting temp.	Temp. after 5 min of heating	Temp. after 5 min of cooling
Soil			
Sand			
Water			

Materials 6 paper cups / scissors / dark-colored soil / light-colored sand / 3 thermometers / lamp

Procedure

A. Cut the tops off three paper cups so that the remaining part is about 4 cm deep. Fill each cup with one of the following materials: dark-colored soil, light-colored sand, and water.

B. Place the cups together as shown. Put a thermometer into each cup. The bulb of the thermometer should be covered by about 0.5 cm of sand, soil, or water. Rest the top of each thermometer on a paper cup that has been turned upside down.

C. Copy this chart. Record the starting temperature in each cup.
   1. Do you think the materials will heat at different rates? Explain your answer.

D. Place a lamp so its light bulb is about 15 cm from the tops of the cups. Turn on the lamp. After 5 minutes read and record the temperature in each cup.
   2. Which material was heated the most? Which was heated the least?
   3. If you turn off the lamp, do you think the materials will cool at different rates? Explain your answer.

E. Turn off the lamp. After 5 minutes read and record the temperature in each cup.
   4. Which material cooled the least? The most?

Conclusion

How does this activity help explain the uneven heating of the earth?

AIR PRESSURE AND WINDS
What causes winds?

Air is made up of particles of matter. Like all matter, air has mass. The mass of the atmosphere above the earth pushes down on the surface. This causes air pressure. The pressure of air changes from day to day and from place to place. The temperature of the air affects the pressure of the air.

When air is heated, it expands. This means that the particles in air move farther apart. When this happens, the air becomes less dense. So there are fewer air particles over a certain part of the earth's surface. This lowers the air pressure in that place.

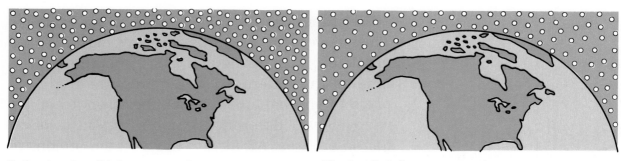

Before heating (higher pressure)   After heating (lower pressure)

Usually when temperature increases, air pressure decreases. Think about equal volumes of warm air and cold air. Would the cold air have higher, or lower, air pressure than the warm air?

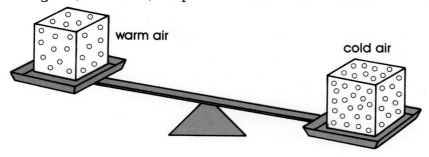

warm air

cold air

The amount of water in the air also affects the air pressure. The more water vapor there is in air, the lower the air pressure. This may seem strange to you. But keep in mind that water vapor is a gas. Water vapor is less dense than air. So 1 L of water vapor has less mass than 1 L of air. Usually the more water vapor in air, the lower the air pressure.

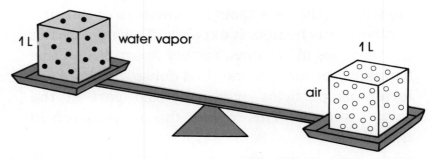

Differences in air pressure cause air to move. This movement of air is wind. Winds may be gentle breezes, or they may be strong gusts. The greater the difference in air pressure from one place to another, the greater the strength of the wind. Small differences in air pressure bring gentle breezes. Air always moves from regions of high pressure, called highs, to regions of low pressure, called lows.

There are different groups of winds. Some winds are local winds. Local winds are caused by local differences in pressure. For example, there are differences in air pressure over land and water. These differences cause winds to change direction along coastal regions.

During the day the air over the land is heated more than the air over the water. So the pressure of the air over the land is lower. The cooler, high-pressure air over the water blows toward the land. It moves under the warm, low-pressure air and pushes it up. This movement of air from water to land is called a **sea breeze.** On a summer day at the beach, you can often feel cool breezes blowing from the sea to the land.

At night the air over the land becomes cooler than the air over the water. So the pressure of the air over the land is higher. This air blows toward the water. It pushes up the warm, low-pressure air over the water. This movement of air from land to water is called a **land breeze.**

Sea and land breezes are local winds. But the earth has large regions of high and low pressure. Air moves from the high-pressure regions to the low-pressure regions. This movement of air, along with the rotation of the earth, creates wind belts, shown in the drawing. These wind belts, which circle the earth, are called global winds. Global winds are another group of winds.

GLOBAL WIND BELTS

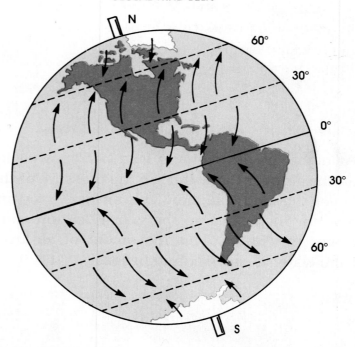

The global winds in each belt blow steadily in the direction shown by the arrows. The winds are named for the direction from which they come. Most of the United States lies within a global wind belt called the westerlies. Because of the direction in which these global winds blow, much of the weather in the United States moves from west to east across the country.

AIR MASSES AND WEATHER
What are the four kinds of air masses?

Have you ever noticed how hot and humid it can be on a summer day? Then, the very next day, the air is cool and dry. This type of change in the weather is caused by the movement of air masses. An **air mass** is a large body of air that has about the same temperature and moisture throughout. When air stays over a region of the earth for a long time, the air takes on the properties of that region.

There are four basic kinds of air masses. Air masses are named for their temperature and for the amount of moisture they contain. The kind of air mass that forms depends on where it forms. Cold, wet air masses form over cold ocean waters. Cold, dry air masses form over cold land areas near the poles. These regions are usually covered by snow and ice.

Warm, wet air masses form over oceans near the equator. Where do warm, dry air masses form? What kind of air mass would form in each place shown on page 269 and this page?

The map shows the six major areas where air masses that affect North America form. It shows the kind of air mass that forms over each area and the path it often follows. During winter a cold, dry air mass will bring clear but very cold weather. In summer a warm, wet air mass will mean hot, humid weather. How long any kind of weather remains in an area depends on how fast an air mass is moving.

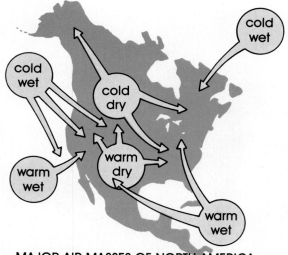

MAJOR AIR MASSES OF NORTH AMERICA

WHEN AIR MASSES MEET
How do cold fronts and warm fronts differ?

You have learned that air masses move. As one air mass moves away from a region, another air mass moves in. The place where two air masses meet is called a **front.** Changes in weather take place at a front.

Fronts are named for the kind of air mass moving into a region. The drawing shows what happens when a cold air mass moves into a warmer air mass. The place where these air masses meet is a **cold front.**

As the dense, cold air mass moves forward, it remains close to the ground. It moves under the less dense, warm air mass. This forces the warm air to rise quite rapidly. As the warm air is forced up, it cools. Water vapor in the air condenses. The water vapor changes to tiny drops of liquid water. These drops form clouds. The clouds that form along a cold front are often dark towering clouds.

cold front

warm air mass

movement of cold air

cold air mass

movement of warm air

Cold front

Thunderstorm

Brief but heavy rain may occur along cold fronts. And wind speed may increase a great deal. Thunderstorms are common along cold fronts. Sometimes very wet, warm air is pushed up by a cold front. This can form a line of thunderstorms ahead of the front. Under certain conditions, tornadoes (tôr nā′dōz) can form along with a line of thunderstorms. A tornado is the most violent kind of storm.

Tornadoes are narrow, funnel-shaped spirals of air. Wind speeds in a tornado may be as much as 800 km/h. Tornadoes hang from the bottom of

Tornado

storm clouds. They move in a twisting path. From time to time, they touch the ground. When they do, they can destroy buildings, uproot trees, and carry cars many meters through the air.

During winter, a blizzard (bliz′ərd) may form along a cold front. Blizzards occur when there are large differences in pressure between two air masses. Blizzards are snowstorms in which temperatures are below freezing and winds are very high.

After a cold front passes, the temperature in the region drops. The sky usually clears and fluffy white clouds may be seen. Why does the temperature drop after a cold front passes?

Now look at the drawing that shows a warm front. A **warm front** is the place where a moving warm air mass meets a colder air mass. The dense, cold air mass remains close to the ground. As the less dense, warm air mass moves forward, it slowly slides up and over the cold air mass. As it

Blizzard

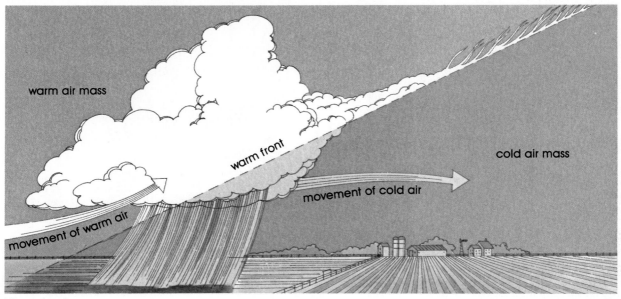

Warm front

273

slowly rises, the warm air cools. Water vapor in the warm air condenses. High thin, feathery clouds may form. They are a sign that a warm front is coming.

A warm front passes through a region more slowly than does a cold front. As the warm front moves, thick low clouds may form ahead of it. Steady, light rain may fall for a day or more. When the warm front passes, the temperature rises and the sky slowly clears.

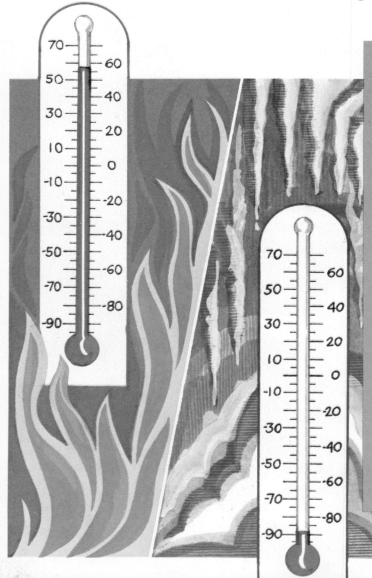

How does the weather change?

Materials   thermometer / barometer

Procedure

A. Scientists observe changes in the weather to help them better understand and predict them. You can also do this. First, you should make a chart on a sheet of paper. The chart should have columns for the day, the temperature, the amount of clouds, the air pressure, wind direction, and the weather conditions.

B. Write what day it is in your chart.

C. Read a thermometer that is in a shady place outside. Record the temperature in your chart.

D. Read a barometer. Most barometers have an indicator that can be moved to line it up with the barometer needle. This indicator helps you determine whether the air pressure has risen, fallen, or remained steady since the last reading. Line up this indicator with the needle. In your chart, indicate whether the air pressure is rising, falling, or steady.

E. Look at the cloud cover. Indicate in your chart whether it is clear, partly cloudy, or cloudy. Also indicate the direction the wind is coming from.

F. Indicate the weather conditions in your chart. You might use terms such as *rainy, clear,* or *hazy.*

G. Repeat steps **B** through **F** at the same time each day for 1 week.

Conclusion

1. On what day was the temperature the highest? On what day was it the lowest?

2. How did the barometer change?

3. Based on how the weather changed during the week and on today's weather conditions, what do you think the weather will be like tomorrow?

CLOUDS

There are many types of clouds. You have learned that different types of clouds form along cold fronts and warm fronts. Clouds are named for their shape. The type of cloud that forms depends on the conditions of the atmosphere. So the type of cloud that you see depends on the weather.

The large fluffy white clouds often seen during fair weather are called **cumulus** (kyü′myə ləs) **clouds.** *Cumulus* means "heap." These clouds are flat on the bottom. Their rounded tops can billow high into the sky.

The thin, wispy clouds that look like feathers or curls of hair are called **cirrus** (sir′əs) **clouds.** *Cirrus* means "curl." Cirrus clouds form high in the sky. The air at this height is very cold. So cirrus

Cumulus clouds

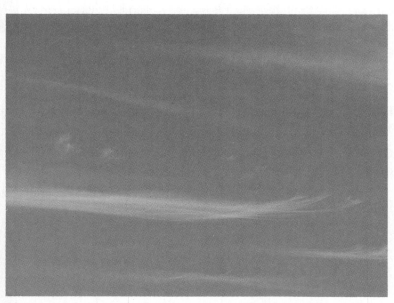

Cirrus clouds

clouds are made up of tiny ice crystals. You often see cirrus clouds in a blue sky. They are sometimes a sign that a warm front is moving in and that the weather will soon change.

Thick low clouds that cover the sky are called **stratus** (strā′təs) **clouds.** *Stratus* means "layer." These sheetlike clouds are a sign of rainy weather. Fog is a stratus cloud near the ground.

Stratus clouds

Date	Cloud Type	Time and Temp.	Forecast

What weather forecasts can you make by looking at clouds? Make a chart like the one shown. For the next 7 days, observe the clouds. Try to identify the types of clouds you see. Find out the temperature at the time you make your observation. What is the weather like? Record all this information in your chart. Using what you know about clouds and fronts, try to forecast the weather for the next day. Predict how the temperature and other weather conditions will change. The next day, look at your forecast and see how accurate it is.

There are many other types of clouds. Sometimes clouds have two names. This is because they have features of two types of clouds. For example, stratocumulus clouds are layers of cumulus clouds that cover the sky. Other word parts are added to the names of clouds. *Nimbo* or *nimbus* means "rain." Cumulonimbus (kyü myə lō-nim'bəs) clouds are dark towering clouds. They usually bring thunderstorms. They form when rapidly rising air causes cumulus clouds to build up. *Alto* is a word part that means "high."

Look at the clouds shown on these two pages. Read the name of each type of cloud. See if you can tell why each cloud was given that name.

Altocumulus clouds

Stratocumulus clouds

Cumulonimbus clouds

Nimbostratus clouds

IDEAS TO REMEMBER

▶ The earth's surface and atmosphere are heated unevenly. Weather is caused by the uneven heating of the atmosphere.

▶ Weather is related to air pressure. Cold, dry air has the highest pressure. Warm, wet air has the lowest pressure.

▶ An air mass is a large body of air that has about the same temperature and pressure throughout. The kind of air mass present determines the weather.

▶ Differences in air pressure cause winds. Sea and land breezes are local winds.

▶ Global winds cause weather to move from west to east across the United States.

▶ Weather changes take place at fronts. A front is the place where two air masses meet.

▶ The type of cloud that forms depends on the weather.

Reviewing the Chapter

SCIENCE WORDS

A. Identify each of the following.

    1. It is a type of cloud. Its name means "curl." It forms high in the sky. It is made up of tiny ice crystals. What is it?

    2. It is a type of cloud. Its name means "layer." It is sheet-like. It is a sign of rainy weather. What is it?

    3. It is a type of cloud. Its name means "heap." It has rounded tops that can billow high into the sky. It is often seen during fair weather. What is it?

B. Copy the sentences below. Use science terms from the chapter to complete each sentence.

    1. When a warm air mass moves into a cold air mass, a/an _____ forms.

    2. The movement of air from water to land is called a/an _____.

    3. A large body of air that has about the same temperature and moisture throughout is called a/an _____.

    4. When a cold air mass moves into a warm air mass, a/an _____ forms.

    5. The movement of air from land to water is called a/an _____.

    6. The place where two air masses meet is called a/an _____.

UNDERSTANDING IDEAS

A. Write the kind of air mass that would form over each place shown in the drawings.

1   2   3

B. Look again at the drawings above. Suppose the air mass that formed over the place in drawing 1 moved into the air mass that formed over the place in drawing 3. What kind of front would form? Describe how air masses move at this kind of front. What weather changes might occur?

C. Describe three factors that cause the uneven heating of the earth's atmosphere.

USING IDEAS

1. Because the moon has no atmosphere, it has no weather. Explain why this is a true statement.

2. When weather announcers predict the temperature range for the next day, they often say, "Daytime temperatures will be cooler for places along the shore." Why is this?

Chapter 12

Beyond the Solar System

Have you ever looked into the night sky and wondered how far it is to the edge of space? On a clear night you can see thousands of stars. Are there any stars so far away you cannot see them?

People have always been interested in space. What do you think this picture shows? It is a cloud of dust and gas in space. Scientists think it was left when a star exploded in the year 1054.

Objects like this are of great interest to people who study space. Scientists are trying to find out what lies beyond the solar system. They are also interested in finding out how far space extends.

In this chapter you will see how to measure distances to objects in space. You will learn about the life cycle of a star. You will also find out how stars are grouped in patterns.

DISTANCES IN SPACE
What is a light-year?

You know that the sun and nine planets make up most of the solar system. The sun is at the center of this system. All the planets move in orbits around the sun. Now imagine how large the solar system must be.

The solar system is very large. But the solar system is only one small part of a much larger system. The sun is just one of billions of stars that make up a large family of stars.

Do you have any idea how far bodies in space are from the earth? Look at the table. It lists the distance from the earth to other bodies in space.

DISTANCES TO BODIES IN SPACE

Body in space	Average distance from the earth (in km)
Sun	150,000,000
Mercury	92,000,000
Venus	42,000,000
Moon	400,000
Mars	79,000,000
Jupiter	632,000,000
Saturn	1,290,000,000
Uranus	2,730,000,000
Neptune	4,520,000,000
Pluto	5,800,000,000
Proxima Centauri (closest star to the earth except the sun)	41,000,000,000,000

How far is it to the moon? To the sun? How far is it to Pluto? You can see that the distances are very large. As the distances get larger, the numbers become more difficult to read.

You are used to traveling much shorter distances. Even if you were to travel across the United States, you would only go about 4,800 km. Therefore, the distances in the table may be too large to fully understand. It may help to think about how long it would take to travel to different bodies in space. Imagine you are in a spacecraft. You are moving at a speed of 40,000 km/h. This is the speed needed to escape gravity once the rocket engines are turned off. It is more than 400 times faster than a car on a highway.

Look at the drawing. It shows how long it would take to reach certain bodies in space. How long would it take to reach the moon? Could you reach Proxima Centauri (prok'sə mə sen tôr'ī) within your lifetime? It would take about 116,906 years to reach this star. It is even more difficult to imagine how long it would take to reach a star that is farther away. Do you think people from the earth will ever visit other stars?

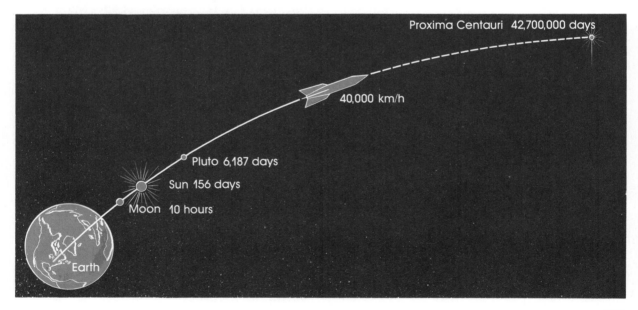

Proxima Centauri 42,700,000 days

40,000 km/h

Pluto 6,187 days

Sun 156 days

Moon 10 hours

Earth

For centuries people have wondered about the size of the universe (yü′nə vėrs). The **universe** includes all of space and all the matter and energy in it. People have wondered how far out space goes. They have wondered *where* it ends and even *if* it ends.

Astronomer looking through telescope

The study of the universe and all the objects in it is a science called **astronomy** (ə stron′ə mē). Astronomy includes the study of stars, planets, moons, and other objects in space. It is one of the oldest sciences. Scientists who study the universe are called **astronomers** (ə stron′ə mərz).

In the picture above, the Italian astronomer Galileo is shown with his telescope. The scene may have occurred in the early 1600s. A modern telescope is shown on page 287.

Sacramento Peak Observatory

You have learned that distances between certain bodies in the universe are very great. How do astronomers work with such great distances? Units such as meters and kilometers are used to measure much shorter distances. A larger unit is needed to measure distances in space.

Astronomers use the speed of light in measuring distances in space. Light travels great distances in a short time. For example, light from the sun reaches the earth in about 8 minutes. Light travels 300,000 km in 1 second (km/s). This is equal to 1,080,000,000 km/h. How much faster is this than a car on a highway? To find out, divide 1,080,000,000 by 100, which is about the speed of a car on a highway (100 km/h).

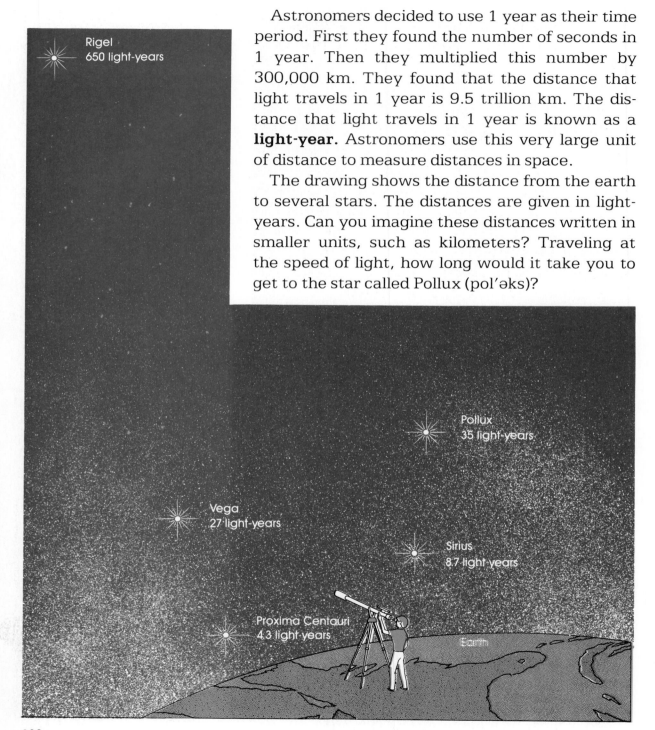

Astronomers decided to use 1 year as their time period. First they found the number of seconds in 1 year. Then they multiplied this number by 300,000 km. They found that the distance that light travels in 1 year is 9.5 trillion km. The distance that light travels in 1 year is known as a **light-year.** Astronomers use this very large unit of distance to measure distances in space.

The drawing shows the distance from the earth to several stars. The distances are given in light-years. Can you imagine these distances written in smaller units, such as kilometers? Traveling at the speed of light, how long would it take you to get to the star called Pollux (pol'əks)?

Rigel
650 light-years

Pollux
35 light-years

Vega
27 light-years

Sirius
8.7 light-years

Proxima Centauri
4.3 light-years

Earth

— CHARACTERISTICS OF STARS —
How are stars different from each other?

You may think all stars look alike. By looking closely you might observe that some seem brighter than others. You may even notice that some appear to be slightly different in color. The great distances between stars and the earth make it hard to see all the differences. The most visible difference is brightness. The measure of the brightness of a star as seen from the earth is known as **magnitude** (mag'nə tüd). In the picture which star is the brightest?

The magnitude of a star depends on three things. The first is the star's distance from the earth. Suppose two stars are exactly alike except for their distance from the earth. The one that is closer will appear brighter. It will have a greater magnitude. You can compare the magnitude of a star to the brightness of the headlights of a car. The closer the car is, the brighter its headlights will seem. The closer a star is to the earth, the brighter the star will appear.

The second thing that affects the magnitude of a star is size. Stars differ greatly in size. Some stars are very small. Many of these stars are smaller than the earth. The sun, with a diameter of 1,392,000 km, is a medium-sized star. There are stars that have a diameter 10 to 100 times that of the sun. Supergiant stars have a diameter 100 to 1,000 times that of the sun.

The third thing that affects the magnitude of a star is temperature. Stars differ greatly in temperature. The temperature of a star also determines its color. Look at the drawing that shows star temperature and color. Notice that red stars are the coolest stars. Which stars are the hottest?

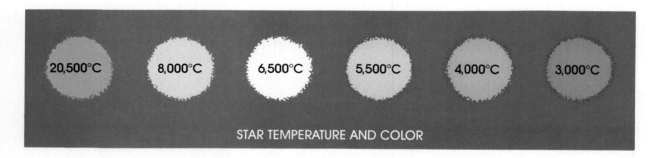

STAR TEMPERATURE AND COLOR

Suppose that two stars are the same distance from the earth. They are also the same size. All that differs is their temperature. One is blue and one is red. Which will appear brighter? The blue star will seem brighter because it is hotter. It will have a greater magnitude.

A star's magnitude, then, depends on its distance from the earth, its size, and its temperature. All three things must be considered. Remember that when scientists speak of magnitude, they mean the brightness of a star as it is seen from the earth.

What things affect brightness?

Materials 3 identical flashlights labeled *X*, *Y*, and *Z* / scissors / cardboard / tape / meterstick

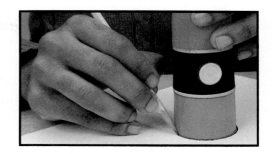

Procedure

A. Cut three circles of cardbord so that each will cover the end of a flashlight. Cut a hole 1 cm in diameter in the center of each circle. Tape the circles to three flashlights labeled *X*, *Y*, and *Z*.

B. Mark three positions on the floor. Position 1 is 1 m away. Position 2 is 10 m away. Position 3 is 20 m away.

C. You will need three of your classmates to help you complete this activity. Give each student a labeled flashlight. Have the students stand in a row at position 1.

D. Ask your teacher to darken the room. Have the students turn on their flashlights.
  1. How would you describe the brightness of each flashlight?

E. Have the student with flashlight *X* stay at position 1. Have the student with flashlight *Y* move to position 2. Have the student with flashlight *Z* move to position 3.
  2. Which flashlight looks brightest? Dimmest?

F. Cut a cardboard circle with a 2-cm hole in the center. Cut another circle with a 3-cm hole in the center. Replace the circles on flashlights *Y* and *Z* with these new circles.

G. Have the three students stand in a row at position 3 and turn on the flashlights.
  3. Which flashlight looks brightest? Dimmest?

Conclusion
What two things affect how bright the flashlights look?

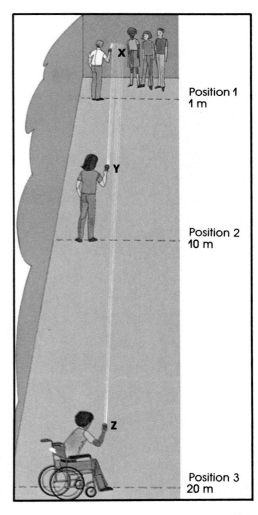

Position 1
1 m

Position 2
10 m

Position 3
20 m

THE LIFE OF A STAR

What is the life cycle of a star?

You may be surprised to know that stars have a life cycle. New stars are being "born" and old stars are "dying." Of course, the life and death of stars does not happen overnight. Changes in stars take place over billions of years. The drawings show the stages in the life cycle of a typical star. Not all stars will go through every stage. As you read, look at the drawings.

1. A star is formed from dust and gas in space. A cloud of dust and gas found in space is called a **nebula** (neb'yə lə). The dust and gas in such clouds come together because of gravitational attraction. A tremendous amount of matter must collect for a new star to form. There must be as much matter as there is in the sun. As the matter in the nebula presses together, it gets hot. When enough matter comes together and the temperature gets high enough, a new star is "born."

Horsehead Nebula

1 nebula

2

3

young star

2. When a star first forms, it has a red glow. In this stage the star is large and cool. The matter of the star continues to come together.

3. When a star is "middle-aged," it may be one of several different colors. It may be blue, white, yellow, or red. The color depends on the temperature. The temperature depends on the amount of matter that collects. The more matter that collects, the hotter the star is. So, a hot, blue star forms when a great deal of matter collects. A cool, red star forms when a smaller amount of matter collects. The sun is a yellow star. It is larger and hotter than a red star but smaller and cooler than a blue star. Which star in the drawing could be the sun?

4. A star beginning "old age" often swells up to form a **red giant.** A red giant is a star that is many times larger than the sun. The temperature of a red giant is lower than that of the sun. Some scientists believe that the sun will enter this stage millions of years from now.

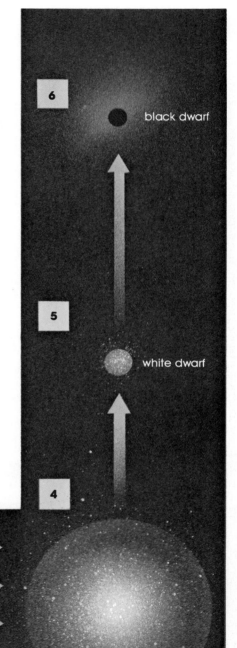

6 black dwarf

5 white dwarf

4

sun

red giant

5. After a while a red giant begins to collapse into a smaller star. It becomes hotter and appears white in color. A small star in this stage is called a **white dwarf.** It may be about as large as the earth. Because it is small, a white dwarf does not appear bright. The drawing of the life cycle of a star on page 293 shows a white dwarf.

6. Once most of a star's fuel is gone, it will enter the last stage of its life. The star will become a **black dwarf.** In this stage the star has no heat or light. It is a cold, dense object in space.

Not all stars follow these stages. Stars that collapse into the white dwarf stage sometimes explode and become very bright. An exploding star of this type is called a **nova.** After the explosion the star will slowly shrink and grow dim. Sometimes a very large star may explode violently. Then it is called a **supernova.** The Crab Nebula shown on pages 282–283 is a supernova.

SUPERNOVA
294

NEUTRON STAR

BLACK HOLE

Stars that explode into supernovas sometimes collapse into very dense stars called **neutron stars.** A neutron star is much smaller than a white dwarf, even though it has more matter packed into it.

Some scientists think that the gravitational pull of a neutron star can be so great that the star disappears. When this happens, a black hole forms. A **black hole** is a region in space that was once occupied by a star. Some people believe that the gravity of a black hole is so great that not even light can escape. The drawing above shows how a black hole might look.

FAMILIES OF STARS

What are the shapes of galaxies?

By this time you probably know that there is gravity everywhere in the universe. Each body in space attracts every other body. Because of gravity, no bodies are all alone in space. Instead, bodies in space collect in families. The sun is one of billions of stars that form the family called the Milky Way. A large group of stars and other bodies in space is called a **galaxy** (gal′ək sē). The Milky Way is a **spiral** (spī′rəl) **galaxy.** This type of galaxy is shaped like a flat disk, or wheel, with curved arms coming out from the center.

Sun

Milky Way

The Milky Way is about 100,000 light-years from edge to edge. The solar system is about one third of the way from the outer edge of the Milky Way. The sun is believed to be one of about 200 billion stars in the Milky Way. Can you find the sun in the drawing of the Milky Way on page 296?

Many scientists believe that all the objects in the Milky Way revolve around its center. This means that the sun and its planets are moving around the center of the Milky Way. The Milky Way is so large that it takes the sun 250 million years to go once around. It is possible that the sun is just now returning to the place where it was before dinosaurs were on the earth.

Do you know?

Astronomers have been studying a group of strange bodies on the outer edges of space. These high-energy bodies look almost like stars. They can give off more energy than 10 trillion suns. They are called quasars (kwā′särz).

Most quasars are studied by the radio waves they give off. The picture shows a radio map of a quasar.

Quasars are so far away that light coming from them takes 12 billion years to reach the earth. When you see light from a quasar, you are actually looking back into the early days of the universe.

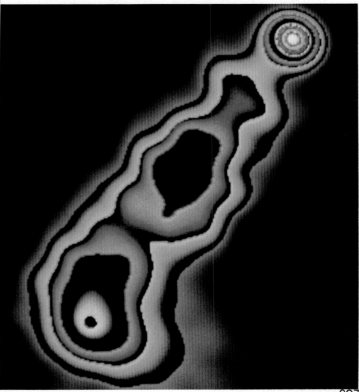

All galaxies are not spiral-shaped. Two other types of galaxies have been discovered. One of these is the **elliptical** (i lip'tə kəl) **galaxy.** An elliptical galaxy is like a spiral one, but it does not have arms. There are more elliptical galaxies than spiral galaxies. But the elliptical galaxies are not as large or as bright. Most of the stars in elliptical galaxies are very old.

Another kind of galaxy is called an irregular (i reg'yə lər) galaxy. An **irregular galaxy** does not have a definite shape or size. Some scientists believe that this type of galaxy may have formed when two or more galaxies bumped into one another.

ELLIPTICAL GALAXY (top); SPIRAL GALAXY (bottom)

Spiral galaxy

Many astronomers believe that entire galaxies are moving. They think that galaxies are moving toward the outer edges of the universe. The galaxies seem to be moving away from each other. The belief that galaxies are moving is part of a theory that suggests that the universe is expanding. No one seems to know why the universe is expanding. No one knows if it will ever stop expanding. What is your theory about the universe?

MOVEMENT OF GALAXIES

Can you make a model of the moving galaxies?

Balloon size	Distance between dots (in mm)			
	V to W	V to X	V to Y	V to Z
Small				
Medium				
Large				

Materials round balloon / felt-tip pen / string / 10-cm twist-tie / metric ruler

Procedure

A. Copy the data chart. Blow up a round balloon to a small size. Tightly twist a twist-tie around the neck of the balloon so that the air does not escape. The balloon represents the universe.

B. Use a felt-tip pen to mark five dots on the balloon. Label the dots V, W, X, Y, and Z. Dot V is in the center. Dots W, X, Y, and Z are an equal distance from dot V. The dots represent the galaxies.

C. Use string to measure the distance from V to each of the other dots. Find these distances in millimeters by placing the measured string against a meterstick. Record these distances.

D. Untie the twist-tie. Blow up the balloon to a medium size. Twist the twist-tie around the neck of the balloon. Repeat step **C.**
  1. Have the distances between dots changed?
  2. Find the difference between the measurements on the small balloon and on the medium balloon.

E. Untie the twist-tie. Blow up the balloon to a large size. Twist the twist-tie around the neck of the balloon. Repeat step **C.**
  3. Have the distances between the dots changed?
  4. Find the difference between the measurements on the medium balloon and on the large balloon.

Conclusion

1. How is the expanding balloon like the universe?

2. If dot V represents the Milky Way and the other dots represent other galaxies, what is happening to the galaxies?

STAR PATTERNS
What is a constellation?

People have always been interested in the objects they could see in the sky. For centuries people have gazed into the night sky and wondered about stars. They have wondered about such things as what stars were made of and how big they were. As people watched, they noticed that stars seemed to form groups. People observed that even though the stars seemed to change position, the groups stayed together.

Ancient people saw patterns in these groups of stars and gave them names. Today we call these star patterns **constellations** (kon stə lā'shənz). One of the best-known constellations is the Big Dipper. Another is Scorpio (skôr'pē ō), shown on page 289. Have you ever seen these constellations? Can you name other constellations?

Finding out

Why do stars seem to move? You may know that the stars seem to move in the sky. But you do not see them moving. They seem to move because the earth moves. You can show how the stars seem to move. You will need a black umbrella and a star chart. Use chalk to draw a few familiar constellations on the underside of the opened umbrella. Be sure to draw the North Star at the point where the handle connects with the ribs of the umbrella. Slowly turn the handle of the umbrella counterclockwise. This shows how the stars seem to move in the sky as the earth turns.

The constellations helped people keep track of certain stars in the sky. People could watch the movements of these stars. They used these star movements to measure time and the seasons.

How did the constellations first get their names? Years ago ancient people named many constellations for people or animals. Some examples are the Great Bear, the Little Bear, and Draco (the Dragon). These names are still used today.

Some constellations are shown on this page. The drawings show the main stars in the constellations. They also show the figure that each star pattern looks like. The main stars in a constellation have names. For example, Sirius (sir′ē-əs) is part of the Big Dog. Sirius is also the brightest star in the sky. Vega (vē′gə) is a star in Lyra (lī′rə). Lyra is a constellation that is the shape of a lyre, a type of harp. Pollux is part of the constellation called the Twins. See if you can find some of these stars in the drawings of the constellations. Do the constellations really look like the things for which they were named?

GREAT BEAR

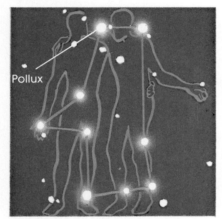

TWINS

Pollux

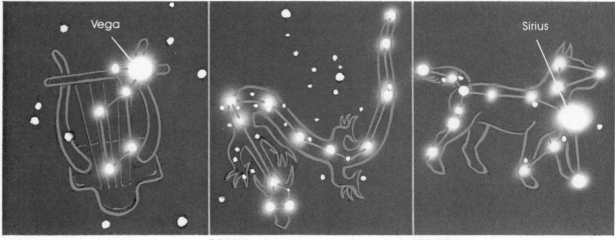

Vega

Sirius

LYRA

DRACO

BIG DOG

IDEAS TO REMEMBER

▶ Astronomy is the study of the universe and all the objects in it. Scientists who study the universe are called astronomers.

▶ The distance to objects in space is measured in light-years. A light-year is the distance light travels in 1 year.

▶ Magnitude is a measure of the brightness of a star as seen from the earth. Magnitude depends on the distance of a star from the earth. Magnitude also depends on the size and the temperature of a star.

▶ The color of a star and its temperature are related. The coolest stars are red; the hottest are blue.

▶ New stars are always forming and old ones are dying. During its life cycle a star may change color, temperature, and size.

▶ A galaxy is a group of billions of stars. A galaxy may be spiral, elliptical, or irregular in shape.

▶ A constellation is a group of stars that seem to form a pattern. Ancient people named constellations for familiar objects.

Reviewing the Chapter

SCIENCE WORDS

A. Use all the terms below to fill in the blanks.

astronomers astronomy light-year universe

  Space and all the matter and energy in it is called the __1__. The study of the stars, planets, moons, and other objects in space is called __2__. Scientists who do this study are called __3__. To measure distances in space, scientists use a unit called a/an __4__.

B. Write the letter of the term that best matches the definition. Not all the terms will be used.

1. A large group of stars and other bodies in space
2. An exploding star
3. Region in space once occupied by a star
4. Last stage in the life cycle of a star
5. Pattern of stars
6. Measure of the brightness of a star as seen from the earth
7. Galaxy shaped like a wheel with arms coming out of center
8. Cloud of dust and gas in space
9. A very dense star
10. Star much larger than the sun

a. magnitude
b. elliptical galaxy
c. black dwarf
d. constellation
e. neutron star
f. galaxy
g. black hole
h. red giant
i. nebula
j. nova
k. spiral galaxy
l. irregular galaxy

UNDERSTANDING IDEAS

A. List three characteristics that determine the magnitude of a star.

B. The drawings below show some of the stages in the life cycle of a star. Write the numbers of the drawings to show the correct order. Describe each stage.

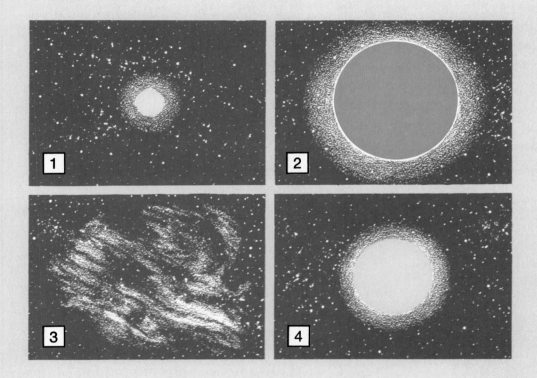

USING IDEAS

1. Choose your favorite constellation. Find out the story behind its name. Draw the constellation.
2. Make up your own constellation. Write a story telling how it got its name.

Science in Careers

Many people are concerned about the condition of the world around them. *Soil conservationists* help farmers make the best use of land without damaging it. If a farmer has a problem with soil erosion, the soil conservationist can help solve it.

As you know, fossil fuels are an important source of energy. So the *petroleum geologist* (pe trō′lē əm jē ol′ə jist) has an important job. This person is a scientist who looks for new sources of oil. The petroleum geologist is usually one of a team of people who carry out this task.

Astronomers

Some people are always seeking answers to questions about the universe. Such people may one day want a career in astronomy.

Most people think of *astronomers* as stargazers. But astronomers of today spend little time gazing at the sky through a telescope. Most of their time is spent examining photographs and studying the information gained through research. Some astronomers work in observatories. An observatory is a building with special equipment for studying objects in space. Almost all astronomers do research or are teachers in colleges.

Soil conservationist

People in Science

Rachel Carson (1907–1964)

Rachel Carson was a biologist and a science writer. In her most famous book, *Silent Spring*, Carson warns about DDT, a chemical that is used to kill insects that feed on crops. She points out that DDT pollutes the environment in a way that affects many living things, including people. She explains how DDT poisons the food supply of animals. As a result of *Silent Spring*, many laws were passed that changed the ways in which DDT could be used. Carson worked for the U.S. Fish and Wildlife Service for many years.

Bird egg damaged by DDT

Developing Skills

WORD SKILLS

Many English words come from Latin, Greek, and other languages. If you know the meanings of words in other languages, you can often understand the meaning of English words. The table lists some word parts that come from other languages and gives their meanings.

Use the table to help you write a definition for each of the following words. You can do this by breaking each word into parts. For example, the word *geothermal* is made up of these parts: *geo-* + *therm* + *-al.* Check your definitions of these words in a dictionary.

1. geothermal
2. astronaut
3. interstellar
4. biomass
5. telescope
6. geology

Word part	Meaning
astro-	star, heavenly body
bio-	life, of living things
geo-	earth
inter-	among, between
tele-	over a long distance
mass	lump
naut	sailor
stella	star
therm	heat
-al	of, like
-ar	of, relating to
-logy	science of
-scope	for seeing

READING A WEATHER MAP

A weather map gives information about the weather in a region on a certain day. A weather map for the United States is shown on the next page. The symbols on the map are explained in the boxes below the map. The numbers next to the cities are temperature readings in degrees Celsius.

Use the weather map to answer these questions.

1. Name two cities in which it rained.
2. What kinds of clouds were over Dallas? Over Atlanta?
3. Describe the cloud cover that was over Los Angeles and Atlanta.
4. What kind of front was north of Miami?
5. What was the temperature in New York? In St. Louis?
6. Name a city in which it snowed.

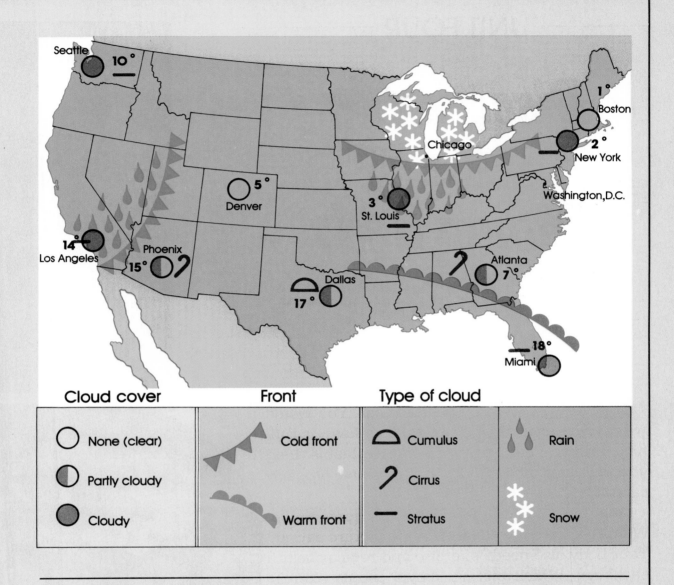

Cloud cover

○ None (clear)

◖ Partly cloudy

● Cloudy

Front

⟩⟩⟩ Cold front

⌢⌢⌢ Warm front

Type of cloud

⌒ Cumulus

∫ Cirrus

— Stratus

Rain

Snow

MAKING A WEATHER MAP

Trace a map of the United States. Show the location of eight major cities. Find a weather map of the United States in a newspaper. Locate the following information for each city that appears on your map: cloud cover, type of cloud, type of front, rain or snow, and temperature. Enter this information on your weather map for the eight cities that you have chosen.

UNIT FOUR

Discovering the Human Body

Suppose you owned a valuable car. You would want to do everything you could to keep it running its best. Your body is the most valuable thing you will ever own. And it too must be properly cared for.

Your body needs the right foods to function. What foods are the children in the picture eating? Your body also needs exercise and regular health checkups. Which picture shows people exercising? Who is giving the child a checkup?

In this unit you will learn about the systems that support and move your body. You will also learn about systems that transport needed materials through your body. You will see how injuries and disease can affect these body systems. And you will learn how to keep your body healthy.

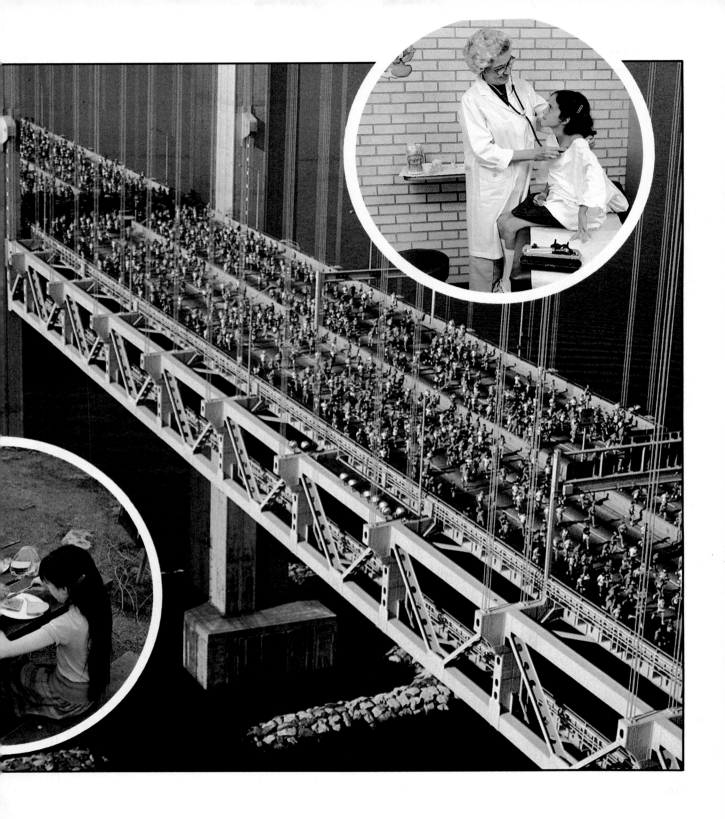

Chapter 13

Support and Movement of the Body

Have you ever played volleyball? Have you ever thought about how your body moves when you run or jump up to hit the ball? Every time your body moves, dozens of muscles and bones are put into action. Muscles and bones work together to move your whole body when you play volleyball. And muscles and bones work together to move your fingers, hand, and arm when you write.

In this chapter you will learn about bones and muscles. You will learn what they look like and how they work together. You will also learn how to keep them healthy.

—YOUR BODY'S FRAMEWORK—
What jobs does the skeleton do?

You may know that some animals have a soft body. Many of them live in water. The water helps support their body. Some animals have a hard outer covering that supports and protects their body. Still other living things have bones inside their body. These bones make up the skeleton. The **skeleton** (skel'ə tən) is the system of bones that supports and protects the body and the organs inside it. The skeleton is also called the skeletal (skel'ə təl) system. What parts of the human skeleton can you name?

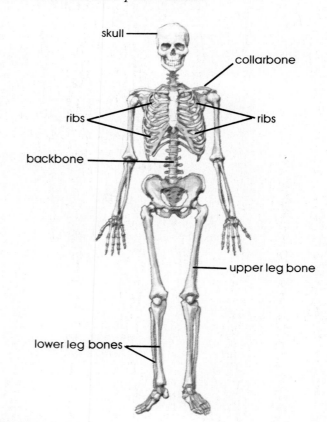

skull

collarbone

ribs — — ribs

backbone

upper leg bone

lower leg bones

THE HUMAN SKELETON

314

The skeleton of your body can be compared with the steel framework of a building. The picture shows a skyscraper being built. The steel beams give the building its shape and support.

The skeletal system forms the framework of the body. It supports the body and gives it shape. But it does other jobs, too. Some parts of the skeleton protect soft parts of the body. For example, the brain, heart, and lungs are protected by the skeleton.

The skeleton is different from the framework of a building in an important way. The steel framework of a building cannot move. But the skeleton can move. It can move because muscles are attached to the bones of the skeleton. Muscles make the bones move.

Many parts of the skeleton help support and protect the body. In fact, the skeleton has 206 bones that help it do its jobs. There are two kinds of bones in the head. They are the bones of the face and the bones that protect the brain. These bones are joined together and form the **skull.**

BONES OF THE SKULL

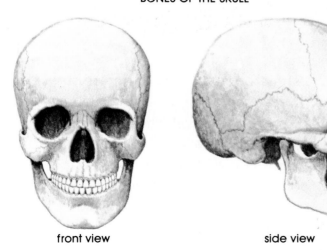

front view   side view

THE BACKBONE

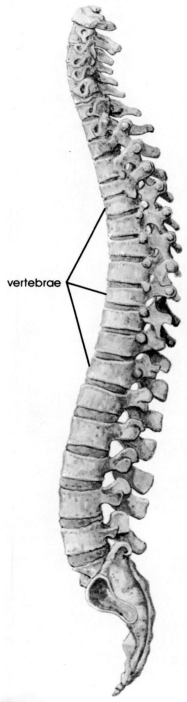

vertebrae

The skeleton in the middle part of the body is made up of the backbone and ribs. You have learned that the backbone is made of many small bones called vertebrae. Run your finger along your backbone. Can you feel the vertebrae? These bones protect many nerves in your back. They also help support your body.

Some of the bones of your backbone are attached to ribs. There are 12 pairs of ribs. The ribs protect organs inside the body. Look at the drawing below. Which organs do the ribs protect?

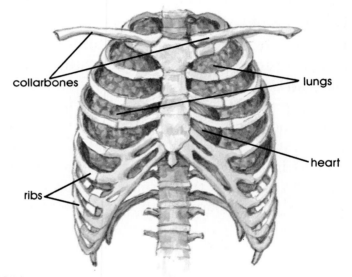

collarbones

lungs

heart

ribs

THE RIBS

The shoulders, arms, hips, and legs are also parts of the skeleton. The shoulders are made of flat bones. These are the collarbones and the shoulder blades. Find the collarbones in the drawing above. Can you find these bones in your body?

The hips are made of bones in the shape of a bowl. The bowl shape of these bones helps support and protect the organs inside the body. Find these bones in the drawing on the next page.

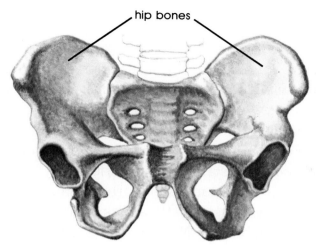

hip bones

Long bones make up the arms and legs. The center of these bones contains a soft material called **bone marrow.** Refer to the drawing below. You may have seen bone marrow inside round bones of beef. The bone marrow inside of some bones produces new blood cells. This is another important job of the skeletal system.

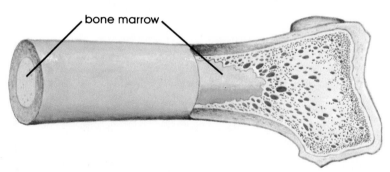

bone marrow

The drawing on the right shows the bones in the arm and the leg. Compare these bones. Notice that the leg bones are longer and heavier than the bones in the arm. The strength of the leg bones allows them to hold the body upright when walking or running. The long bone in the thigh is called the femur (fē′mər). It is the longest and heaviest bone in the body.

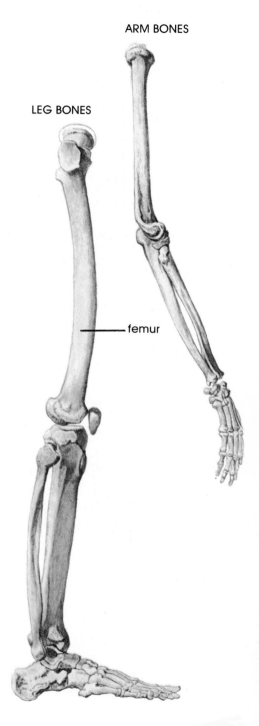

ARM BONES

LEG BONES

femur

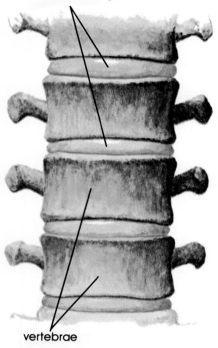

pads of cartilage

vertebrae

When you were born, your skeleton was made of a soft, bonelike material that bends. This material is called **cartilage** (kär'tə lij). As you grow older, much of this cartilage changes to hard bone. Not all the cartilage in the body changes to bone. Feel the tip of your nose. Feel your ears. These body parts are made of cartilage.

Cartilage is important in other places in your body. You know that the backbone is made of many small bones. Nerves travel out from between these bones. If the bones were able to rub against one another, they would also rub against the nerves. This would be very painful. But there are pads of cartilage between the bones. These pads prevent the bones from rubbing against the nerves. Pads of cartilage are also found at the ends of the long bones in your arms and legs. The pads act as cushions, or shock absorbers.

Do you know?

Some scientists believe that human cartilage may one day be used to prevent, treat, and even cure some diseases. Research shows that cartilage contains a special substance called anti-invasion factor (AIF). Scientists have removed AIF from cartilage. They have found that AIF stops the growth of cancer. They believe that AIF may also prevent blindness caused by diabetes. And it may also cure some gum diseases. Scientists hope that they will one day be able to produce AIF in the laboratory.

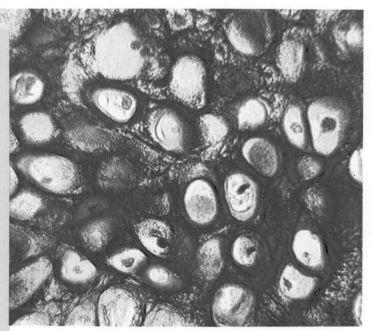

Cartilage seen through a microscope

WHERE BONES MEET
What are four kinds of joints?

You know that parts of your skeleton can move. They can move because of the way bones are joined together. The place where two or more bones are joined together is called a **joint**. Most joints in the body allow the body to move. Bones are held together at joints by strong cords of tissue called **ligaments** (lig′ə mənts). The drawing on the right shows ligaments in the knee joint.

THE KNEE

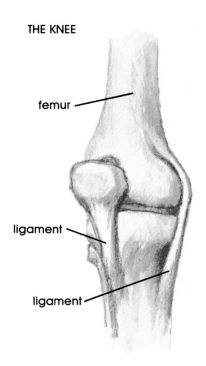

femur

ligament

ligament

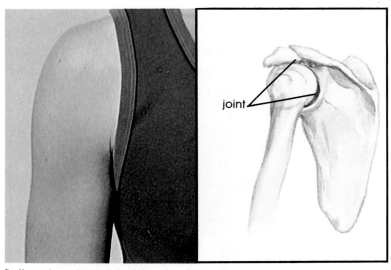

Ball-and-socket joint of the shoulder

joint

Move your arm around. How many different ways does it move? Your arm can move in many directions. The kind of joint that allows the most movement of bones is a **ball-and-socket joint**. This joint is formed by a round knob at the end of one bone. The knob fits into a hollow cavity, or socket, at the end of another bone. The drawing above shows the ball-and-socket joint that connects the upper arm to the shoulder.

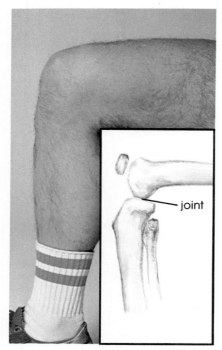

Hinge joint of the knee

A ball-and-socket joint allows bones to move in many directions. But some bones can only move back and forth. This is because they are connected by another kind of joint. A **hinge joint** allows bones to move back and forth. Your knee is a hinge joint. Move the bottom part of your leg. How is this movement different from the way your upper arms can move? Where else do you have a hinge joint?

Turn your head from side to side. Your skull is attached to your backbone by a pivot joint. This joint is between the first two vertebrae. A **pivot joint** allows for movement from side to side.

You have learned that the bones of the skull are joined together. But the bones of the skull cannot move. The kind of joint between bones that cannot move is called a **fixed joint.**

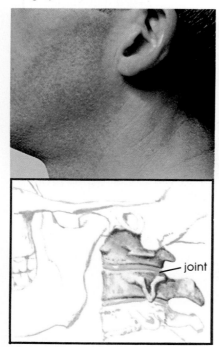

Pivot joint of the neck

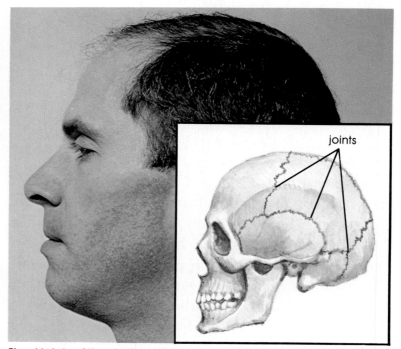

Fixed joints of the skull

MUSCLES MOVE BONES

How do muscles move bones?

You have learned that bones form the framework of your body. You also know that bones move. Bones are able to move because muscles move them. The whole skeletal system is covered with muscles. Muscles are made of soft but strong tissue. The muscles in the body make up the muscular system. You have more than 600 muscles. The drawing shows the muscles of someone who is running.

Muscles are attached to bones by tough cords called **tendons** (ten'dənz). You can feel tendons in your hand and wrist. You can also feel the big tendon that connects the large muscle in the calf of your leg to your heel. The drawing below shows this tendon.

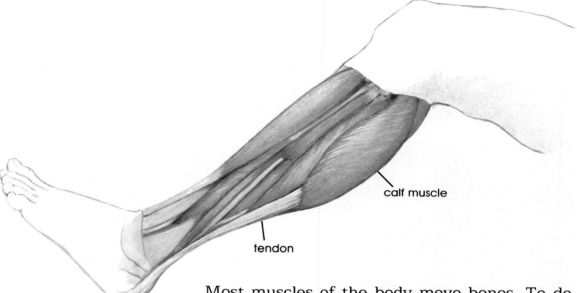

calf muscle

tendon

Most muscles of the body move bones. To do this, the muscles must contract. When a muscle contracts, the muscle becomes shorter and thicker. Muscles also relax. When a muscle relaxes, the muscle becomes longer and thinner. Muscle is the only kind of tissue that can contract and relax. The contracting and relaxing of muscles causes them to move.

Most muscles that move bones work in pairs. One muscle pulls a bone in one direction. The other muscle of the pair pulls the bone in the opposite direction. Muscles can only pull. They cannot push. To make a bone move, one muscle shortens, or contracts. This pulls the bone and moves it. The other muscle of the pair relaxes.

You can observe how pairs of muscles contract and relax to move a bone in your body. Place your left hand over the muscle on the top of your upper right arm. Move the lower half of your right arm upward, as shown in the drawing below. You should feel the muscle in your right arm bulge. This muscle bulges because it is contracting. As it contracts, it pulls the bones in your lower arm upward. Now feel the muscle on the underside of your right arm. This muscle should feel soft. It is soft because it is relaxed.

Now lower your arm. Again feel the pair of muscles on the top and underside of your upper arm. Which one contracts? Which one relaxes? The drawings show what these muscles look like as you raise and lower your arm.

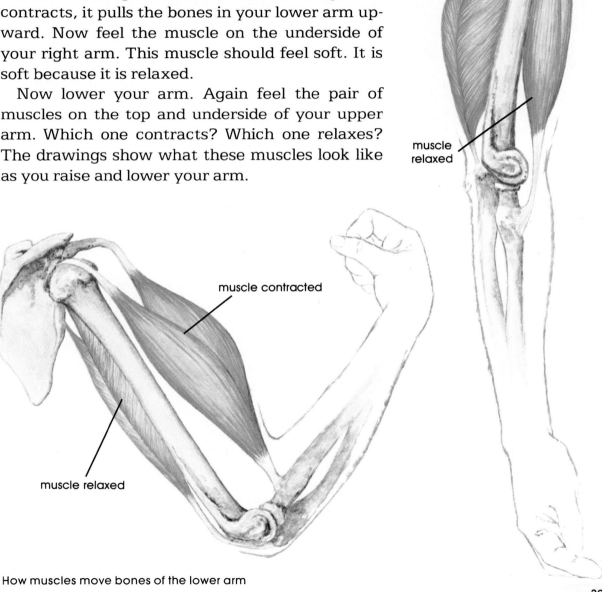

muscle contracted

muscle relaxed

muscle contracted

muscle relaxed

How muscles move bones of the lower arm

What happens when muscles become tired?

Materials clock or watch with second hand

Procedure

A. Copy a paragraph from any page in this book. Then move the fingers of your writing hand quickly, as though you were playing a piano. Keep moving your fingers until your fingers or arm become tired. Now copy the same paragraph again. Compare the way your handwriting looks in the two samples.

    1. Was it harder to write when your fingers were tired?

    2. How do your two handwriting samples differ?

B. While seated, raise one leg as shown. Record the time you begin. Keep your leg raised until it becomes tired. Record the time when you put your leg down. Rest for 30 seconds.

    3. How long did you keep your leg raised?

C. Repeat step **B** at once.

    4. How long did you keep your leg raised this time?

    5. How do the results for step **B** compare with these results?

Conclusion

1. How do tired muscles affect how well you can do a task?

2. How do tired muscles affect how long you can do a task?

Using science ideas

Repeat steps **B** and **C** five times in a row. Graph your results. Suppose someone rides a bicycle every day for an hour. How might this affect that person's results for steps **B** and **C**?

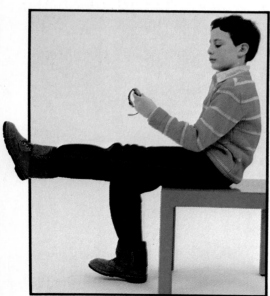

TWO GROUPS OF MUSCLES

What are two groups of muscles?

You can control some of the muscles in your body. You can control muscles that help you walk, run, sit down, get up, or jump. The muscles that you can control are in a group called **voluntary muscles.** Voluntary muscles are attached to bones and other muscles. They move these bones and muscles. The pictures show some of the many activities that are possible because of voluntary muscles.

Muscles that you cannot control are in a group called **involuntary muscles.** You need these muscles to stay alive. Suppose you had to control your heartbeat. You would have to think about moving your heart muscle every moment of your life. Other involuntary muscles are in the stomach and intestines. They move food through these parts of the body. Involuntary muscles also move blood through the blood vessels. They even cause you to blush or to turn pale.

Finding out

Are your eyelids controlled by both voluntary and involuntary muscles? Look at your eyes in a mirror. See how long you can keep from blinking. What kind of muscles cause you to blink? Blink your eyes four times in a row. What kind of muscles allow you to do this?

Now look in the mirror at the pupil of one eye. The pupil is the dark circular opening in the center of the eye. It controls the amount of light that enters the eye. As you look in the mirror, have another student shine a dim flashlight beam on the pupil of one eye. What happens to the size of the pupil? What kind of muscle controls the pupil?

Skeletal muscle

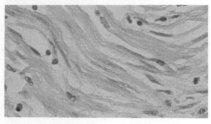

Smooth muscle

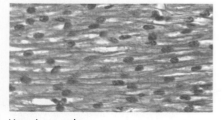

Heart muscle

There are three kinds of muscles. Most muscles that move bones are made of long fibers. These are voluntary muscles called **skeletal muscles.** The picture shows what skeletal muscle looks like under a microscope.

The involuntary muscles that make up most body organs are another kind of muscle. They are called **smooth muscles.** These muscles make up the inside of the blood vessels, stomach, intestines, and other organs. Smooth muscles, as seen through a microscope, are shown.

A third kind of muscle is found in the heart. This special kind of muscle, called **heart muscle,** is also involuntary. The picture shows heart muscle, as it appears under a microscope. The heart is the hardest working muscle in the body. It beats between 2 billion and 3 billion times during an average lifetime. You can see why the muscle of the heart is a special kind of muscle.

—BONE AND MUSCLE INJURIES—
What are some common injuries of bones and muscles?

Even though bones are strong, they can be damaged. Have you ever had a broken bone? Because most young people are very active, they often break bones. A crack or a break in a bone is called a **fracture** (frak′chər). There are different kinds of fractures.

Usually when a bone breaks it does not push through the muscle and skin. This is called a **simple fracture.** Sometimes the broken end of a bone pushes through the muscle and skin. This is called a **compound fracture.** Look at the drawing of a compound fracture. Compare it with the drawing of a simple fracture. Why do you think there is a great danger of infection with a compound fracture?

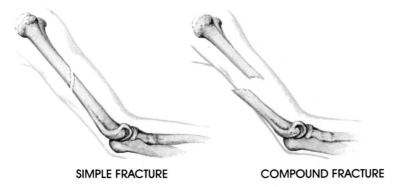

SIMPLE FRACTURE   COMPOUND FRACTURE

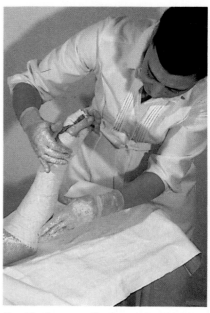

Cast being applied

Because bones contain living tissue, they can repair themselves. The parts of broken bones are put back in place, or set, by a doctor. Then the broken parts will grow back together. A cast holds the broken bones in place. The picture shows a cast being put on a broken arm.

The ligaments that connect bones can also be injured. A **sprain** is an injury in which a ligament is stretched or torn. This happens when a joint is forced to move in a way other than the way it normally moves. Football players often suffer torn ligaments of the knee joint when they are hit from the side. Ankle and wrist sprains are also a result of torn or stretched ligaments.

Sometimes muscles are injured. Some muscle injuries are caused by overuse of a muscle. A muscle **strain** is an injury caused by overstretching a muscle or tendon. Muscle strain often results when someone lifts a heavy object in the wrong way. The pictures show the correct way to lift a heavy object.

Did you ever wake up in the middle of the night with a cramp in your leg or foot? A **cramp** is a sudden strong contraction of a muscle. It can be very painful. But it does not usually last long. Often you can help get rid of a cramp by rubbing the muscle.

Proper way to lift a heavy object

- CARE OF BONES AND MUSCLES -
How can you keep bones and muscles healthy?

There are three important things you can do to keep your bones and muscles healthy. You can eat a proper diet. You can get enough of the right kind of exercise. And you can get enough rest.

Eating a proper diet means eating the foods needed for healthy bones and muscles. There are four main groups of foods that make up a proper diet. The meat group contains protein foods needed for cell growth and to make new cells. The dairy group includes foods that contain minerals that make bones hard. The foods in the fruit and vegetable group contain needed vitamins. The bread and cereal group foods provide energy needed for muscles to move bones. What foods do you see in the pictures of each group?

Meat group

Dairy group

Fruit and vegetable group

Bread and cereal group

What happens to bones when minerals are removed from them?

Materials   leg or thigh bone from uncooked chicken / jar / vinegar / paper towel

Procedure

A. Remove all the meat from a chicken bone. Wash the bone in water and then dry it with a paper towel. Feel the bone. Then gently try to bend the bone.

    1. Does the bone feel hard or soft?

    2. Does the bone bend?

B. Half fill a jar with vinegar. Place the bone in the jar. Allow the bone to remain in the vinegar for 5 days. Vinegar removes minerals from bone.

C. After 5 days, remove the bone from the jar. Wash the bone in water and then dry it with a paper towel. Feel the bone. Gently try to bend the bone.

    3. How does the bone feel now compared with the way it felt in step **A**?

    4. Does the bone bend?

Conclusion

1. If you did not eat foods containing minerals, what would your bones be like?

2. How would a lack of minerals affect the ability of your skeleton to support your body?

Using science ideas

Vitamin D is needed for strong bones and teeth. Find out why this vitamin is often called the sunshine vitamin.

In addition to a proper diet, exercise is important for the growth and development of muscles. When muscles are not used, they shrink. This means they become smaller and weaker. Exercise keeps muscles strong.

While exercise is important, there is a problem created by exercise. As energy is used in exercising, food is burned. When the body burns food, waste products are left behind in the muscles. Rest helps get rid of these wastes. Rest also keeps muscles from being overused. Sleep helps to relax muscles and rid them of waste materials.

IDEAS TO REMEMBER

► The skeletal system forms the framework of the body and protects soft body parts.
► Most joints allow the body to move. The main kinds are ball-and-socket joints, hinge joints, and pivot joints. Fixed joints do not allow movement.
► Bones are moved when muscles contract and relax.
► Skeletal muscle is voluntary muscle. Smooth muscle and heart muscle are involuntary muscle.
► Injuries to the skeletal system include fractures and sprains.
► Injuries to the muscular system include strains and cramps.
► Muscles and bones can be kept healthy with proper diet, exercise, and rest.

Reviewing the Chapter

SCIENCE WORDS

A. Use all the terms below to complete the sentences.

simple fracture   skull   compound fracture   cartilage
bone marrow   skeleton

The system of bones that supports and protects the body and the organs inside it is the __1__. The bones of the face are part of the __2__. New blood cells are made by a soft material called __3__. Pads of __4__ prevent the small bones of the back from rubbing together. A break in a bone in which the broken end pushes through muscle and skin is a/an __5__. A break in a bone in which this does not happen is called a/an __6__.

B. Write the letter of the term that best matches the definition. Not all the terms will be used.

1. Attaches muscles to bone
2. Injury that is caused by over-stretching a muscle or tendon
3. The place where two or more bones are joined together
4. Any crack or break in a bone
5. Muscle that you can control
6. Holds bones together at a joint
7. Muscle that you cannot control
8. Sudden strong muscle contraction
9. Injury in which a ligament is torn or stretched

a. involuntary muscle
b. sprain
c. cramp
d. ligament
e. fracture
f. skull
g. strain
h. tendon
i. bone marrow
j. voluntary muscle
k. joint

USING IDEAS

A. Identify each of the following.

1. It is a kind of muscle. It makes up the hardest working muscle in the body. What is it?
2. It is a kind of muscle. It makes up the inside of the blood vessels, stomach, and other organs. What is it?
3. It is a kind of muscle. It is muscle that moves bones. What is it?

B. Write the name of each kind of joint in the drawings.

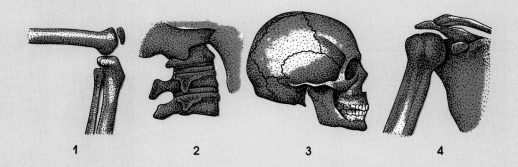

1   2   3   4

C. Name the four food groups.

1. Identify three different foods in each group.
2. Write what each food group provides that keeps your bones and muscles healthy and working properly.

UNDERSTANDING IDEAS

1. Prepare three menus—one for breakfast, one for lunch, and one for dinner. Be sure each meal includes foods from all four food groups.
2. Use a reference book to find out what type of injury a dislocated bone is. Write a brief description of this injury and the type of treatment that is given.

Chapter 14

Transport Systems of the Body

This man is having a special kind of test. The doctor sitting at the machine is testing the man's heart. The man with the clipboard is watching the man while he exercises. This test can give much information about the health of the man's heart and blood vessels.

The heart and blood vessels carry food and oxygen throughout the body. They also remove certain wastes. The heart and blood vessels form a transport system.

In this chapter you will learn about the three main transport systems of the body. You will learn about the structures of these systems and how they work. You will also learn about some of the diseases that affect these systems.

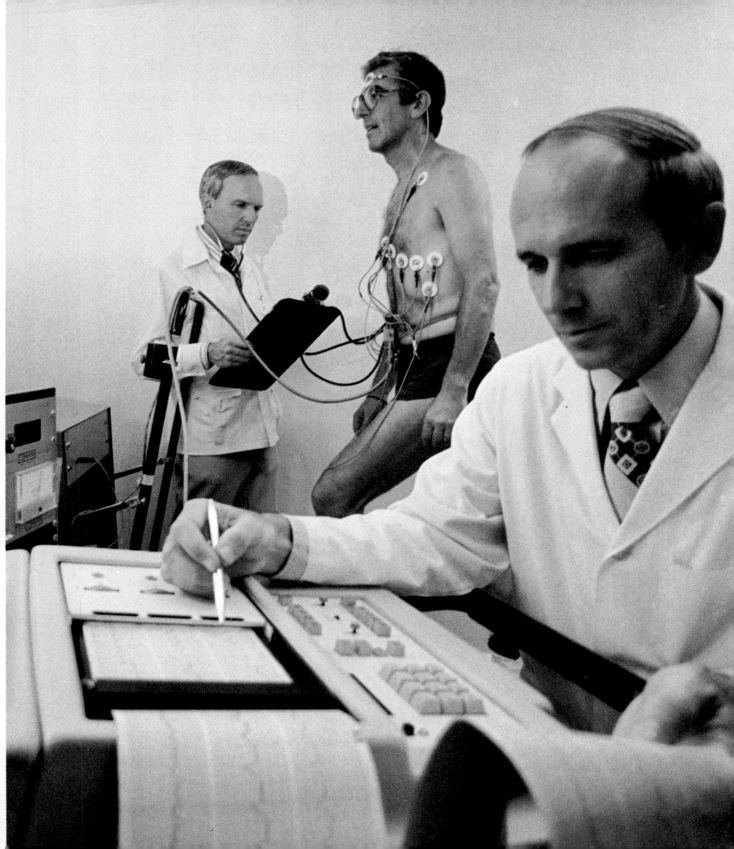

THE CIRCULATORY SYSTEM

What are the two jobs of the circulatory system?

The **circulatory** (sėr'kyə lə tôr ē) **system** is one of the body's transport systems. It carries needed materials, such as food and oxygen, to the cells of the body. It also carries away waste products. Another important job of the circulatory system is to protect the body from disease. It serves as a defense system. The circulatory system has three main parts that help it perform its jobs. These parts are the blood, the heart, and the blood vessels.

How much blood is in the body? An average adult has 5 L of blood. This amount is about the same as the amount of liquid contained in the five bottles shown in the picture.

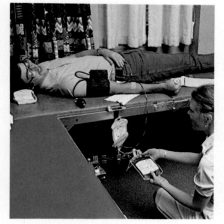

Donating blood

Blood is a liquid with solid parts floating in it. The liquid part of the blood is called **plasma** (plaz'mə). Plasma is yellowish in color and is mostly water. It contains many important chemicals. Plasma makes up over half of the blood.

There are three different kinds of solid parts in the blood. The first solid part of the blood is the red blood cells. **Red blood cells** carry oxygen to

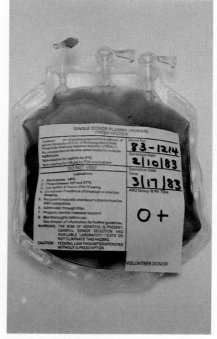

Container of plasma

336

all the cells of the body. They can do this because they contain a special chemical called hemoglobin (hē′mə glō bən). The hemoglobin in red blood cells contains iron and makes blood look red.

A red blood cell looks something like a doughnut without a hole. This shape is shown in the picture. A red blood cell is very small. A single drop of blood contains about 5 million red blood cells.

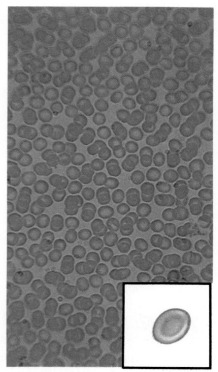

Red blood cells

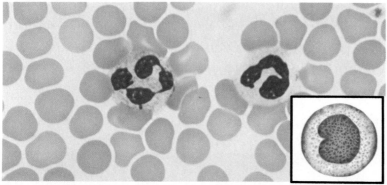

Red and white blood cells under microscope   White blood cell

White blood cells are the second solid part of the blood. They help the body fight infection. Some white blood cells are shown above. White blood cells do not contain hemoglobin. Although they are called white cells, they really have no color. White blood cells can change shape as they move. Sometimes they even squeeze through the walls of blood vessels. They move out into infected parts of the body where they destroy bacteria and other harmful things. White blood cells surround and digest the bacteria.

Platelets (plāt′lits) are the third solid part of blood. Platelets are not whole cells. They are parts of cells that control bleeding. Like white blood cells, they have no color. They are much smaller than red blood cells. Have you ever had a

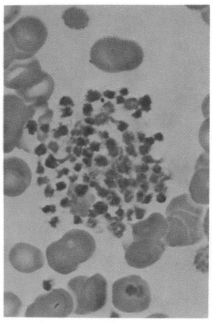

Platelets

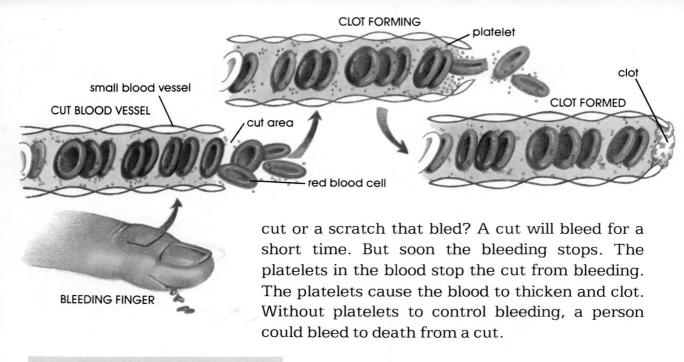

CLOT FORMING

platelet

clot

CLOT FORMED

small blood vessel

CUT BLOOD VESSEL

cut area

red blood cell

BLEEDING FINGER

cut or a scratch that bled? A cut will bleed for a short time. But soon the bleeding stops. The platelets in the blood stop the cut from bleeding. The platelets cause the blood to thicken and clot. Without platelets to control bleeding, a person could bleed to death from a cut.

Do you know?

On December 2, 1982, a medical miracle took place. The first permanent artificial heart was placed in a human being. Made of plastic and aluminum, the heart was built to run on electricity. It was named the Jarvik-7, after its inventor, Dr. Robert Jarvik. A 61-year-old man, Dr. Barney Clark, was the lucky person to receive the heart. Without the heart he would have died within a few hours.

The artificial heart replaced the two diseased lower chambers of the heart. It was attached to the two upper heart chambers. Dr. Clark lived 112 days with the artificial heart. He died on March 24, 1983.

CIRCULATION OF BLOOD

How does blood move through the body?

The second main part of the circulatory system is the heart. The heart is a strong, hollow muscle about the size of a fist. It is located in the center of the chest. As long as you are alive, your heart never stops working. A normal heart beats about 70 to 80 times per minute.

There are four cavities, or hollow chambers, in the heart. Each upper chamber of the heart is called an **atrium** (ā'trē əm). There is a right atrium and a left atrium. Blood collects in these thin-walled chambers. Each lower chamber of the heart is called a **ventricle** (ven'trə kəl). There is a right ventricle and a left ventricle. Ventricles have thick, muscular walls. They are the pumping chambers of the heart. Between the upper and lower chambers is a flap of tissue. This tissue acts as a valve. The valve keeps the blood from flowing backward. The drawing to the right shows the heart chambers and valves.

There are three kinds of blood vessels: arteries, veins, and capillaries. An **artery** (är'tər ē) is a thick-walled blood vessel that carries blood away from the heart. It usually carries blood that is rich in food and oxygen. A **vein** (vān) is a blood vessel that carries blood back to the heart from the body cells. This blood usually carries only waste products. A **capillary** (kap'ə ler ē) is a tiny blood vessel that connects an artery and a vein. Capillaries are the smallest blood vessels in the body. They allow food, oxygen, and wastes to pass directly between the blood and the cells.

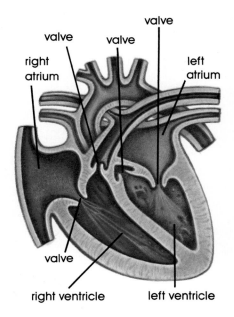

INSIDE THE HEART

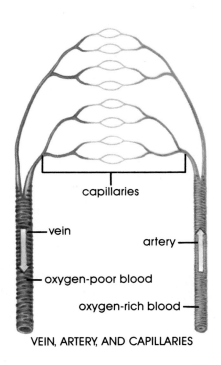

VEIN, ARTERY, AND CAPILLARIES

The drawing shows the path of blood through the circulatory system. Refer to the drawing as you read the steps.

1. Begin in the left atrium. The blood has just left the lungs. It has a rich supply of oxygen.

2. Blood passes from the left atrium through a valve into the left ventricle. From here the blood is pumped into a large artery.

3. The large artery branches into smaller and smaller arteries. These arteries go to all parts of the body.

4. Blood from the arteries enters the capillaries. Food and oxygen in the blood pass through the capillary walls into the cells.

5. Carbon dioxide and waste products from the cells pass through the capillary walls into the blood.

6. From the capillaries blood enters the smallest veins. The blood flows from the smallest veins into larger and larger veins.

7. Blood passes into the largest of the veins.

8. The largest veins return blood that is poor in oxygen to the right atrium.

9. Blood passes from the right atrium through a valve to the right ventricle. Then the blood is pumped into a large artery to the lungs.

10. In the lungs the blood loses carbon dioxide and picks up a fresh supply of oxygen.

11. Oxygen-rich blood from the lungs returns through veins to the left atrium.

12. The whole cycle begins again.

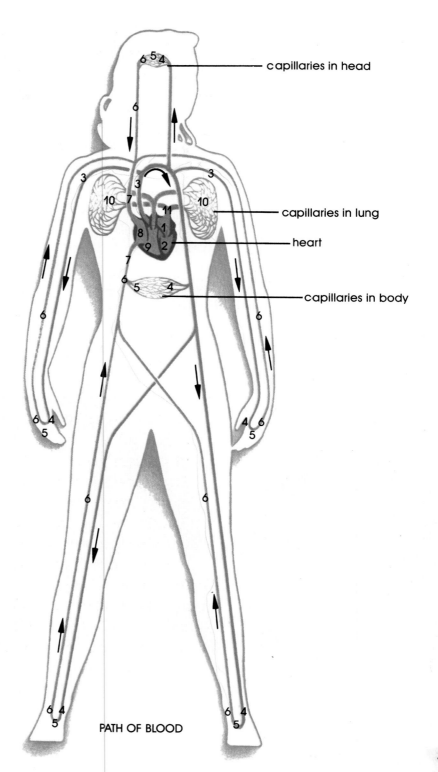

capillaries in head

capillaries in lung

heart

capillaries in body

PATH OF BLOOD

341

DISEASES AND CARE OF THE CIRCULATORY SYSTEM

What are some circulatory problems?

Severe cuts can cause a loss of blood. No one can afford to lose large amounts of this substance. The best way to stop bleeding is to apply direct pressure to the wound. A clean cloth should be used to apply the pressure. To prevent infection, the wound should be covered with a bandage. A large, deep cut should be checked by a doctor.

Blood can also be lost in a nosebleed. The best way to stop a nosebleed is to hold the head straight and pinch the nostrils together. Sometimes a severe nosebleed must be treated in a doctor's office or a hospital.

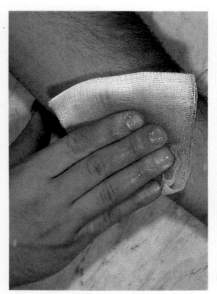

Applying direct pressure

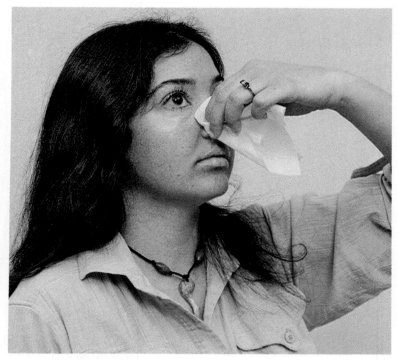

Treating a nosebleed

Each of the three main parts of the circulatory system can become diseased. For example, fat may build up in the walls of arteries. The inside of the arteries may then become clogged. The clogging of an artery is similar to the clogging of a water pipe with minerals. The drawings show how clogged arteries and clogged pipes are alike.

Normal artery

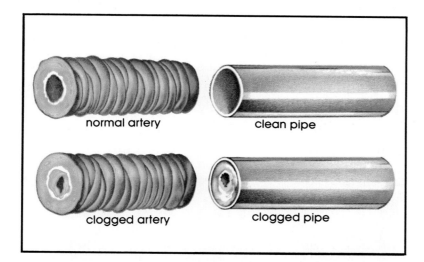
normal artery   clean pipe

clogged artery   clogged pipe

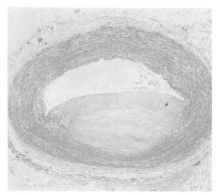
Clogged artery

Heart attack is a common heart problem. It occurs when the supply of blood to part of the heart is cut off. Usually the blood cannot reach the heart because the arteries that carry blood to the heart are clogged. If the blood supply is cut off too long, the heart can be permanently damaged. A person can die from a heart attack. It is a leading cause of death in the United States.

High blood pressure is another serious problem. Blood flowing through the arteries presses against the artery walls. This pressure is called the blood pressure. It can be measured with a special device. The picture shows a person having his blood pressure tested. Sometimes the blood

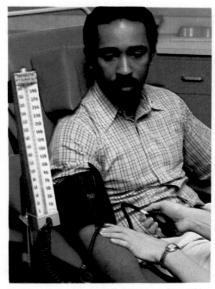
Taking blood pressure

343

pressure is too high. This causes the heart to work harder than it should. High blood pressure can often be controlled with certain kinds of medicine.

A longer and healthier life can be enjoyed by people who take care of themselves. Certain studies have shown that foods high in fat can clog the arteries. Clogged arteries make the heart work harder. This condition can also cause high blood pressure. Some people are more likely than others to get clogged arteries from fats in food. So, they should eat foods that are low in fats. Some diseases of the circulatory system are less likely to appear in thin people. It is a good idea to watch your diet to avoid becoming overweight.

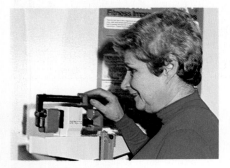

Checking weight

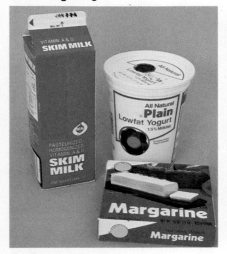

Low-fat foods

Runners

Exercise is also important for a healthy circulatory system. Like other muscles, the heart benefits from exercise. Making the heart work harder with exercise helps to make it stronger. Exercise like swimming, jogging, and jumping rope is good for the heart.

How does exercise affect the pulse rate?

Materials   stopwatch or wristwatch with second hand

Procedure

A. Work with a partner. Sit quietly and find your pulse as shown. Hold your index finger and middle finger against your wrist at the base of the thumb. Press firmly. Make sure you can feel the pulse.

B. Take your pulse for 1 minute. Have your partner tell you when 1 minute has passed. Record your pulse.
   1. What was your pulse rate?

C. Take and record your pulse rate two more times. Find and record the average rate. (Add the three readings and divide by 3.)
   2. What was your average pulse rate?

D. Jog in place for 1 minute. Then take your pulse rate again.
   3. What is your pulse rate after jogging?

E. Take your pulse rate after jogging two more times. Be sure there is a rest period before each 1-minute period of jogging.

F. Record your pulse rate after jogging. Find and record the average pulse rate after jogging.
   4. What is your average pulse rate after jogging? How does it differ from your average pulse rate while sitting quietly?

	1	2	3	Average
Pulse rate while sitting				
Pulse rate after jogging				

Conclusion

1. When is your pulse rate greater, while sitting or after jogging?

2. What is the difference between the average sitting pulse rate and the average jogging pulse rate?

THE RESPIRATORY SYSTEM

How does air move in and out of the lungs?

A healthy person can live several weeks without food. It is also possible for a healthy person to live a few days without water. But a person can live only a few minutes without air. A constant supply of air is necessary for life.

When you breathe, air enters your body through your respiratory (res′pər ə tôr ē) system. The **respiratory system** is another transport system of the body. It works closely with the circulatory system to put to use the oxygen in the air you breathe.

Receiving oxygen

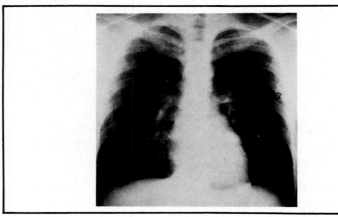

Recall that oxygen from the air is needed by living cells to release energy from food. The oxygen combines with food to release energy. This is called respiration. Respiration is the process by which each body cell gets oxygen and releases energy from food. Carbon dioxide and water are also given off. The respiratory and circulatory systems work together during the process of respiration.

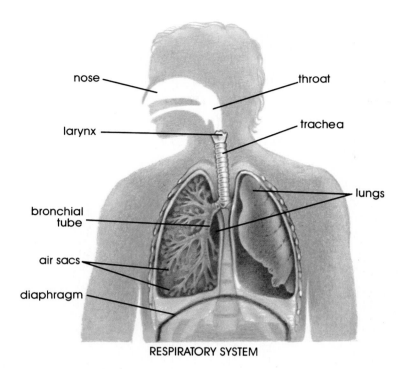

nose

throat

larynx

trachea

bronchial
tube

lungs

air sacs

diaphragm

RESPIRATORY SYSTEM

The drawing shows the respiratory system. The steps below tell how oxygen in the air travels from outside the body to the cells inside the body.

1. When a person breathes in, air enters the nose. From the nose the air travels to the throat. The air then enters a soft tube with rings of cartilage around it. This tube is the windpipe, or **trachea** (trā'kē ə). The voice box, or **larynx** (lar'ingks), is at the top of the trachea. Air passing through the larynx lets a person make sounds for speaking or singing.

2. The trachea divides into two tubes. These tubes are called the **bronchial** (brong'kē əl) **tubes.** They lead to the lungs.

3. The lungs are made of spongy tissue. In the lungs the bronchial tubes divide many times into smaller branches. The smallest branch is thinner than a human hair.

4. At the ends of the tiny branches in the lungs are the air sacs. The air sacs look something like a bunch of grapes. They have very thin walls. Each sac is surrounded by a capillary. Gases can pass from the sacs into the capillaries and from the capillaries into the sacs.

5. Every time a person breathes in, the air sacs fill with air. Oxygen from the air leaves the air sacs and enters the blood through capillaries.

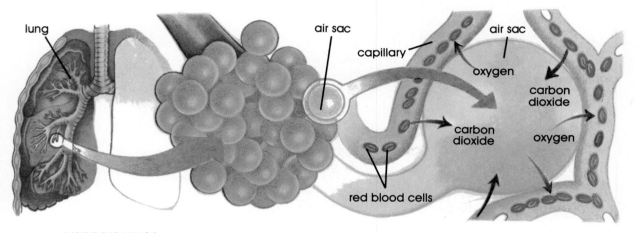

INSIDE THE LUNGS

The oxygen that reaches the body cells from the lungs is used to break down food. When food is broken down, energy is released. Carbon dioxide is also released from the cell as a waste product. The carbon dioxide passes into the blood and is carried to the lungs. In the lungs the carbon dioxide passes from the capillaries into the air sacs. When a person breathes out, the carbon dioxide passes from the air sacs to the bronchial tubes. From there it goes to the outside air.

The **diaphragm** (dī′ə fram) is a thick sheet of muscle at the bottom of the chest cavity. It moves down when a person breathes in. This movement spreads the ribs and allows the lungs to expand.

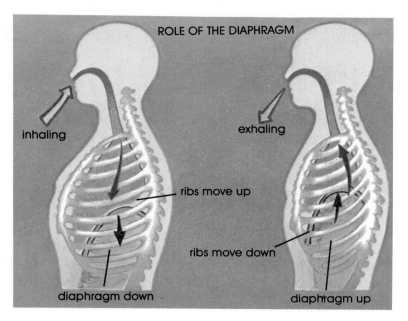

ROLE OF THE DIAPHRAGM

inhaling

exhaling

ribs move up

ribs move down

diaphragm down

diaphragm up

This process is called **inhaling** (in hāl'ing). When a person breathes out, the diaphragm moves up and the ribs come together. This movement pushes air out of the lungs. This process is called **exhaling** (eks hāl'ing). The drawings help show how air enters and leaves the lungs.

Finding out

How does the diaphragm help to fill up the lungs?
You will need a 2-L plastic bottle, two round balloons, scissors, and 2 rubber bands. Cut the bottle in half. Place one of the balloons through the opening of the bottle. Stretch the balloon opening over the bottle opening. Hold the balloon in place with a rubber band. Think of this balloon as the lungs. Cut the neck off the other balloon. Stretch this balloon across the bottom of the bottle. Hold the balloon in place with a rubber band. Think of this balloon as the diaphragm. Pull down on the stretched balloon. What happens to the balloon inside the bottle? Explain how this action is like that of the lungs and the diaphragm.

349

How much air do your lungs hold?

Materials large empty plastic milk jug with cap / plastic dishpan / rubber tubing / drinking straw / masking tape / grease pencil / graduate

Procedure

A. Work with a partner. Place a piece of masking tape on a plastic milk jug from top to bottom as shown.

B. Fill the jug with water. Screw the cap on the jug. Fill a dishpan about one third full of water. Place the jug upside down in the water. Carefully remove the cap. Do not let air bubbles enter the jug.

C. Ask your partner to hold the jug so that it does not tip over. Place one end of the tubing inside the jug. Put a straw in the other end of the tubing. Take a deep breath and blow through the straw.
   1. What happens to the water in the jug?
   2. Where did the air in your lungs go?

D. Replace the cap on the jug. Do not let any extra water out of the jug.

E. Remove the jug from the dishpan. Turn the jug right side up. Mark the level of water on the tape.

F. Use a graduate to fill the jug with water.
   3. How much water did you add? What does this water represent?

G. The amount of water you just added to the jug is equal to the amount of air you blew into the jug.
   4. How much air did you blow into the jug?

H. Repeat steps **B–F** two more times. Take an average of the three volumes of air collected.
   5. What was the average volume of air blown into the jug?

Conclusion
How much air do your lungs hold?

DISEASES AND CARE OF THE RESPIRATORY SYSTEM

What are some common respiratory diseases?

Think back to the last time you had a cold. Colds are one of the most common diseases of the respiratory system. Colds are easily spread from one person to another. Every time a person sneezes or coughs, germs are sprayed into the air. People nearby may breathe in the germs. Then they may get the cold. Always cover your nose and mouth when you sneeze or cough. Always wash your hands. Why should you do this?

Ragweed—a plant that causes allergies

Do you know someone who has allergies? An allergy is a strong reaction to a substance that is not normally in the body. Plant pollen and dust are such substances. They often enter the body through the respiratory system. These materials can cause sneezing, headaches, or difficult breathing. Many people are allergic to the pollen of ragweed, shown in the picture.

Bronchitis (brong kī′tis) is another respiratory disease. In this disease the bronchial tubes become red and swollen. Sometimes bronchitis can lead to other diseases of the lungs.

Another disease of the respiratory system is lung cancer. Lung cancer has several causes. One cause is breathing polluted air. Another cause is smoking cigarettes. The pictures show a lung from a person who did not smoke and a lung from a smoker. Which would you rather have in your body? Over half the people with lung cancer smoked cigarettes. Because of the dangers of smoking, every package of cigarettes must carry a warning label.

Warning labels on cigarettes

Exercising for good health

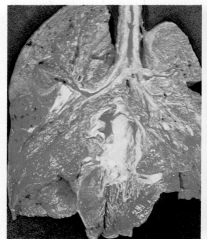
Healthy lung

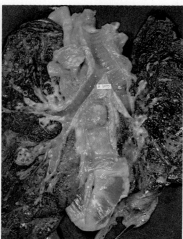
Smoker's lung

Regular exercise is needed for a healthy respiratory system. When strenuous exercise is done, the diaphragm becomes stronger. A stronger diaphragm allows a person to take in more air. With more air in the lungs, more oxygen can be sent to the body cells. Then the cells can work better to release energy from food.

THE EXCRETORY SYSTEM
What waste products are removed by the excretory system?

The **excretory** (eks'krə tôr ē) **system** is the transport system that removes waste products from the body. Waste products are the unwanted materials left over from life processes such as respiration. Living things will die if they do not get rid of waste products.

Many body parts get rid of waste products. The kidneys are among the main organs of the excretory system. But the lungs and the skin may also be thought of as parts of the excretory system.

The lungs get rid of one main waste product. This product is carbon dioxide. They also get rid of some moisture. These materials leave the body each time a person exhales. You may be surprised to learn that the skin is also a part of the excretory system. One layer of the skin contains sweat glands. Find them in the drawing. When a person sweats, water leaves the body. This water contains many waste materials. Sweating gets rid of extra water and wastes.

Replacing lost fluids

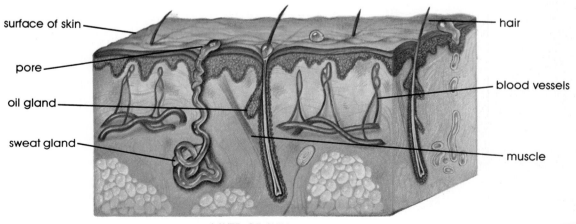

surface of skin

pore

oil gland

sweat gland

hair

blood vessels

muscle

LAYER OF SKIN

Most of the waste water in the body is removed by the kidneys. Normally, a person has two kidneys. They are located in the lower back, one on each side of the backbone. The drawing shows where the kidneys are located.

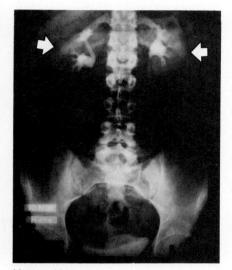

X ray of kidneys

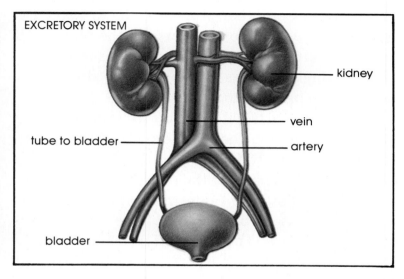

EXCRETORY SYSTEM

kidney

vein

tube to bladder

artery

bladder

All the blood passes through the kidneys. As it does, the kidneys take out waste materials and excess water. These dissolved wastes and excess water are taken through small tubes to the bladder for storage. Finally, the water and wastes leave the body as **urine** (yur'ən). Urine is water with wastes and salts dissolved in it. Solid human waste is removed from the body by the large intestine, which is part of the digestive system.

If the kidneys become diseased, they may stop working properly. Harmful waste products will then build up in the body. People with diseased kidneys can use a special machine to remove wastes from the blood. A person using one of these machines is shown in the picture. These machines have saved many lives.

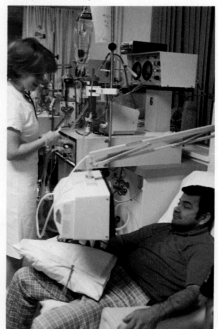

Person using kidney machine

To keep the excretory system healthy, a person should drink several glasses of water each day. The water will replace water that is lost when waste products are removed. Water can be supplied to the body by various foods. It is found in such foods as milk, soup, and juice, as well as in juicy fruits and vegetables.

IDEAS TO REMEMBER

▶ The transport systems of the body are the circulatory system, the respiratory system, and the excretory system.

▶ The blood, the heart, and the blood vessels are parts of the circulatory system.

▶ The circulatory system carries food and oxygen to cells and carries away wastes. It also protects the body from disease.

▶ The nose, the trachea, the bronchial tubes, the lungs, and the air sacs are parts of the respiratory system.

▶ The respiratory system brings oxygen into the body and removes carbon dioxide and some water.

▶ The parts of the excretory system include the kidneys, the skin, and the lungs.

▶ The excretory system gets rid of waste products.

Reviewing the Chapter

SCIENCE WORDS

A. Identify each of the following.

1. It is a type of blood vessel. Its walls are thin. It carries blood from the body cells back to the heart. What is it?
2. It is a thick sheet of muscle. It is found at the bottom of the chest cavity. It helps in breathing. What is it?
3. It is one of the solid parts of the blood. It helps fight infection. What is it?
4. It is one of the body's transport systems. It carries food and oxygen to the body cells. It defends the body against disease. What is it?

B. Write the letter of the term that best matches the definition. Not all the terms will be used.

1. Lower chamber of the heart
2. Windpipe
3. Cell that helps in clotting
4. Waste formed of water and dissolved salts
5. Thick-walled blood vessel
6. Cell shaped like doughnut without hole
7. Process of breathing out
8. Upper chamber of heart
9. Voice box
10. Smallest blood vessel

a. capillary
b. inhaling
c. red blood cell
d. atrium
e. larynx
f. exhaling
g. trachea
h. ventricle
i. urine
j. platelet
k. artery
l. white blood cell

UNDERSTANDING IDEAS

A. Make a chart like the one shown. Write each science term under the correct heading of the chart.

kidneys   air sacs   bronchial tubes   skin

trachea   atrium   diaphragm   lungs

bladder   nose   ventricle   artery

Circulatory system	Respiratory system	Excretory system

B. Write the correct term for each number in the diagram. Then describe the process of respiration.

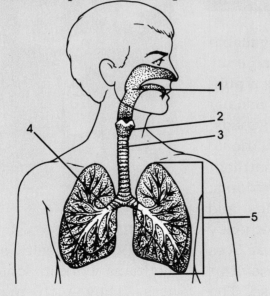

USING IDEAS

1. Use clay, paper, or other material to make a model of the heart. Label the parts of the model.

Science in Careers

Emergency medical technicians

There are many careers available in the health field. An *emergency medical technician* (EMT) is a public-health worker. EMTs usually work in teams on rescue squads. They give aid in many situations. They give on-the-scene treatment to victims of automobile accidents, heart attacks, near drownings, and poisonings. This type of emergency treatment saves thousands of lives each year. An EMT must have at least an 80-hour basic course. The need for additional training varies.

Physical therapists help people with diseases or injuries of muscles, bones, joints, or nerves. They test the strength of muscles and develop treatment programs, such as special exercises. They help disabled people adjust to physical problems.

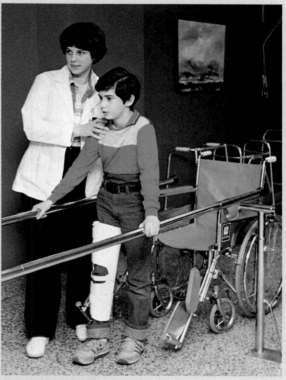

Physical therapist

Dietitians (dī′ə tish ənz) provide an important health service. Some dietitians work in schools and business. They plan menus so that meals have the proper amounts of foods from each food group. Many dietitians plan special diets for people in hospitals and nursing homes.

People in Science

William DeVries (1943–)

Dr. DeVries is the skillful young surgeon who placed the first permanent artificial heart into the chest of a human being. Dr. DeVries prepared over 3 years for the task. He practiced the operation 200 times on sheep and calves. For more information about this operation, see *Do you know?* on page 338.

Dr. DeVries enjoys the challenge of surgery. "You have to pay attention to a million different things at once," he says. "You know you're doing something really important."

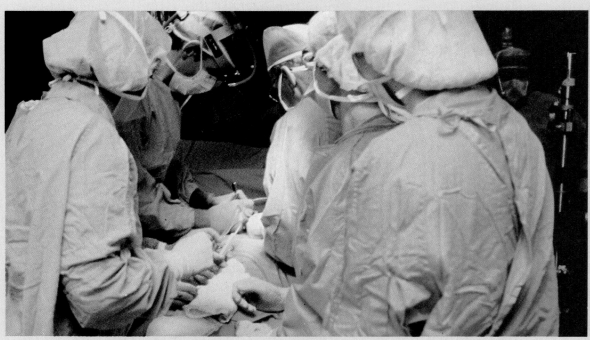

Dr. DeVries and staff placing artificial heart in patient

Developing Skills

WORD SKILLS

The table lists some word parts that come from other languages and gives their meanings. Use the table to help you write a definition for each of the following words. You can do this by breaking each word into parts. For example, the word *hemophilia* is made up of these parts: *hemo- + -philia.*

Word part	Meaning
bronch-	bronchial tubes
cardio-	heart
erythro-	red
hemo-	blood
leuko-	white
trans-	across, to the other side
-cyte	cell
-graph	instrument that writes or records
-itis	swelling of
-logy	science of
-philia	tending toward
-port	to carry
-stasis	stopping, slowing

1. hemophilia
2. cardiology
3. leukocyte
4. bronchitis
5. erythrocyte
6. hemostasis
7. cardiograph
8. transport

READING NUTRITION PANELS

Many packaged foods have a nutrition panel on their label or box. The nutrition panels on the next page show how much of each nutrient is in a certain amount of food. Nutrients are materials that are needed for good health.

Use the nutrition panels to answer these questions.

1. What does *U.S. RDA* mean?
2. How much magnesium does each cereal provide?
3. What is the amount of carbohydrates in 1 oz of each cereal?
4. How much fat is in ½ cup of whole milk?
5. Which cereal provides more vitamin C? How much more?
6. Both cereals provide less than 2 percent of which nutrient?
7. How much vitamin A is provided by one serving of each cereal with whole milk? How much vitamin A is still needed to have 100 percent of the U.S. RDA?
8. For cereal *A*, which nutrients are supplied by the cereal alone?

CEREAL A

NUTRITION INFORMATION PER SERVING
SERVING SIZE: 1 OZ. (28.4 g)

	CEREAL A	
	1 OZ. (28.4 g)	WITH ½ CUP WHOLE MILK
CALORIES	110	190
PROTEIN	2 g	6 g
CARBOHYDRATE	25 g	30 g
FAT	0 g	5 g
SODIUM	75 mg (265 mg per 100 g)	135 mg (90 mg per 100 g)

PERCENTAGE OF U.S. RECOMMENDED DAILY ALLOWANCES (U.S. RDA)

	CEREAL A	
	1 OZ. (28.4 g)	WITH ½ CUP WHOLE MILK
PROTEIN	2	10
VITAMIN A	25	30
VITAMIN C	25	25
THIAMIN	25	30
RIBOFLAVIN	25	35
NIACIN	25	25
CALCIUM	*	15
IRON	10	10
VITAMIN D	10	25
VITAMIN B_6	25	25
FOLIC ACID	25	25
PHOSPHOROUS	4	15
MAGNESIUM	4	8
ZINC	2	6
COPPER	2	2

*CONTAINS LESS THAN 2 PERCENT OF THE U.S. RDA OF THIS NUTRIENT.

CARBOHYDRATE INFORMATION

	CEREAL A	
	1 OZ. (28.4 g)	WITH ½ CUP WHOLE MILK
STARCH AND RELATED CARBO-HYDRATES	10 g	10 g
SUCROSE AND OTHER SUGARS	15 g	20 g
TOTAL CARBOHY-DRATES	25 g	30 g

CEREAL B

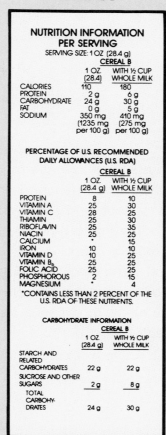

NUTRITION INFORMATION PER SERVING
SERVING SIZE: 1 OZ. (28.4 g)

	CEREAL B	
	1 OZ. (28.4)	WITH ½ CUP WHOLE MILK
CALORIES	110	180
PROTEIN	2 g	6 g
CARBOHYDRATE	24 g	30 g
FAT	0 g	5 g
SODIUM	350 mg (1235 mg per 100 g)	410 mg (275 mg per 100 g)

PERCENTAGE OF U.S. RECOMMENDED DAILY ALLOWANCES (U.S. RDA)

	CEREAL B	
	1 OZ. (28.4 g)	WITH ½ CUP WHOLE MILK
PROTEIN	8	10
VITAMIN A	25	30
VITAMIN C	28	25
THIAMIN	25	30
RIBOFLAVIN	25	35
NIACIN	25	25
CALCIUM	*	15
IRON	10	10
VITAMIN D	10	25
VITAMIN B_6	25	25
FOLIC ACID	25	25
PHOSPHOROUS	2	15
MAGNESIUM	*	4

*CONTAINS LESS THAN 2 PERCENT OF THE U.S. RDA OF THESE NUTRIENTS.

CARBOHYDRATE INFORMATION

	CEREAL B	
	1 OZ. (28.4 g)	WITH ½ CUP WHOLE MILK
STARCH AND RELATED CARBOHYDRATES	22 g	22 g
SUCROSE AND OTHER SUGARS	2 g	8 g
TOTAL CARBOHY-DRATES	24 g	30 g

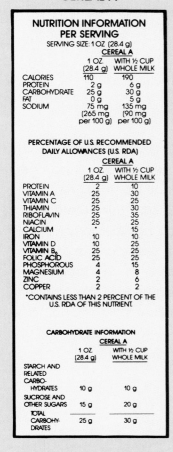

USING NUTRITION PANELS

Look at and compare the nutrition panels on two similar foods. For example, you could compare a packaged white bread with packaged whole-wheat bread. Or you could compare grape juice with grape drink. Answer these questions about the foods you compare.

1. Which of the foods contains more nutrients?

2. Of the nutrients that are the same for both foods, which food supplies more of the U.S. RDA of each nutrient?

3. Compare the price of food per ounce, fluid ounce, or gram. Does one food cost more than the other? If so, which food costs more? In your opinion, which food is the better buy? Explain your answer.

Units of Measurement

Two systems of measurement are used in the United States, the metric system and the English system. Feet, yards, pounds, ounces, and quarts are English units. Meters, kilometers, kilograms, grams, and liters are metric units. Only metric measurements are used in science. The following tables list some metric and English units. The tables show what each unit is approximately equal to in the other system. The metric mass/English weight relationships hold true for objects on the earth.

MEASUREMENT	METRIC UNITS (symbol)	EQUAL TO IN ENGLISH UNITS (symbol)
Length	1 millimeter (mm)	0.04 inch (in.)
	1 centimeter (cm)	0.4 inch (in.)
	1 meter (m)	39.4 inches (in.) or
		1.1 yards (yd)
	1 kilometer (km)	0.6 mile (mi)
Mass (weight)	1 gram (g)	0.035 ounce (oz)
	1 kilogram (kg)	2.2 pounds (lb)
Volume	1 liter (L)	1.06 quarts (qt)

MEASUREMENT	ENGLISH UNITS (symbol)	EQUAL TO IN METRIC UNITS (symbol)
Length	1 inch (in.)	2.5 centimeters (cm) or
		25 millimeters (mm)
	1 foot (ft)	30.5 centimeters (cm)
	1 yard (yd)	0.91 meter (m)
	1 mile (mi)	1.6 kilometers (km)
Weight (mass)	1 ounce (oz)	28.4 grams (g)
	1 pound (lb)	0.45 kilogram (kg)
Volume	1 quart (qt)	0.95 liter (L)

Lesson Questions

To the student

Reading your book will help you learn more about the world around you. Your book will provide answers to many questions you may have about living things, the earth, space, matter, and energy.

On the following pages you will find questions from each lesson in your book. These questions will help test your understanding of the terms and ideas you read about.

There are two kinds of questions. You can answer the first kind by using the information you read in each lesson. Careful reading will help answer these questions.

The second type of question is called "Thinking like a Scientist." These questions are more challenging. The answer may not be found just by reading the lesson. You may have to think harder.

1 *Activities of Green Plants*

LIVING THINGS ARE ALIKE
(pp. 4–5)

1. Name three things that plants and animals need to stay alive.
2. Name the five life processes.

Thinking like a Scientist
Life processes are activities that keep living things alive. Why is reproducing a life process?

TRANSPORTING MATERIALS
(pp. 6–11)

1. What three things do green plants need to make food?
2. Describe the role of root hairs.

Thinking like a Scientist
Gardeners sometimes dig around the base of a plant to loosen the soil. How does this benefit the plant?

FOOD MAKING IN A LEAF
(pp. 12–15)

1. Define the term *photosynthesis*.
2. Identify the three parts shown in the drawing. Describe the role of each part in photosynthesis.

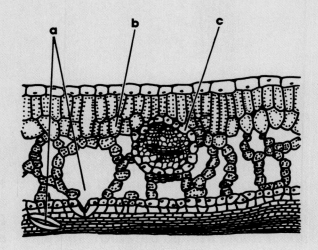

Thinking like a Scientist
Scientists do experiments to test their ideas. Suppose a scientist believed that the leaves of plants were the most important structure for absorbing water. How might the scientist test this idea?

USING THE ENERGY IN FOOD
(pp. 16–17)

1. Define the term *respiration*.
2. Look at the chart on page 17. Compare photosynthesis and respiration in terms of where the processes take place and what happens to sugar and carbon dioxide.

Thinking like a Scientist

Certain plants can be grown in rich, moist soil in sealed glass containers called terrariums. Plants grown in this way do not need to be watered. How can the plants carry on photosynthesis and respiration in the closed containers?

PRODUCING NEW PLANTS
(pp. 18–23)

1. Define the term *reproduction.*
2. Identify the four parts shown in this drawing. In what part do pollen grains form? Which parts contain the female reproductive cells?

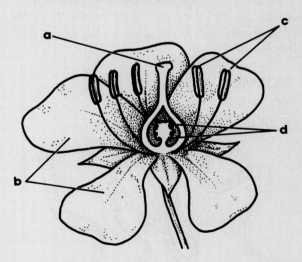

3. Identify the parts shown in this drawing. Explain what happens after germination.

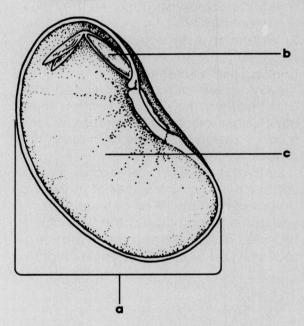

Thinking like a Scientist

Many people are allergic to pollen dust. They might sneeze, have itchy noses, or have trouble breathing. How does pollen get into these people's lungs? During which seasons are the people more likely to be bothered by the allergy? During which seasons are they less likely to be bothered by it?

2 Animals Without a Backbone

CLASSIFYING LIVING THINGS
(pp. 28–29)

1. What do scientists do when they classify animals?
2. What is an invertebrate?

Thinking like a Scientist

Animals are grouped as vertebrates and invertebrates. Scientists often draw conclusions about large groups of animals by observing a few animals in the groups.

Look at pictures of vertebrates and invertebrates. Compare sizes of these two groups of animals. What conclusions can you make by comparing the sizes of vertebrates and invertebrates? What reasons can you give for your observations?

SPONGES
(pp. 30–31)

1. Where do sponges live?
2. For many years, scientists mistakenly believed that sponges were plants. Why, do you think, did this happen?

Thinking like a Scientist

How do you suppose sponges attach themselves to rocks on the ocean bottom?

ANIMALS WITH STINGING CELLS
(pp. 32–33)

1. Identify the opening, hollow sac, and tentacle on this hydra.

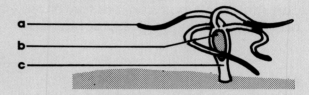

2. How do stinging cells help a hydra capture food?

Thinking like a Scientist

When jellyfish die and wash up onto the shore, they disappear much faster than do fish that die and wash up onto the shore. Why, do you think, does this happen?

WORMS
(pp. 34–38)

1. Identify the animals shown here.

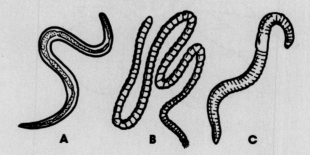

2. How is a parasite related to a host?

Thinking like a Scientist

A storybook for little children contained the following paragraph.

Little Wendell Worm was crawling happily through the desert searching for a new place to make a nest in the sand. He had been moving along at a fast pace when suddenly he looked up and spotted a fat robin. "Oh no!" squeaked Wendell. "I'm in trouble now!" And he dashed over to the nearest bush and hid under a large green leaf.

What is scientifically wrong in this paragraph?

ANIMALS WITH SPINY SKIN
(pp. 39–40)

1. Define the term *enchinoderm.*
2. What are two uses of the tube feet on a starfish?

Thinking like a Scientist

A starfish has light-sensitive spots at the tips of its arms. Why wouldn't it be better for the starfish to have the spots in the center of its body? What disadvantages can you think of for having spots at the tips of the arms?

ANIMALS WITH A SOFT BODY
(pp. 41–44)

1. Define the term *mollusk.*

2. Name three two-shelled mollusks.
3. How do snails and slugs move?

Thinking like a Scientist

If animals were classified simply on appearance, the jellyfish, octopus, and squid might all be grouped together. Why aren't these animals in the same group?

ANIMALS WITH JOINTED LEGS
(pp. 45–53)

1. Define the term *arthropod.*
2. What is an exoskeleton?
3. Identify the three main parts of this insect's body.

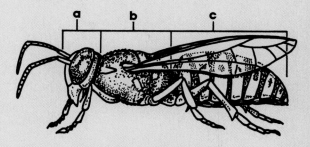

4. Explain what an insect's antennae do.

Thinking like a Scientist

Most types of invertebrates live in water. Most arthropods do not. What parts of their bodies enable arthropods to live on land?

3 Animals With a Backbone

FISH
(pp. 58–60)

1. Define the term *cold-blooded*.
2. Explain how a fish breathes.
3. Identify the parts of this fish.

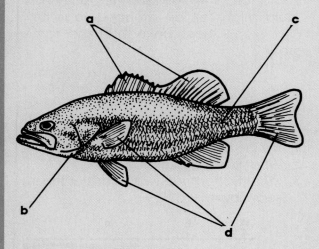

Thinking like a Scientist
Do you think it is possible to catch fish through a hole in a frozen lake? Explain your answer in scientific terms.

AMPHIBIANS
(pp. 61–62)

1. Name three common amphibians.
2. What changes occur in a tadpole as it gets older?

Thinking like a Scientist
Scientists can draw conclusions about what an animal eats by looking at where it lives and what it looks like. What conclusions can you make about what a tadpole eats and what a frog eats?

REPTILES
(pp. 63–66)

1. What are the characteristics of a reptile?
2. Name four groups of reptiles.
3. How is it possible for a snake to eat an animal larger than its mouth?

Thinking like a Scientist
An animal called the horned toad is often mistaken for an amphibian. But the horned toad is a reptile. What things might you observe about the horned toad that would tell you it is a reptile?

BIRDS
(pp. 67–71)

1. Define the term *warm-blooded*.
2. Why are a bird's bones and the central shafts of its feathers hollow?
3. Why must some birds spend most of their time hunting for food?

Thinking like a Scientist

You can tell something about how a bird flies by looking at its wings and the size and shape of its body. Think about a sparrow, a chicken, a hawk, a duck, an ostrich, a hummingbird, and a goose. Which of those birds can soar for long periods of time? How do the wings of these birds compare to their body size? Which of the birds can travel long distances? How do the wings of these birds compare to their body size? Which birds do not fly very well? How do the wings of these birds compare to their body size?

MAMMALS
(pp. 72–75)

1. In what two ways are mammals different from other vertebrates?
2. Use the following chart to compare the length of time needed by a hamster and a dog to develop.

MAMMAL	LENGTH OF TIME TO DEVELOP (days)
Dog	63
Whale	450
Hamster	16
Giraffe	442

3. What is the relationship between the mass of a mammal and the time needed for its young to develop?
4. What is the function of a pouch in a kangaroo and an opossum?

Thinking like a Scientist

Most land-dwelling mammals have tails. Name a mammal that uses its tail in each of the following ways: as a warning device, to grasp tree limbs, for balance, for protection from insects, for keeping warm.

4 Living Communities

THE LIVING AND NONLIVING WORLD
(pp. 82–83)

1. Name at least three living things and three nonliving things in your school environment.
2. What is ecology?
3. Explain how fish and plants in a fish tank affect each other.
4. Define the term *ecosystem*.

Thinking like a Scientist
Many scientists must become experts in more than one area of science. Why would an ecologist become an expert in chemistry?

2. Define the term *niche*.

Thinking like a Scientist
What problems would plants and animals living in a cave ecosystem have? What features might these living things have that would help them overcome the problems?

LIVING THINGS IN ECOSYSTEMS
(pp. 84–90)

1. Identify six populations in this desert community. Tell the habitats of at least three of the living things shown.

CHANGES IN POPULATIONS
(pp. 91–94)

1. When ecologists study a community, what are three things they try to learn?
2. Name three things that may affect the death rate of a population.
3. Explain the relationship between a predator and its prey.

Thinking like a Scientist

Most states have hunting laws that limit which animals can be hunted as well as when and where they can be hunted. Why do most hunters support this practice?

CHANGES IN COMMUNITIES
(pp. 95–100)

1. Define the term *succession*. Name the first and last stages of succession.

2. Write the letters of the drawings to show succession in a pond community from first stage to last. Then briefly describe each stage shown.

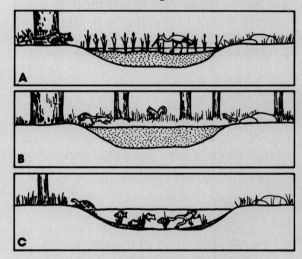

Thinking like a Scientist

In some places in the world there are islands that are battered by hurricanes every two or three years. What would succession be like on such an island?

5 *Building Blocks of Matter*

STUDYING MATTER
(pp. 112–115)

1. Define the term *matter.*
2. Choose five objects. List them in order from the object with the least mass to the object with the greatest mass.
3. What is meant by *indirect evidence*?

Thinking like a Scientist

Long ago, scientists used indirect evidence to conclude that the earth is round. Today, we have direct evidence of this. What is this direct evidence?

THE ATOM
(pp. 116–117)

1. Identify the parts of this atom.

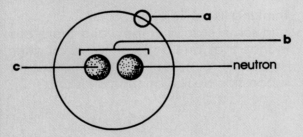

2. Is an entire atom a tightly packed group of particles? Explain your answer.
3. Why do scientists create models?

Thinking like a Scientist

In what ways is a model of an atom like a model of the solar system? How are they different?

ELEMENTS
(pp. 118–121)

1. Define the term *element.*
2. Explain one way elements are different from one another.
3. What are the symbols for calcium, cobalt, sulfur, carbon, iron, and sodium?
4. Why do scientists use symbols for writing names of elements?

Thinking like a Scientist

Scientists throughout the world use the same names and symbols for the elements. Why is this important?

MOLECULES AND COMPOUNDS
(pp. 122–129)

1. Define the term *compound*.
2. Two atoms of oxygen can combine to form a molecule of oxygen. But a molecule of oxygen is not a compound. Why?
3. Identify the parts of this water molecule.

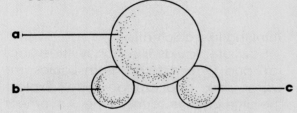

4. What is the formula for the molecule shown here? Explain what the letters and numbers in the formula stand for.

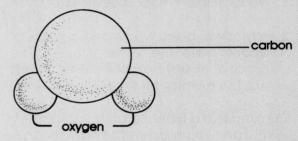

Thinking like a Scientist

Soda water is made by adding carbon dioxide to water. Is soda water a compound? Explain your answer.

6 Physical Changes in Matter

PHYSICAL PROPERTIES
(pp. 134–135)

1. Name five physical properties of matter.
2. A block of balsa wood and a block of ebony have the same volume. The block of ebony has more mass. Which has the greater density? Why?

Thinking like a Scientist
   Why do helium balloons float?

PHYSICAL CHANGES
(pp. 136–141)

1. Why is getting a haircut an example of a physical change?
2. These drawings show particles of water in three states. Identify each state of matter. Tell what water in each state is called.

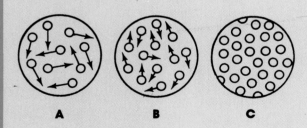

3. What must be done to change a solid to a liquid or a liquid to a gas?
4. Define the term *melting*.
5. At what temperature does water change from a liquid to a solid? At what temperature does it change from a liquid to a gas?
6. How is the melting point of a substance different from its freezing point?

Thinking like a Scientist
   How are liquids like honey, tree sap, tar, and glue different from liquids like water, milk, and orange juice? Explain the difference in terms of the movement of particles.

MIXTURES
(pp. 142–144)

1. Define the term *mixture*.
2. How is a mixture different from a compound?

Thinking like a Scientist
   Air contains the gases oxygen, nitrogen, argon, and carbon dioxide. Scientists describe air as being a mixture. What does this tell you about the gases in air?

TWO KINDS OF MIXTURES
(pp. 145–148)

1. What is a solution?
2. Name the two parts of a solution. Explain what each part is.
3. What is a suspension?

Thinking like a Scientist
Two boys decide to paint their bicycles. They have four unmarked cans of paint. Two of the cans have water as a basic ingredient. The other two cans have oil. The boys mix two cans. How will they know if they have mixed a can of paint containing water with a can containing oil?

ANOTHER KIND OF CHANGE
(pp. 149–150)

1. How is a chemical change different from a physical change?

2. Write whether each drawing shows a physical change or a chemical change.

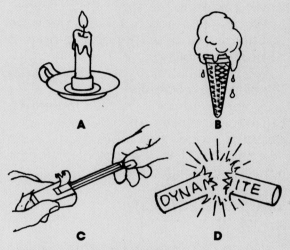

Thinking like a Scientist
What physical changes and chemical changes take place to make a bowl of hot buttered popcorn?

7 Understanding Electricity

ELECTRICITY
(pp. 156–158)

1. Is electricity matter or energy? How do you know?
2. If an atom has 6 protons, what else will it need to have a neutral charge? What will it need to have a negative charge? What will it need to have a positive charge?

Thinking like a Scientist

Benjamin Franklin observed the effects of static electricity on objects. He proposed a theory that there must be an ''electric fluid'' in the objects. Was he right? Explain your answer.

KINDS OF ELECTRICITY
(pp. 159–162)

1. Name two kinds of electricity. Explain how they differ.
2. Name three metals through which current moves easily.

Thinking like a Scientist

Suppose you attend a magic show. The magician takes a page of newspaper and waves a wand over it. Then he walks over to a clean blank wall, places the paper on the wall, and rubs the paper with a wool cloth. Presto! The paper stays on the wall! Explain this so-called magic act in scientific terms.

ELECTRIC CIRCUITS
(pp. 163–166)

1. Define the term *circuit.*
2. What is a closed circuit?
3. Identify the two types of circuits shown here.

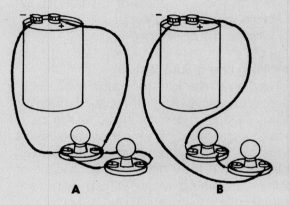

A   **B**

Thinking like a Scientist

What type of circuit does this flashlight have? How does the flashlight work?

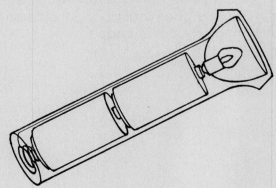

PRODUCING ELECTRICITY
(pp. 167–170)

1. What did Michael Faraday discover about electricity?
2. Define the term *generator*.
3. What does an electric cell do?

Thinking like a Scientist
Many electric companies are working hard to produce solar-powered generators. How do you think a solar-powered generator might work?

USING ELECTRICITY
(pp. 171–172)

1. What does an electric motor do?
2. Name three appliances that contain motors.

Thinking like a Scientist
Many people are trying to produce an electric car that will run as well as a gasoline-powered car. What problems do you think an electric car would have? What advantages would it have?

MEASURING ELECTRICITY
(pp. 173–174)

1. What units are small amounts of electric power measured in?
2. What shows how much electricity has been used in your home?

Thinking like a Scientist
Suppose your electric company charges 10 cents for every kilowatt-hour of electricity. How much would you owe if you used a 200-watt motor for 10 hours?

USING ELECTRICITY SAFELY
(pp. 175–176)

1. What do fuses and circuit breakers do?
2. Which of these pictures shows a possible danger? Explain your answers.

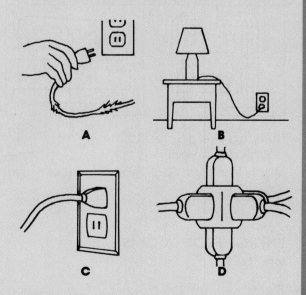

Thinking like a Scientist
Why are houses safe places to be during a lightning storm?

8 Sources of Energy

ENERGY FROM FOSSIL FUELS
(pp. 182–185)

1. Define the term *fossil fuel*.
2. Name three fossil fuels.
3. Write the numbers of the drawings in the correct order to show how a fossil fuel is used to produce electricity.

Thinking like a Scientist
Why did Americans 200 years ago use much less fossil fuel than Americans use today?

ENERGY FROM ATOMS
(pp. 186–189)

1. What is nuclear energy?
2. Explain the difference between fission and fusion.

3. What is radiation?
4. Describe one advantage and one disadvantage in the use of nuclear energy.

Thinking like a Scientist
Energy from nuclear fusion can come from combining the nuclei of two hydrogen atoms. What common substance on earth contains hydrogen atoms? Why would fusion be a good alternative to fossil fuels?

ENERGY FROM THE SUN
(pp. 190–194)

1. Explain the greenhouse effect.
2. How is a solar collector different from a solar cell?

Thinking like a Scientist
What advantages are there to having solar collectors on orbiting satellites?

ENERGY FROM WATER
(pp. 195–196)

1. In what two ways can energy be produced from water?
2. Describe a disadvantage of both ways.

Thinking like a Scientist

Scientists are often hired by private companies to make recommendations on important decisions. Suppose you were hired to help recommend a location for a hydroelectric power plant. What information about a location would you want to know before you could recommend it?

ENERGY FROM HEAT IN THE EARTH
(pp. 197–198)

1. What is geothermal energy?
2. Use the terms *well, steam, magma, generator, natural crack,* and *turbine* to identify the parts of this drawing.

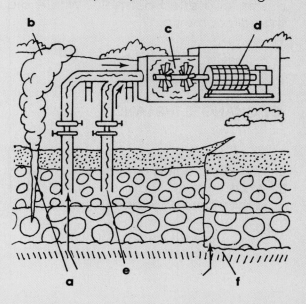

Thinking like a Scientist

Geothermal energy plants are almost always found near active volcanoes, where the heat is close to the surface. What else must be present in these areas to produce geothermal energy?

ENERGY FROM THE WIND
(pp. 199–200)

1. How can wind energy produce electricity?
2. Why is wind energy not a major energy source?

Thinking like a Scientist

People found wind energy to be very useful for more than 1000 years. Why isn't this form of energy used more often today?

ENERGY FROM LIVING THINGS
(pp. 201–203)

1. What is bioconversion?
2. How can bacteria be used to make energy?

Thinking like a Scientist

Scientists warn that fossil fuels will be used up in the near future. Why, then, don't we return biomass into the ground so that it can change into coal, oil, or gas?

9 Changes in the Earth

WEATHERING CHANGES THE LAND
(pp. 214–217)

1. What is meant by *weathering*?
2. Define the term *physical weathering*.
3. How do plants cause physical weathering?

Thinking like a Scientist
Why must engineers who design bridges be experts in frost action?

ANOTHER KIND OF WEATHERING
(pp. 218–219)

1. What is chemical weathering?
2. Why is chemical weathering common in places where there are large amounts of limestone and water?
3. How do mosses and lichens cause chemical weathering?

Thinking like a Scientist
Which do you think would be damaged by chemical weathering faster—statues in Washington, D.C., or statues in Egypt? Explain your answer.

WATER CHANGES THE LAND
(pp. 220–225)

1. How do moving water, moving ice, and moving air cause erosion?
2. How does runoff cause problems for farmers?
3. What are sediments?

Thinking like a Scientist
In 1884 gold was discovered in a stream at Sutter's Mill in California. Within a year 80,000 people rushed to California to look for gold. Many of these people simply dipped a pan into a stream and sifted out gold. Where did this gold come from?

ICE CHANGES THE LAND
(pp. 227–230)

1. What are glaciers?
2. How did glaciers form lakes?
3. What would happen if glaciers spread across the earth again?

Thinking like a Scientist

Describe two ways in which glaciers might have helped make farming in New England difficult.

WIND CHANGES THE LAND
(pp. 231–233)

1. How does wind cause physical weathering?
2. How does wind cause sand dunes?
3. How can wind erosion damage farm-land?
4. Identify this method of preventing erosion. Explain why it is helpful.

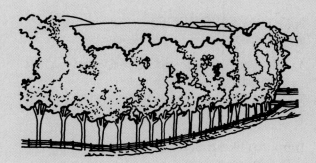

Thinking like a Scientist

Suppose a space probe sent back pictures of a cold, lifeless planet without an atmosphere. What would you look for in the pictures to tell whether the planet once had an atmosphere?

10   Cleaning Up the Earth

NATURAL RESOURCES
(pp. 238–239)

1. Why are trees, air, land, and water called natural resources?
2. Name three renewable resources.
3. Define the term *pollution.*

Thinking like a Scientist

Sometimes natural resources are destroyed by careless human beings. Forest fires are often caused by carelessness. How can forest fires be prevented?

AIR POLLUTION
(pp. 240–244)

1. Name two waste products given off by burning fuels.
2. Explain how acid rain is formed.
3. How does smog develop?
4. This graph shows the parts of the air. Oxygen makes up 21% of the air, nitrogen makes up 78%, argon makes up 0.94%, carbon dioxide makes up 0.03%, and other gases make up the rest. Identify the gases that make up air in the graph.

THE PARTS OF AIR

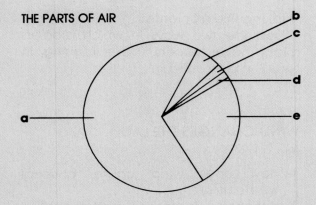

Thinking like a Scientist

What parts of North America are most likely to be affected by acid rain? Explain your answer.

WATER POLLUTION
(pp. 245–252)

1. Define the term *sewage.*
2. What does a sewage-treatment plant do?
3. What chemical is used to kill harmful living things in water?
4. How does the use of chemical sprays or fertilizers by farmers cause water pollution?

5. How does the growth of algae in lakes affect fish and other animals in the lakes?
6. What is thermal pollution?
7. Why are oil spills harmful to the environment?

Thinking like a Scientist

Scientists are constantly searching for new and better ways to clean up oil spills. One scientist has developed a strain of superbacteria that eat oil. It has been shown that these bacteria can eat an entire 40-liter oil spill in 6 hours. What advantages does this method have? What problems could come from using these bacteria?

LAND POLLUTION
(pp. 253–255)

1. What are toxic wastes?
2. What are biodegradable materials? Give three examples.
3. What are nonbiodegradable materials?
4. Why are nonbiodegradable materials more harmful to the environment than biodegradable materials?

Thinking like a Scientist

On an average day in Yellowstone National Park, campers produce about 24,500 kg of trash. What kinds of trash do you think cause the greatest disposal problems? Explain your answer.

11 Changes in the Weather

HOW WEATHER BEGINS
(pp. 260–264)

1. What kind of energy causes weather?
2. What happens to the sun's energy as it enters the atmosphere?
3. Name three reasons why the earth's surface is heated unevenly.

Thinking like a Scientist

What causes sunburn? Why do snow skiers often get sunburn on their faces?

AIR PRESSURE AND WINDS
(pp. 265–268)

1. What causes air pressure?
2. How does the amount of water vapor in the air affect air pressure?
3. What causes wind?
4. What is a sea breeze?
5. What is a land breeze?
6. Describe how warm air and cold air move in each picture.

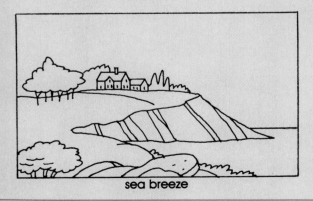
sea breeze

land breeze

Thinking like a Scientist

Is it possible to have a sea breeze and a land breeze at a lake? Explain your answer.

AIR MASSES AND WEATHER
(pp. 269–270)

1. What is an air mass?
2. Name four kinds of air masses and tell where they form.
3. Describe six major areas where air masses that affect North America form. Describe three of the air masses.

Thinking like a Scientist

Plains states such as Kansas and Arkansas have suffered from droughts that have turned huge areas into swirling dust bowls. Why are the plains states more likely to have droughts than states such as Oregon and Washington?

WHEN AIR MASSES MEET

(pp. 271–275)

1. What is a front? What happens at a front?
2. Identify the kind of front shown in each drawing. Describe the kind of weather that may occur with each front.

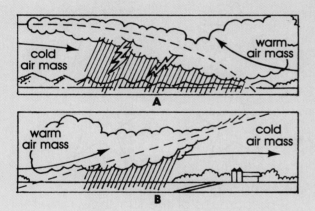

Thinking like a Scientist

Why can cold fronts cause special problems for people who are fishing from small boats?

CLOUDS

(pp. 276–278)

1. What affects the type of clouds that form?
2. Name and describe three main types of clouds.

Thinking like a Scientist

Airport traffic controllers inform pilots about the "cloud ceiling" before take-offs and landings. What do you think a cloud ceiling is? What do you think a ceilometer measures?

12   *Beyond the Solar System*

DISTANCES IN SPACE
(pp. 284–288)

1. Define the term *universe*.
2. Why is the distance that light travels in a year used to measure distances in space?

Use this table to answer questions 3–5.

BODY IN SPACE	APPROPRIATE DISTANCE FROM THE EARTH (km)	TIME TO REACH THE BODIES (at 40,000 km/h)
Sun	150,000,000	156 days
Moon	400,000	10 hours
Pluto	5,800,000,000	6,187 days
Proxima Centauri	41,000,000,000,000,000	42,700,000 days

3. Which of the bodies listed in the table is closest to the earth?
4. Which of the bodies could you reach in your lifetime, traveling at a speed of 40,000 km/h?
5. How long would it take to reach the only planet listed in the table?

Thinking like a Scientist
Several space probes have been launched containing information about Earth. It is hoped that the information will tell whoever finds the probes about our planet. What three pieces of information about Earth do you think should be included on a space probe traveling beyond our solar system?

CHARACTERISTICS OF STARS
(pp. 289–291)

1. Describe three things on which the magnitude of a star depends.
2. The four stars below are of different colors. Rank them in order from the coolest (1) to the hottest (4).

white

yellow

red

blue

Thinking like a Scientist
Photographs of the sun show that it is brighter at the center than at the edges. What conclusion can you draw from this information?

THE LIFE OF A STAR
(pp. 292–295)

1. What is a star made up of before it is "born"? What is it called?
2. Define the term *nova*.
3. What is a neutron star?

4. What is a black hole?
5. Make a chart like the one below. Complete the chart.

STAGE	COLOR	SIZE	TEMPERATURE
Young star			
Middle age			
Old age			
White dwarf			
Black dwarf			

Thinking like a Scientist

What do you suppose it would be like to enter a black hole?

FAMILIES OF STARS
(pp. 296–300)

1. Define the term *galaxy*.
2. Identify the types of galaxies shown here.

A

B

Thinking like a Scientist

Why is it more difficult to observe the Milky Way in cities today than it was during colonial times?

STAR PATTERNS
(pp. 301–302)

1. Define the term *constellation*.
2. How did constellations get their names?

Thinking like a Scientist

The North Star is a very special star to people north of the equator. It is the only star in the sky that does not appear to move. Why is this information useful? Is this information useful to people south of the equator? Explain your answer.

13 Support and Movement of the Body

YOUR BODY'S FRAMEWORK
(pp. 314–318)

1. What two important jobs does the skeletal system do?
2. What is the skull?
3. Explain what cartilage is. Why is cartilage in the backbone important?

Thinking like a Scientist

Did you know that you are slightly taller in the morning than you are at night? Why is this so? (*HINT:* Think about the cartilage found between the vertebrae in your backbone.)

WHERE BONES MEET
(pp. 319–320)

1. Define the term *joint.*
2. Copy and complete this chart.

JOINT	DESCRIPTION OF BONE MOVEMENT	EXAMPLE
Ball-and-socket		
		Knee
Pivot		
	Cannot move	

Thinking like a Scientist

Is there any advantage in having hinge joints at knees and elbows? What would the movement of legs and arms be like if ball-and-socket joints were at knees and elbows?

MUSCLES MOVE BONES
(pp. 321–324)

1. What attaches muscles to bones?
2. Explain how a pair of muscles moves bones.

Thinking like a Scientist

Put your right elbow on your desk. Use your right hand to lift a book off the desk. Your arm is working like a simple machine. Which simple machine is it working like? Explain your answer.

TWO GROUPS OF MUSCLES
(pp. 325–326)

1. What are the two groups of muscles?
2. Give an example of an activity controlled by voluntary muscles.
3. Give an example of an activity controlled by involuntary muscles.
4. What are the three kinds of muscles?

Thinking like a Scientist

When you are cold your muscles contract and you shiver. Your teeth may even chatter. What do you think the purpose of these movements is? Are they voluntary or involuntary movements?

BONE AND MUSCLE INJURIES
(pp. 327–328)

1. Define the term *fracture*.
2. How is a simple fracture different from a compound fracture?
3. What is a sprain? What causes a sprain?
4. What is a muscle strain?
5. What is a cramp?
6. Describe the proper way to lift a heavy object.

Thinking like a Scientist

A broken bone in a child heals faster than a broken bone in an adult. Why, do you think, does this happen?

CARE OF BONES AND MUSCLES
(pp. 329–331)

1. What three things are needed to keep your bones and muscles healthy?
2. Copy this chart on another sheet of paper. Under each food group write what the food does for the bones and muscles. Give one example of a food in each food group.

DAIRY	MEAT	FRUIT AND VEGETABLE	BREAD AND CEREAL

Thinking like a Scientist

What would happen to astronauts on long space missions if they did not exercise? Design a piece of exercise equipment that could be used by astronauts in the weightless environment of space.

14 Transport Systems of the Body

THE CIRCULATORY SYSTEM
(pp. 336–338)

1. What three things does the circulatory system do for the body?
2. What is plasma?

Thinking like a Scientist
When a doctor orders a blood test on a patient, one thing that might be done is a white blood cell count. What might be indicated if the doctor finds a high number of white blood cells?

CIRCULATION OF BLOOD
(pp. 339–341)

1. What is the heart?
2. Identify the chambers of the heart in this drawing.

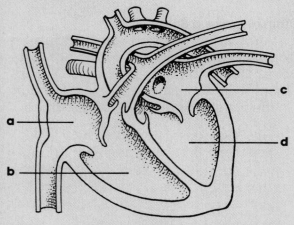

3. Name three kinds of blood vessels.

Thinking like a Scientist
Oxygen-rich blood is red in color. Oxygen-poor blood appears slightly bluish. Suppose you saw a person begin to turn a bluish color around the lips. What would this indicate?

DISEASES AND CARE OF THE CIRCULATORY SYSTEM
(pp. 342–345)

1. What is the best way to stop bleeding?
2. How does a heart attack occur?

Thinking like a Scientist
In China and other countries people mostly eat fish, rice, and vegetables. Fewer people living in these countries have clogged arteries than do people living in America. How can you explain this?

THE RESPIRATORY SYSTEM
(pp. 346–350).

1. Describe the path air follows from outside the body to the cells inside the body.
2. What is the diaphragm? What does it do?

Thinking like a Scientist

Why do you breathe more rapidly when you are exercising than when you are sleeping?

DISEASES AND CARE OF THE RESPIRATORY SYSTEM
(pp. 351–352)

1. How are colds spread?
2. What is bronchitis?

Thinking like a Scientist

Why do people who smoke often have a more difficult time breathing when they exercise than do people who do not smoke?

THE EXCRETORY SYSTEM
(pp. 353–355)

1. What is the main organ of the excretory system? What does this organ do?
2. What is urine?

3. Identify the parts of the skin in this drawing.

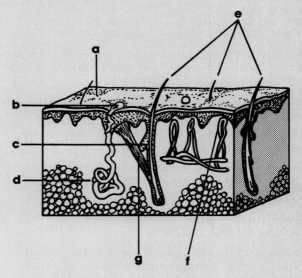

Thinking like a Scientist

In an adult, the kidneys filter about 180 L of blood each day. But there are only about 6 L of blood in an adult's body. Where do the other 172 L come from?

GLOSSARY

Key to Pronunciation

a	apple, bat	i	if, pig	sh	she, wish	ə	stands for:
ā	ate, page	ī	idea, fine	th	think, moth		a in asleep
ã	air, care	ng	ring, sink	ᴛʜ	the, bathe		e in garden
ä	father, star	o	ox, top	u	uncle, sun		i in pencil
ch	chest, such	ō	owe, no	ů	pull, foot		o in button
e	egg, bed	ô	orbit, saw	ü	glue, boot		u in circus
ē	even, me	oi	oil, joy	zh	usual, vision		
ėr	earn, bird	ou	out, mouse				

This Key to Pronunciation is adapted from *Scott, Foresman Intermediate Dictionary,* by E. L. Thorndike and Clarence L. Barnhart. Copyright © 1983 by Scott, Foresman and Company. Reprinted by permission.

abdomen (ab′də mən) The rear part of an insect's body. *p. 48*

acid rain Weak acids that fall as rain or snow. Acid rain can kill living things and damage structures. *p. 241*

agents of erosion Moving water, moving ice, and wind. *p. 220*

air mass A large body of air that has about the same temperature and moisture throughout. *p. 269*

amphibian (am fib′ē ən) A cold-blooded vertebrate that lives part of its life in water and part on land. *p. 61*

antennae (an ten′ē) The two feelers on the head of an insect. *p. 49*

artery (är′tər ē) A thick-walled blood vessel that carries blood away from the heart. *p. 339*

arthropod (är′thrə pod) An invertebrate that has a segmented body, jointed legs, and a hard outer covering. *p. 45*

astronomer (ə stron′ə mər) A scientist who studies the universe. *p. 286*

astronomy (ə stron′ə mē) The science that includes the study of stars, planets, moons, and other objects in space. *p. 286*

atom (at′əm) The basic unit of all matter; the smallest particle of an element. *p. 116*

atrium (ā′trē əm) The upper chamber of the heart. *p. 339*

ball-and-socket joint The kind of joint that allows the most movement of bones. *p. 319*

bioconversion (bī ō kən vėr′zhən) The process of changing biomass into usable energy. *p. 201*

biodegradable (bī ō di grā′də bəl) **material** Material that decays, or is broken down by living things. *p. 254*

biomass (bī′ō mas) Plant and animal matter. *p. 201*

bird A warm-blooded vertebrate that has feathers and wings. *p. 67*

black dwarf The last stage in the life cycle of a star; a star with no heat or light. *p. 294*

black hole A region in space that was once occupied by a star. *p. 295*

boiling point The temperature at which a liquid changes to a gas. *p. 140*

bone marrow   A soft material inside the long bones of the arms and legs. Old blood cells are repaired and new blood cells are made in the bone marrow. *p. 317*

bristles (bris′əlz)   The stiff, strong hairs on an earthworm that are used for moving and clinging. *p. 37*

bronchial (brong′kē əl) **tubes**   The two tubes into which the trachea branches. *p. 347*

bronchitis (brong kī′tis)   A respiratory disease in which the bronchial tubes become red and swollen. *p. 352*

canyon   A deep valley with steep sides. *p. 222*

capillary (kap′ə ler ē)   A tiny blood vessel that connects an artery and a vein. *p. 339*

cartilage (kär′tə lij)   A soft, bonelike material that bends; it makes up the skeleton of some fish, such as sharks. *p. 58*   In people, a soft, bonelike material in the tip of the nose, the ears, and between the small bones that make up the backbone. *p. 318*

cell   The basic unit of all living things. *p. 4*

chemical change   A change in matter in which one or more different kinds of matter form. *p. 149*

chemical weathering   All the processes that break apart rock by changing its chemical makeup. *p. 218*

chlorophyll (klôr′ə fil)   Green-colored material in plant cells needed by a plant to make food. *p. 13*

chloroplast (klôr′ə plast)   A small green body in plant cells. *p. 12*

circuit (sėr′kit)   The path through which an electric current flows. *p. 163*

circuit breaker   A safety device with a switch that turns off to break the flow of electricity when wires become too hot. *p. 175*

circulatory (sėr′kyə lə tôr ē) **system**   One of the transport systems of the body. It carries food and oxygen to the cells and carries away waste products. *p. 336*

cirrus (sir′əs) **clouds**   Thin, wispy clouds that look like feathers or curls of hair. Cirrus clouds form high in the sky and are often a sign that a warm front is moving in. *p. 276*

classify (klas′ə fī)   To arrange in groups by features that are alike. *p. 28*

climax (klī′maks) **stage**   The last stage in the process of succession. *p. 99*

cold front   The place where a moving cold air mass meets a warmer air mass. *p. 271*

cold-blooded animal   An animal whose body temperature changes with the temperature of the water or air around it. *p. 58*

combustion (kəm bus′chən)   The process by which oxygen from the air combines with a fuel, producing heat and light. *p. 184*

community (kə myü′nə tē)   All the plants and animals that live and interact with each other in a place. *p. 84*

compound (kom′pound)   A new substance that forms when atoms of different elements combine. *p. 122*

compound fracture   A break in a bone in which the broken end of the bone pushes through the muscle and skin. *p. 327*

conductor (kən duk′tər)   Matter through which an electric current flows easily. *p. 160*

constellation (kon stə lā′shən)   A group of stars that seems to form a pattern. *p. 301*

cramp   A sudden strong contraction of a muscle. *p. 328*

crude oil Oil that has not been refined; oil that is taken from the earth. *p. 183*

crustacean (krus tā′shən) One of a group of arthropods that includes animals such as shrimps, lobsters, and crayfish. *p. 47*

cumulus (kyü′myə ləs) **clouds** Large fluffy white clouds that are often seen during fair weather. *p. 276*

current electricity The movement of electrons. *p. 160*

delta A fan-shaped landmass formed by sediments deposited at the mouth of a river. *p. 225*

deposition (dep ə zish′ən) The dropping of sediments by the agents of erosion. *p. 223*

diaphragm (dī′ə fram) A thick sheet of muscle at the bottom of the chest cavity. *p. 348*

down Small fluffy feathers near a bird's body that trap air and help to keep the bird warm. *p. 68*

dry cell A type of electric cell that uses a chemical paste and two kinds of metal to produce a flow of electrons. *p. 170*

echinoderm (i kī′nə dèrm) A spiny-skinned invertebrate that lives in the ocean. *p. 39*

ecology (ē kol′ə jē) The study of how living and nonliving things affect each other. *p. 82*

ecosystem (ē′kə sis təm) A group of living things and their nonliving environment. *p. 83*

electric cell A device that changes chemical energy to electrical energy. *p. 169*

electric discharge (dis′chärj) The movement of extra electrons. *p. 160*

electric motor A machine that changes electrical energy to mechanical energy. *p. 172*

electron (i lek′tron) A tiny, negatively charged particle that travels around the nucleus of an atom. *pp. 117, 157*

element (el′ə mənt) Matter that is made up of only one kind of atom. *p. 118*

elliptical (i lip′tə kəl) **galaxy** A galaxy shaped like a flat disk. *p. 298*

embryo (em′brē ō) The tiny young plant in a seed. *p. 22*

environment (en vī′rən mənt) Everything that surrounds and affects a living thing. *p. 82*

erosion (i rō′zhən) The movement of weathered rock and soil from one place to another. *p. 220*

excretory (eks′krə tôr ē) **system** The transport system that removes waste products from the body. *p. 353*

exhaling (eks hāl′ing) The process of breathing out, during which air leaves the lungs. *p. 349*

exoskeleton (ek sō skel′ə tən) A hard outer covering that is like a skeleton on the outside of an animal's body. *p. 45*

femur (fē′mər) The long bone in the thigh; it is the longest and heaviest bone in the body. *p. 317*

fertilization (fèr tə lə zā′shən) The joining of male and female reproductive cells. *p. 22*

fertilizer (fèr′tə lī zər) A substance that helps plants grow. *p. 247*

filament (fil′ə mənt) A thin coil of wire. *p. 172*

fin A structure on a fish that helps it move through the water. *p. 58*

fish A cold-blooded vertebrate with fins. *p. 58*

fixed joint The kind of joint between bones that cannot move. *p. 320*

formula (fôr′myə lə) A group of symbols and numbers that stands for a compound. *p. 128*

fossil fuel A fuel that forms from the remains of dead plants and animals. Coal, oil, and natural gas are fossil fuels. *p. 182*

fracture (frak′chər) A crack or a break in a bone. *p. 327*

front The place where two air masses meet. *p. 271*

frost action A kind of physical weathering in which the daily freezing and melting of water causes large rocks to break up into smaller pieces. *p. 215*

fuse (fyüz) A safety device with a metal strip that melts to break the flow of electricity when wires become too hot. *p. 175*

galaxy (gal′ək sē) A large group of stars and other bodies in space. *p. 296*

generator (jen′ə rā tər) A machine that changes energy of motion into electrical energy. *p. 168*

geothermal (jē ə thėr′məl) **energy** Energy from natural heat trapped beneath the earth's surface. *p. 197*

germination (jėr mə nā′shən) The growth of a plant embryo from a seed. *p. 22*

gills Thin, feathery structures filled with blood and used for breathing. *p. 59*

glacier (glā′shər) A slow-moving mass of ice on land. *p. 227*

greenhouse effect The buildup of heat that occurs when solar energy strikes material and is trapped. *p. 190*

habitat (hab′ə tat) The special place in a community in which a plant or animal lives. *p. 87*

heart muscle A special kind of involuntary muscle that makes up the heart. *p. 326*

hinge joint The kind of joint that allows bones to move back and forth. *p. 320*

host The animal or plant in or on which a parasite lives. *p. 35*

hot spot An area of geothermal energy; an area beneath the earth's surface in which magma collects. *p. 197*

hydroelectric (hī drō i lek′trik) **power plant** A place in which the energy of moving water turns turbines attached to generators that produce electricity. *p. 195*

indirect evidence (in də rekt′ ev′ə dəns) A set of clues that scientists use to make guesses about things they cannot see or test directly. *p. 114*

inhaling (in hāl′ing) The process of breathing in, during which air enters the lungs. *p. 349*

insulator (in′sə lā tər) Matter through which an electric current does not flow easily; matter that is not a good conductor. *p. 161*

invertebrate (in vėr′tə brit) An animal without a backbone. *p. 29*

involuntary muscles The group of muscles that cannot be controlled. *p. 325*

irregular (i reg′yə lər) **galaxy** A galaxy that does not have a definite shape or size. *p. 298*

joint The place where two or more bones are joined together. *p. 319*

kilowatt (kil′ə wot) A unit of measure of large amounts of electric power. A kilowatt is 1,000 watts. *p. 173*

kilowatt-hour A unit equal to 1,000 watts of electricity used for 1 hour. *p. 174*

land breeze The movement of air from land to water. *p. 267*

larynx (lar′ingks) The voice box. *p. 347*

life processes The activities that keep living things alive. *p. 5*

ligament (lig′ə mənt) A strong cord of tissue that holds bones together at a joint. *p. 319*

light-year The distance that light travels in 1 year. *p. 288*

lungs The organs through which animals get oxygen from the air. *p. 62*

magma (mag′mə) Melted rock inside the earth. *p. 197*

magnitude (mag′nə tüd) The measure of the brightness of a star as seen from the earth. *p. 289*

mammal A warm-blooded vertebrate that is usually covered with fur or hair. *p. 72*

mass A measure of the amount of matter in an object. *p. 112*

matter Anything that has mass and takes up space. *p. 112*

mechanical (mə kan′ə kəl) **energy** Energy of moving machine parts. *p. 172*

melting point The temperature at which a solid changes to a liquid. *p. 140*

mineral Any pure hard material found in the earth's crust. *p. 217*

mixture (miks′chər) A material formed by the physical combining of two or more different materials. *p. 142*

molecule (mol′ə kyül) The simplest particle of many compounds. *p. 122*

mollusk (mol′əsk) An invertebrate with a soft body. Some have two outer shells; some live in a one-piece shell; others have no shell at all. *p. 41*

molt (mōlt) To shed a hard outer covering. *p. 52*

natural resource A useful material found in or on the earth. *p. 238*

nebula (neb′yə lə) A cloud of dust and gas found in space. *p. 292*

neutron (nü′tron) A particle in the nucleus of an atom. *p. 117*

neutron star A very dense star; what remains after a supernova collapses. *p. 295*

niche (nich) The role that each living thing plays in a habitat. *p. 89*

nonbiodegradable (non bī ō di grā′də bəl) **material** Material that cannot be broken down by living things. *p. 254*

nova An exploding star. *p. 294*

nuclear (nü′klē ər) **energy** The energy stored in the nucleus of an atom. *p. 186*

nuclear fission (fish′ən) The process by which the nucleus of an atom is split, releasing energy. *p. 186*

nuclear fusion (fyü′zhən) The process by which the nuclei (nü′klē ī) of atoms are combined, releasing energy. *p. 187*

nuclear reactor A special structure in which fission takes place. *p. 187*

nucleus (nü′klē əs) The central part of an atom. *p. 117*

organ A body part that does a certain job. *p. 34*

ovary (ō′vər ē) The bottom part of the pistil that contains the ovules. *p. 19*

ovule (ō′vyül)   A small round body in a flower that contains the female reproductive cells. Ovules grow into seeds. *p. 19*

parallel (par′ə lel) **circuit**   A circuit in which current can follow more than one path. *p. 164*

parasite (par′ə sīt)   An animal or plant that depends on and harms another animal or plant. *p. 35*

petals   The leaflike outer parts of a flower that protect the inner reproductive parts. *p. 19*

photosynthesis (fō tə sin′thə sis)   The process by which green plants make food. *p. 12*

physical change   A change in the size, shape, or state of matter. *p. 136*

physical property   A property that can be used to identify matter. Color, shape, and hardness are physical properties. *p. 134*

physical weathering   All the processes that break apart rock without changing its chemical makeup. *p. 215*

pioneer (pī ə nir′) **stage**   The first stage in the process of succession. *p. 99*

pistil   The female reproductive part of a flower. *p. 19*

pivot joint   The kind of joint that allows bones to move from side to side. *p. 320*

planarian (plə när′ē ən)   A common flatworm found in fresh water. *p. 34*

plasma (plaz′mə)   The yellowish, liquid part of the blood. *p. 336*

platelet (plāt′lit)   A solid part of the blood that controls bleeding. *p. 337*

pollen (pol′ən) **grain**   A tiny body in a flower that contains the male reproductive cell. *p. 19*

pollination (pol ə nā′shən)   The process by which pollen grains move from the stamen to the pistil of a flower. *p. 21*

pollutant (pə lü′tənt)   A substance that causes pollution. *p. 239*

pollution (pə lü′shən)   The presence of waste or other unwanted materials in a resource. *p. 239*

population (pop yə lā′shən)   A group of the same kind of living thing in a community. *p. 84*

pores   The small holes in the body of a sponge. *p. 30*

power   The amount of work done in a certain period of time. *p. 173*

predator (pred′ə tər)   An animal that hunts other animals for food. *p. 93*

prey (prā)   An animal that is hunted by a predator. *p. 93*

proton (prō′ton)   A positively charged particle in the nucleus of an atom. *pp. 117, 157*

red blood cell   A solid part of the blood; it carries oxygen to all the cells of the body. *p. 336*

red giant   One of the stages in the life cycle of a star. During this stage a star expands and is many times larger than the sun. *p. 293*

refinery (ri fī′nər ē)   A place where crude oil is changed to useful products. *p. 183*

regenerate (ri jen′ə rāt)   To regrow. *p. 35*

renewable (ri nü′ə bəl) **resource**   A resource that can be replaced after it is used. *p. 239*

reproduction (rē prə duk′shən)   The process by which living things produce new living things of the same kind. *p. 18*

reptile (rep′tīl)   A cold-blooded vertebrate that has lungs and dry skin. *p. 63*

respiration (res pə rā'shən)   The process by which living things use oxygen to release energy in food. *p. 16, p. 346*

respiratory (res'pər ə tôr ē) **system**   One of the transport systems of the body. It works closely with the circulatory system to put to use oxygen that is taken in during breathing. *p. 346*

root hair   The part of a single cell that grows from a root into the soil. *p. 7*

roundworm   A worm that has a long tube-shaped body with a digestive system. *p. 36*

runoff   Water from rain and melting snow that flows over the earth's surface. *p. 220*

sand dune   A pile of sand formed by the deposition of wind-carried sand. *p. 231*

sea breeze   The movement of air from water to land. *p. 267*

sediments (sed'ə mənts)   The materials carried by the agents of erosion. Sediments include sand, soil, and rock. *p. 223*

seed   A tiny young plant and its stored food. *p. 22*

segmented worm   A worm whose body is divided into segments, or sections. *p. 36*

series (sir'ēz) **circuit**   A circuit in which current can follow only one path. *p. 164*

simple fracture   A break in a bone in which the bone does not push through the muscle and skin. *p. 327*

skeletal muscles   Voluntary muscles that move bones. Skeletal muscles are made of long fibers. *p. 326*

skeleton (skel'ə tən)   The system of bones that supports and protects the body and the organs inside it. The skeleton is also called the skeletal (skel'ə təl) system. *p. 314*

skull   The bones of the face joined together with the bones that protect the brain. *p. 315*

smog   A mixture of smoke and fog. *p. 242*

smooth muscles   Involuntary muscles that make up the blood vessels, stomach, intestine, and other organs. *p. 326*

solar cell   A device that changes solar energy into electrical energy. *p. 192*

solar collector   A device that collects sunlight and changes it to heat energy. *p. 191*

solar (sō'lər) **energy**   Energy from the sun. *p. 190*

solute (sol'yüt)   The substance in a solution that dissolves. *p. 146*

solution (sə lü'shən)   A mixture that forms when one substance dissolves in another. *p. 145*

solvent (sol'vənt)   The substance in a solution that does the dissolving. *p. 146*

spiral (spī'rəl) **galaxy**   A galaxy shaped like a flat disk, or wheel, with curved arms coming out from the center. *p. 296*

sponge   An invertebrate with a simple body full of holes. *p. 30*

sprain   An injury in which a ligament is stretched or torn. *p. 328*

stamen (stā'mən)   The male reproductive part of a flower. *p. 19*

stinging cell   A special structure used to capture food. Jellyfish and hydras have stinging cells. *p. 32*

static (stat'ik) **electricity**   An electric charge that does not move. *p. 159*

stomata (stō'mə tə)   The openings in a leaf through which air enters the leaf. *p. 10*

strain   An injury caused by overstretching a muscle or a tendon. *p. 328*

stratus (strā'təs) **clouds**   Thick low clouds

that cover the sky. Stratus clouds are a sign of rainy weather. *p. 277*

succession (sək sesh′ən) The series of changes in the communities of an ecosystem. *p. 98*

suspension (sə spen′shən) A mixture in which particles of a substance do not dissolve in another substance. *p. 148*

supernova A large star that has exploded violently. *p. 294*

symbol A short way to write the name of an element. *p. 119*

tadpole The fishlike stage in the life cycle of the frog. *p. 62*

tendon (ten′dən) A tough cord that attaches muscle to bone. *p. 322*

tentacle (ten′tə kəl) A long, armlike part of an animal with stinging cells. *p. 32*

thermal (thėr′məl) **pollution** The dumping of heated materials into water. *p. 249*

thorax (thôr′aks) The middle part of an insect's body. *p. 48*

tidal (tī′dəl) **energy** The energy of rising and falling tides. Tidal energy can be used to produce electricity. *p. 196*

tides The daily movements of the water level along the shore. *p. 196*

toxic (tok′sik) **wastes** Waste materials that are poisonous. *p. 253*

trachea (trā′kē ə) The windpipe. *p. 347*

tube foot A hollow structure with a sucker at the end. Most echinoderms have tube feet. *p. 39*

turbine (tėr′bin) A device that is made up of a wheel and blades. *p. 168*

universe (yü′nə vers) All of space and all the matter and energy in it. *p. 286*

urine (yür′ən) Water with body wastes and salts dissolved in it. *p. 354*

vein (vān) A small thin tube in a leaf that carries water and food to and from leaf cells. *p. 10* A blood vessel that carries blood back to the heart from the body cells. *p. 339*

ventricle (ven′trə kəl) Lower chamber of the heart. *p. 339*

vertebrae (vėr′tə brā) The small bones linked together to form the backbone. *p. 29*

vertebrate (vėr′tə brit) An animal with a backbone. *p. 29*

voluntary muscles The group of muscles that can be controlled. *p. 325*

warm front The place where a moving warm air mass meets a colder air mass. *p. 273*

warm-blooded animal An animal whose body temperature stays the same even when the temperature of the air or water around it changes. *p. 67*

watt (wot) A unit of measure of small amounts of electric power. *p. 173*

weathering All the processes that break rock into smaller pieces. *p. 214*

wet cell A type of electric cell that uses acid and water, which react with metal plates, to produce a flow of electrons. *p. 170*

white blood cell A solid part of the blood; it helps the body fight infection. *p. 337*

white dwarf One of the stages in the life cycle of a star; a hot white star about the size of the earth. *p. 294*

windbreak Something that blocks the force of the wind. *p. 233*

INDEX

CREDITS

7 8 9 10 -VH—90 89 88 87